the 60-Minute Flower Garden

the 60-Minute Flower Garden

have a yard full of dazzling flowers in one hour a week

Jeff Ball and Charles O. Cresson

Rodale Press, Emmaus, Pennsylvania

Printed in the United States of America

Book Design by Linda Jacopetti

Color Illustrations by Michell Muldoon

Black-and-White Illustrations by Kathi Ember

Black-and-White Photography by Liz Ball

Color Photography by Liz Ball, David Cavagnaro, Charles O. Cresson, Jill Elliot, Derek Fell, John P. Hamel, J. Michael Kanouff, Alison Miksch, Gary Mottau, Joanne Pavia, Rodale Press Photography Department, and Pat Seip.

Library of Congress Cataloging in Publication Data

Ball, Jeff.
    The 60-minute flower garden.

    Bibliography: p.
    Includes indexes.
    1. Flower gardening.   2. Organic gardening.
I. Cresson, Charles O. II. Title. III. Title: Sixty-minute flower garden.
SB405.B248   1987   635.9   86-20427
ISBN 0-87857-636-3 hardcover
ISBN 0-87857-637-1 paperback

2 4 6 8 10 9 7 5 3   hardcover
2 4 6 8 10 9 7 5 3   paperback

Contents

Acknowledgments

Writing a book is always a challenge, but having two people write a book can often lead to tension, arguments, and sometimes broken relationships. We hereby acknowledge that we have become good friends and look forward to new projects in the future. We have learned much from each other in developing the ideas we present in this book.

We are both indebted to Jeff's wife, Liz, for her firm but always supportive first-draft editing, and we appreciate the highly professional guidance we have received from Suzanne Nelson, our editor at Rodale.

We are grateful for the enormous amount of time and energy Liz spent taking many of the photographs that are in the book. In addition, we appreciate the gracious welcome we received from so many gardeners in the Delaware Valley as we took our photographs.

One of the special pleasures in writing this book was working with Michell Muldoon, who painted the exciting color illustrations of Charles's garden plans. Her dedication to detail and accuracy is overshadowed only by her wonderful talent as a painter.

Charles wishes to thank J. Liddon Pennock, Jr., owner of Meadowbrook Farm near Jenkintown, Pennsylvania, and John Story, manager of Meadowbrook, for all he has learned from them and for their strong support and extended patience as Charles labored over this project, which often took him away from his duties there. Thanks also go to Princeton Nursery, Conard-Pyle Company, Brent Heath of the Daffodil Mart, Darrel Apps of the American Hemerocallis Society, Warren Pollock of the American Hosta Society, and Anita Kistler of the American Rock Garden Society for their helpful information.

We both want to thank Bill Cresson, Charles's father, for stepping in and taking care of Charles's garden while he was inside writing this book.

Introduction

When *Jeff Ball's 60-Minute Garden* came out in 1985, people with only a little space in their yards and not too much spare time learned how it was possible to grow over 400 pounds of vegetables in only 200 square feet of garden. And this productive garden took only 60 minutes a week to manage! Now that same group of people with small yards and limited time can learn how to have a splendid flower garden. With *The 60-Minute Flower Garden*, anybody can design and build a lovely flower garden anywhere in the yard—in the sun or even in the shade, on a rocky bank or in a soggy, poorly draining spot, as well as in less challenging sites. All you have to do is follow the simple steps outlined in this book by us—Jeff Ball and Charles Cresson. And best of all, you'll spend at most 60 minutes a week taking care of your flower garden.

We make a big distinction between the time it takes to develop and build a garden in the beginning and the time it takes later on to maintain it and keep it attractive. You may spend a weekend or two to build the garden in the first place, but then that job is done. From then on the maintenance will take you only 60 minutes a week, year in and year out. That's what we mean by the "60-Minute Flower Garden."

What makes a 60-Minute Flower Garden possible are the low-maintenance features that are built right into the garden design. Low maintenance doesn't mean the flower garden is plain or boring or unattractive. We give you a way to have the best of both worlds—a flower garden with reduced maintenance needs that provides you with an abundance of color and beauty throughout the season. One of our secrets is to use a mixture of perennial and annual flowers, tender and hardy bulbs, bright, eye-catching foliage plants, and flowering shrubs in a proportion that is laborsaving and as stunning as any flower garden you could wish to create. We also provide techniques that save on time, water, fertilizer, and pest control. Drip irrigation and mulch essentially eliminate any time spent on watering and weeding your garden. Our garden is designed to be ecologically stable, so it requires little supplemental fertilization and chemical pest control.

The 60-Minute Flower Garden can be enjoyed by beginning gardeners and experienced horticulturists alike. The directions for designing and preparing a garden are simple and straightforward. We've tried to eliminate the confusion and simplify the overly complex directions that can sometimes intimidate beginners. We also share some innovative ideas and techniques that should whet the interest of more experienced gardeners. Because of Charles's extensive experience in horticulture and Jeff's skills as a researcher, this book is filled with information about the latest ideas for flower gardening.

The Key Players in This Book

When Jeff finished his book about 60-minute vegetable gardening, he decided to adapt his timesaving techniques to suit flower gardens. Although he knew all about the key elements of low-maintenance gardening, he realized that he didn't have enough experience with flowers to get the job done properly. That's when Charles came into his life. Charles is a professional horticulturist at Meadowbrook Farm greenhouse and nursery near Jenkintown, Pennsylvania, a specialty garden shop where he has created display flower gardens to educate the public. He is also a private garden consultant. In that capacity he has helped people solve many of the same problems dealt with in this book. Over the years he has had the opportunity to work with many master gardeners throughout England, Europe, and the United States. Since we met, Charles has been teaching Jeff about flower gardens and Jeff has been teaching Charles about natural pest control and how computers can help manage gardens (and write a book). It has been a very productive relationship for both of us. This book is the product of the sharing of our respective specialties.

Liz, Jeff's wife, played several major roles in this book. She spent time behind the camera taking some of the photographs that appear on these pages. She also spent time seated at the computer, acting as the first line editor of the manuscript. More important, she took over the major responsibilities for developing and managing the flower gardens on the Ball suburban homestead, under the close but loving supervision of Charles. Every idea and recommendation made in this book has been tried and proven by either Jeff, Liz, or Charles. We have made lots of mistakes in the process, and we hope that by sharing our lessons we can help you avoid some of those same mistakes. We want you to be able to get started with few problems so that you'll gain confidence and fall in love with flower gardening. As you advance in skill, you'll be able to learn more by making your own mistakes.

Designing a 60-Minute Flower Garden

The first five chapters of our book will take you through the design process in such a clear and understandable fashion that it will be almost impossible not to have a successful 60-Minute Flower Garden in your yard. Here we'll give you a sneak preview of what's to come in the book. In Chapter 1 we get you started by having you look at your entire yard as a series of "garden rooms." Just as you would remodel the rooms in your house, we are suggesting you can remodel these garden rooms. And of course the essential ingredient in this remodeling is the creation of a 60-Minute Flower Garden. We think this concept of remodeling a garden room is a handy way to figure out where you can put a flower garden. By the end of Chapter 2 you should be able to select the best spot in a garden room for a flower garden that is just the right size to stay within the 60-minute-a-week time frame. In Chapter 3 you'll be introduced to the five basic flower garden models we propose you use as the starting point for your own garden design. Then, in Chapter 4, you will find a series of easy-to-understand planning principles that will help your garden take shape—a garden with maximum beauty and minimum inputs of time.

The part of the book that will help you select the flowers for your garden is Chapter 5. Here is where you'll find a series of plant lists in which we recommend the best plants, in our opinion, to include in your flower garden design. At the end of the chapter, in the Gallery of Flower Garden Designs, Charles has created nine sample plans for different types of gardens for both sunny and shady areas. For each you'll find a "blueprint" to show the layout and a list of the plants included in the garden. You could copy these exactly or vary them to suit your particular taste and garden situation.

The important thing about these lists

of recommended flower garden plants is that we've reduced the potentially numbing assortment of possibilities to a manageable number of the best candidates from which you can choose. If you've ever thumbed through catalogs or visited nurseries, you know that there are thousands of flowering plants available. Charles used his professional judgment to narrow down the selection. First he sorted through and kept only those that are easy to find and easy to grow. Of those, he selected nearly 500 with the best qualities for a low-maintenance and attractive flower garden. Next he narrowed the field to those he thought were the absolute best of their kind. These are the plants that show up in the lists in Chapter 5 and also in the chart The Best Plants for the 60-Minute Flower Garden at the back of the book. We've already done the hardest part of the selection process; you get to do the fun part of making up your own list, confident that you're working with the best possible choices.

New Types of Flower Gardens in America

In this book we talk about five basic types of flower garden models. Two of these represent new ideas for flower gardens in America.

Decorative Home Garden

The idea for the Decorative Home Garden was born while the gardens on Jeff and Liz's property were being developed. There are over 20 million homes in America that have very similar front yards. This common front yard includes a lawn that is anywhere from 5 to 30 feet deep and almost invariably has shrubbery of some sort planted across the front of the house. Flowers are seldom seen in this typical American front yard.

We've come up with a very simple method for "remodeling" that front yard to create a beautiful flower garden. We start by using those existing shrubs as the foundation for the flower garden's design. By simply digging a bed in front of those shrubs and following the simple planning steps we provide, you can have a breathtaking flower garden across the front of your home that will be the envy of the neighborhood. The best part is that once you've built it, the garden won't take more than 60 minutes a week to maintain.

If just half the people with this typical front yard built a Decorative Home Garden, there would be a virtual explosion of color and beauty across America. It wouldn't take much to start this gardening "revolution," since all that's missing in these front yards are the flowers and foliage plants, arranged in a tasteful fashion to create a lovely flower garden. Our 60-minute gardening approach starts with the shrubs and guides you in building the rest of the flower garden with ease and confidence and relatively little money. We hope this new garden design changes the way we all look at our front yards.

Bank Garden

In some part of our property, many of us have a slope or a bank that presents a problem area for any kind of landscaping, much less a flower garden. Charles has taken the design principles for a traditional rock garden and translated them into what we are calling a Bank Garden. This design is intended to solve the thorny problem of what to do on that bank to make the yard look more attractive. You'll be pleased to know there's a nice array of colorful flowering plants that can dress up a slope.

Maintaining a 60-Minute Flower Garden

In Chapter 6, flower gardeners will find a new way to think about the soil in which their flowers grow. You'll begin to think about "managing" your garden's soil, and you won't ever take it for granted. You'll learn some surprising things about soil that can help you have a better flower garden.

In Chapter 7, you'll probably learn a few things you didn't know about how to deliver just the right amount of water to your flowers with minimal effort on your part. The key to this is drip irrigation. Drip irrigation isn't a new idea in commercial agriculture, but it's still a very new concept in most home flower gardens in this country. We think its time has come and that more flower gardeners should take advantage of all the benefits it has to offer. In Chapter 7 we show you how to determine which of the many drip irrigation systems are best for your flower garden and give you tips on how to make the best use of a system.

Feeding the flower garden using a mist spray is another relatively new idea for home gardeners. Foliar feeding offers a number of advantages over the traditional method of applying fertilizer to plant roots. After reading Chapter 7, we hope you decide to try foliar feeding in your garden.

Weeds, insects, and diseases, not to mention animal pests, can be discouraging even to the most experienced flower gardeners. In Chapter 8 we offer a rational approach to pest control called Backyard Pest Management (BPM). This is our adaptation of Integrated Pest Management (IPM), used widely by commercial growers. Our BPM approach is scaled down to suit the requirements of backyard gardeners and emphasizes prevention rather than frantic control measures after the pests have done their damage.

And finally, Chapter 9 helps you put all the pieces together by giving you pointers on how to plant and manage a successful 60-Minute Flower Garden.

Special Features

The Appendix of this book is loaded with valuable information that will make your flower gardening easier and a lot more enjoyable. The chart we mentioned earlier, The Best Plants for the 60-Minute Flower Garden, provides handy, easy-to-use growing information for 173 flowering plants. The Appendix also gives you a Resources Guide so you can track down any tools and garden accessories we talk about in the text. We also provide a Recommended Reading list of other books that you may find helpful over the course of your flower gardening adventures.

Some Final Thoughts

Our final words concern the two traditional professions that occupy themselves with yards and flowers, namely the landscape architect and the horticulturist. In our book there is a blurring of the lines between the traditional turf (pardon the pun) of the landscape architect and the domain of the horticulturist. This book is *not* about landscaping. It *is* about flower gardens, but it isn't a traditional flower garden book. All of our 60-Minute Flower Garden models, especially the Decorative Home Garden, combine some of the elements that are commonly considered "landscaping" with elements that are generally thought to be "flower gardening" to create a form of gardening that falls between these two specialties. For example, the Decorative Home Garden is a flower garden and more because it includes shrubs and is designed to fit into its surrounding landscape. We hope that both the landscape architect and the horticulturist will include the Decorative Home Garden as well as our other flower garden concepts in their kitbags of tricks.

So now let's get down to business and the 60-Minute Flower Garden. Get ready as you turn the page to start thinking about your yard in ways that should help you design and build a spectacular flower garden.

Chapter 1

Taking an Educated Look at Your Property

Choosing a spot in your yard for a 60-Minute Flower Garden shouldn't be a prolonged, nerve-wracking undertaking, but neither should it be a spur-of-the-moment selection. There are a number of mistakes you might make right in the beginning that could create some complicating and time-consuming problems later as you build your garden. If the site you select for the garden is too large, if it requires too much preparation, or if it offers challenging growing conditions, you can be set back even before you get started.

In this chapter we will help you take an educated look at your entire property to see what kinds of uses can be made of its space and how these uses, in turn, help determine the kind of flower garden you'll have. We offer some simple steps to help you assess all of the options you have on ways to use your property. We'll also help you make sure you've made the right decision in this first stage of choosing the area for your 60-Minute Flower Garden.

Analyzing Your Property

Once you've decided you would like to have a flower garden, one of the first deci-

sions you face is where to put it. Most property owners have more than one place in the yard where a flower garden might look attractive. To narrow this selection, it helps to be able to visualize how a garden might enhance any particular site when it is finished. Unfortunately, no flower garden can be instantly created on location with flowers in full bloom, shrubs all the right size, and ground cover all filled in around the plants. You must rely on your imagination. An added complication is the need to be able to visualize how your garden will look in each season of the year. What makes this exercise even more challenging is the need to be able to see into the future and imagine how your garden will look five years from now when the perennial flowers and any accompanying trees and shrubs have matured. Some people draw a blank when it comes to doing all this mental garden designing. Fortunately, this chapter and the next will give you some tips that we have developed to simplify this conceptual process.

"Remodeling" the Yard

To start, we'd like to suggest that you think about your yard in the same way you

1

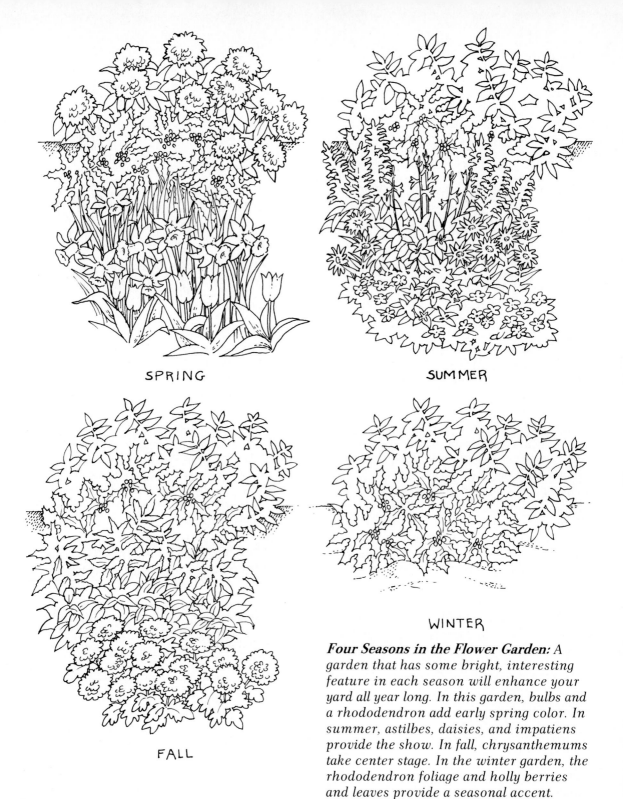

SPRING

SUMMER

FALL

WINTER

Four Seasons in the Flower Garden: *A garden that has some bright, interesting feature in each season will enhance your yard all year long. In this garden, bulbs and a rhododendron add early spring color. In summer, astilbes, daisies, and impatiens provide the show. In fall, chrysanthemums take center stage. In the winter garden, the rhododendron foliage and holly berries and leaves provide a seasonal accent.*

think about your house—as a space composed of a number of rooms. We define a garden room as an area of the yard having apparent natural and physical boundaries that separate it from all the other parts of the property. Rooms in the yard can be remodeled just like rooms in your house. You know it is much easier to remodel a house one room at a time than it is to redo the whole house at once. The same principle applies to your yard.

If you try to build a flower garden, establish a vegetable garden, reseed your whole lawn, and cut back every overgrown shrub on your entire property all at the same time, you are in for a job that may be so overwhelming that you won't get any of it done. Jeff and Liz have watched a neighbor try this overload approach, with this result: All her vegetable and flower beds have reverted to lawn, and a lot of hard work has gone down the drain.

We suggest that you tackle this remodeling of your yard in gradual stages. In a single growing season select only one garden room in which to establish a lovely flower garden. By following our low-maintenance pointers, you'll have a garden that will not be difficult to handle, nor will it take more than 60 minutes of your time each week once it is constructed. Over a period of years you can comfortably remodel your entire property, one room at a time.

Remodeling a house is a multistep process, with decisions to be made every step of the way. The same holds true for remodeling a yard and designing a flower garden. Starting in this chapter and continuing through the next four, we'll help you make important decisions through all the stages of the process that begins with the desire to have a flower garden and ends with your selection of a gorgeous array of plants to fill your own personal flower garden design. In this chapter we'll help you decide in which

garden room to locate your flower garden. The next step, picking the actual site for the garden within the room, is covered in Chapter 2. Chapter 3 will show you how to analyze the conditions in your garden site that will ultimately affect the final garden design and the types of plants you'll be able to grow. General planning principles that will influence how you design your garden are presented in Chapter 4. Finally, in Chapter 5 we'll help you decide which plants will appear in your 60-Minute Flower Garden.

Analyzing the Garden Rooms on Your Property

There are a number of criteria to consider when analyzing your yard and selecting the first garden room to be devoted to a flower garden. These criteria include the room's location in the yard, the purpose or use of each room, the topography of your property, the existing plants in your yard, and any special functional areas such as driveways and sidewalks.

Most properties are divided up into a front yard, a backyard, and one or two side yards. If your property is fairly small, these designations may make up your three or four rooms and all you have to do is pick one for your flower garden. We feel that most people are naturally going to want to have their first flower garden in the front yard, as Jeff and Liz did, but let's look at the other alternatives before you make the final decision.

If the front yard or backyard is a particularly large area, you may have two or more distinct rooms in each of those spaces alone. For example, Liz and Jeff have a fairly large backyard that divides naturally into five rooms. They have an ample area with a deck, a large vegetable and fruit garden, a good-sized bit of lawn, a woodland garden, and a utility area where they store wood for their woodstove.

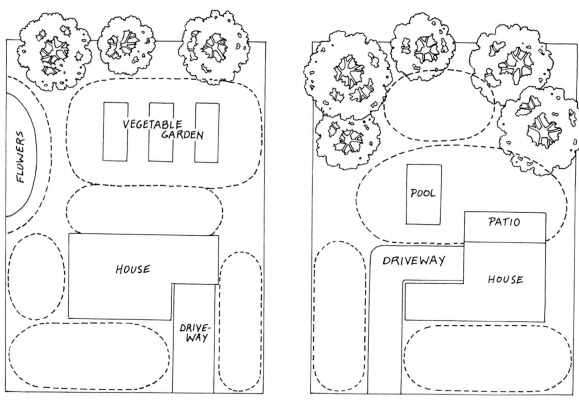

Rooms in a Yard: *Here are two examples of how a yard can be divided into rooms. (The areas within the dotted lines represent different garden rooms.) Although both yards are the same size, the yard on the left divides naturally into six rooms, while the one on the right accommodates four rooms.*

The first exercise is to think about the different areas or rooms of your property in terms of their purpose or use. When we talk about the purpose of your garden room, we are looking at how you use that particular area of your yard. If you haven't thought about how you want to use each room, you may not locate your flower garden in the best spot within that room. Let's spend a few moments reviewing the various functions garden rooms can serve. A garden room can create an attractive view; it can be an outdoor living space; it can serve as an area for strolling; or it can attract wildlife. (There may be other purposes for a garden room besides the four we discuss here, but these are probably the most common.) Each of these purposes causes you to design your garden room just a bit differently and influences the kind of flower garden you can develop within the room's boundaries.

Obviously, these four purposes for a garden room are certainly not exclusive of one another. You can have a garden room with an attractive view that is also designed to attract some wildlife. A garden room that is designed to be an outside living space can also create an attractive view from inside the house. Our point here is that you'll have a better flower garden design and you'll make better plant selections if right from the start you have a clear idea of how you want to use the garden room in which you'll build your 60-Minute Flower Garden.

A Room with a View

Perhaps the most common function for a garden room is to create an attractive view—from both inside and outside the house. In many cases, the view of your home from the street is your primary concern in designing a garden for the front yard. On the other hand, you could have a similar type of room in the backyard because it creates a pleasant view from the kitchen window or from the sliding glass door in the family room. This sort of garden room is designed for its beauty and the way it fills a space, creates a pleasing frame for the house, or dresses up the front of the home. Since the view is so important, you should try to design a 60-Minute

Flower Garden in that room that is attractive through all four seasons of the year.

A flower garden intended to contribute to the attractive view in the front of the house is usually used to focus on the entrance of the home. You want this sort of garden to welcome visitors as they come up the walk. As you'll see in Chapter 4, there are ways you can arrange your plants so that the view beckons to visitors and says, "this is a nice place to visit."

In any case, no matter whether your garden room with an attractive view is in the front of the house or in the backyard, you want to keep in mind the view of the room from inside the house as well as from the outside. Jeff and Liz eat all their meals in a country kitchen that looks out over the front yard onto the street. The view of their flower garden from where they sit in the kitchen is as important as the view of that garden from the street. The importance of this "insider's" view is one of the reasons we feel strongly about not blocking windows with large shrubs. If you block the windows, you will leave your garden for

Attractive View: *This flower garden is in an ideal spot to be enjoyed either from inside the house or from the street.*

Scenic Retreat: *Mealtimes and moments of relaxation are even more enjoyable when there's a beautiful flower garden in sight. The lush and colorful flowers in this garden room brighten the view from inside the screened porch.*

A Garden for Daily Viewing: *As you survey garden rooms in your yard, keep in mind those that you and your family see most often. A flower garden in a room adjacent to the driveway can provide a pleasant scene every time you get in and out of the car.*

everyone passing by to enjoy but cheat yourself of the same pleasure. If you're going to spend 60 minutes a week to keep the flowers in your garden room pretty, you shouldn't have to go outside the house to appreciate them yourself.

You'll find that there may be other, less obvious views you need to consider. For example, if you park your car in a driveway that will be right next to the new flower garden, you might want to keep that view from the driveway in mind as you design the garden. When you get in and out of your car each day, you'll enjoy the special pleasure of a colorful scene in your garden room. Don't underestimate the power of a gorgeous flower garden to delight family members daily.

An Outdoor Living Space

Another purpose a garden room may serve is as an outdoor living space. This kind of room will be used and decorated in much the same manner as you would decorate a room inside your home. The classic example of a garden room with this purpose is a patio or deck that is surrounded by flowers, low shrubs, and pretty plants in containers. You want this setting to be attractive because this is where you entertain friends, spend leisurely Sunday mornings reading the paper, or just simply sit down and take a few minutes' break from your hectic routine.

While this garden room function naturally leads to a flower garden that is attractive, the primary concern here is to have a design that is in keeping with the way the space is used. For example, a flower garden that surrounds or adjoins a recreation space such as a children's play area or a swimming pool can enhance the outdoor living space quite nicely. But you must be practical when you design your space, so the plants aren't endangered by running feet or flying volleyballs. Privacy is something that people often seek to create in outdoor living spaces, and you can build this into the design of your 60-Minute Flower Garden. In addition to tall-growing flowers, you may wish to enclose the perimeter of your outdoor living room with taller shrubs and trees.

A flower garden established to help create an outdoor living space will often have more annuals than perennials in it. Annuals tend to have a longer blooming season than perennials, so they'll put on a more sustained show of color. Since you'll be using this space often, you're likely to want the brighter colors and extended flowering period provided by annuals. The trade-off is that you'll have to water a bit more frequently and do a bit more transplanting than if you filled the garden with perennials. A flower garden in this sort of garden room will also make wide use of portable plants in containers and hanging baskets. Mobile plants make it easy for you to rearrange the elements in this garden in much the same way that you move the furniture in your indoor living room.

Outdoor Living Space: An outdoor "living room" like this one is a natural place for a flower garden. Instead of wallpapering and carpeting this garden room, you use flowers to beautify the "decor." Note in particular the ornamental eulalia grass to the right that adds an exotic touch to the poolside setting.

An Area for Strolling

This is the garden room you might find at the side of the house and enjoy when you are walking from the front yard to the backyard. This type of garden room is often the connecting link between two other rooms in your yard. Or your garden room for strolling might be the area in the very back of your property that's not visited every day but is pleasant to wander through on the way to the compost pile or other outposts in the yard. Charles has two such garden rooms in his large backyard. He has a woodland garden in a room that connects his immediate backyard with his far backyard, which is divided by a stream. His far backyard contains a meadow garden that fills the entire garden room. Both areas are a pleasure to walk through.

A flower garden in this sort of garden room is designed to require relatively little maintenance. It will include more trees, shrubs, perennials, bulbs, and ground covers than annuals. Because it is easy to care for, it can be larger than other 60-Minute Flower Gardens and stay within the accept-

able time frame. Other gardens will rely on lots of blossoming plants with bright colors that change throughout the season for their visual interest. A garden for strolling contains plenty of flowers, but it relies less on blossom color and more on the variety of stunning plant shapes, textures, and colors to catch your eye. As you design this garden, you'll be paying less attention to the details of each plant and more to the overall shape of the garden. What you want to create are appealing changes in shapes and textures within the overall view. A garden for strolling very often includes an area of lawn that has been shaped to make an inviting pathway as you walk through the garden room.

A Room to Attract Wildlife

Gardeners often spend so much time chasing wildlife out of the yard that they overlook the pleasures of creating habitats for creatures where they won't be seen as nuisances. Here the term wildlife includes songbirds, hummingbirds, squirrels, chipmunks, toads, garter snakes, honeybees, lady-

Garden Room for Strolling: This inviting pathway beckons you to come take a walk and enjoy all the beautiful flowering plants, shrubs, and trees that are arranged throughout the garden room.

bugs, and butterflies. No matter what kind of wildlife you're interested in attracting and observing, the garden room must provide four basic requirements: food, water, cover, and an area in which to reproduce. The plants you include in a flower garden can provide these things and at the same time beautify your garden room.

Naturally, all flower gardens will attract some form of wildlife. But you can build into the design of your 60-Minute Flower Garden a number of elements that will increase the desirable wildlife population on your property. Flowers are a source of nectar to feed honeybees, butterflies, and hummingbirds. In your garden design for this wildlife room you'll want to be sure to include the flowers that are most attractive to your wild friends. Besides the flowers, you might also have shrubs that bear seeds and berries to attract and nourish wild creatures. A birdbath or even a small man-made pond will provide water (and a nice accent for the garden design). Trees, shrubs, and foliage plants provide cover, safe places for breeding, and shelter from the weather.

Selecting a Room for the 60-Minute Flower Garden

Our advice is to choose a garden room that is relatively small and simple to remodel for the first year. Since the general size of a flower garden that can be maintained in only 60 minutes a week is 100 to 200 square feet, look for a garden room that has at least that much area. As you'll read in Chapter 3, some of the 60-Minute Flower Gardens can be a bit larger, but 100 to 200 square feet is a good general guide. Remember, the larger the garden room, the more details you'll need to attend to during the remodeling in addition to developing the flower garden.

Some Factors to Consider

You don't have to look very hard to see the shape of a garden room. Property lines and the topography of your yard may naturally define the borders of some of your garden rooms. The general topography of your property will be a consideration if there are a lot of shifts in elevation. For example, large rock formations, natural or man-made terraces, steep slopes, or creek beds are likely to influence the natural boundaries of a garden room. There may even be an area that naturally divides into two rooms because one part basks in full sun and another part lies in full shade.

Any garden room that requires significant physical changes is less desirable as a site for your first 60-Minute Flower Garden than a room that is ready to go. Some natural elements can be changed with minimal work. For example, soil that's in less than prime condition can be improved with the addition of soil amendments and conditioners. Some natural elements may be attractive enough that there's no need to change them—you can incorporate them right into the garden. Liz and Jeff built a small woodland garden around a huge sycamore tree stump and some large rock outcroppings that would have been extremely difficult and costly to move. They were able to turn a problem area into an attractive garden room for strolling. However, things like major grading changes can be very challenging and time-consuming. Assuming that we are talking about your first flower garden, choose a room that requires the least physical change to get it ready for the plants. If you already have some experience gardening with flowers, you may feel better prepared to take on the challenge of making major physical changes in the room.

An important consideration in choosing a room is the existing plants it contains.

In some cases it can be an advantage to work with the greenery already on the site. You may have some trees or shrubs that are in great condition, are properly placed, and need only to be pruned and have some flowers tucked in among them to make a terrific Decorative Home Garden. On the other hand, an area that is bare of trees and shrubs may be easier to work with than an area that is thick with shrubs or full-sized trees and other plants that may require extensive moving. Each of these sites has potential for a wonderful garden, but one takes more time than the other.

Before you select the garden room for your flower garden, you must think about any future plans you have for your property. If you're planning to build a garage, patio, or toolshed, it makes sense not to locate your flower garden in the midst of a potential construction site.

Making Your Choice

After going through this exercise of analyzing your entire property, you'll probably be able to define anywhere from three to six rooms. They aren't all necessarily candidates for flower gardens, but you might have more than one that would look nice with some flowers. We recommend that for the first year you select the room that is modest in size, requires the least physical change, and requires minimum moving of existing trees and shrubs. Building the flower garden will take up some time, so you may not wish to burden yourself with other landscaping tasks that are also time-consuming.

The following year, after you have some experience building a 60-Minute Flower Garden, you may feel ready to tackle a second flower garden in another room that is more challenging. Or you may want to spend time on the landscaping tasks that remain to be done in the remodeling of the garden room that holds your first flower garden. These might include repaving a sidewalk with bricks or attractive stones, adding some trees, or building a wall. However, don't succumb to the all-too-common temptation of overly ambitious plans. Jeff and Liz started a small orchard project in a backyard garden room at the same time they began building their flower garden in the front yard. Remodeling two garden rooms was too much to do in the time they had. Now that their flower garden has been built, Jeff and Liz plan to tackle that small orchard next year. And once they've gotten the orchard under way, they'll still have a number of garden rooms to develop in seasons to come. Charles, on the other hand, has his entire property grandly organized with at least six different types of flower gardens in about eight garden rooms. He also spends considerably more than 60 minutes a week keeping them all so elegant and inviting. But then Jeff is quick to point out that that is what a horticulturist does, and mere "normal" people, like himself, are very happy to find the time and ability to have just one splendid 60-Minute Flower Garden.

Chapter 2

Looking at Your New Garden Room

Now that you've selected the garden room for your first 60-Minute Flower Garden, what's the next step? You have a few things to think about concerning the basic environment of the room before you can pick the precise spot of ground for your flower garden. You need to consider the general features of the space and get a feel for its potential for a flower garden. Then you need to identify the exposure and orientation of the room and evaluate the condition of the soil within the room. These characteristics, with the addition of prevailing winds and available light, make up what is called the microclimate of your garden room. This chapter will help you identify and understand the special microclimate in your newly chosen garden room so that you'll be able to pick the best spot to break ground for the flower garden.

General Characteristics of the Space

Take a few moments to think about how your garden room functions now on your property. How is the space used? Is it a part of the yard where your family spends a lot of time? Think about where you walk in the space, and then think about how that might change depending on where you place your flower garden. Will the new flower garden cause some access problems? Will it block bringing the lawn mower or the garden cart into the room? Will it make the use of the existing sidewalks or paths awkward? Do you want to use the garden to stop foot traffic in some way? For example, you can place a garden in a location that will prevent people from taking a shortcut to your front door and wearing a path in the lawn. Try to anticipate how a flower garden's location might alter normal day-to-day activities around your home. Jeff and Liz eliminated a driveway that was no longer needed and replaced it with their 60-Minute Flower Garden. When they finished, they realized that they had changed the pattern of traffic coming up to their front door. What that means is that they will eventually have to change the direction of the front walk that leads to the door. This isn't a crisis, but they should have thought about all the possible implications before beginning the garden design.

11

Many Ways of Looking at a Flower Garden

As you search for a good location within the garden room, always think about the various views you'll have of the finished flower garden. A garden isn't like a painting, where there's a side you always see and a side that's always hidden. As we mentioned in Chapter 1, there isn't just one fixed view but many vantage points from which to gaze upon a flower garden. You must consider those different views as you create the ultimate plan of the garden. One of the easiest techniques for analyzing the potential views of a flower garden in a garden room is to look from the vantage points of three different locations.

Different Points of View: There are three ways of looking at a flower garden in a garden room. One is from inside the house, another is from within the garden room itself, and the third is from outside the garden room.

Three Vantage Points

- Check the view of the flower garden site while standing in the garden room itself.
- Check the view while standing outside the garden room (for example, out in the street or in the neighbor's yard).
- Check the view while standing inside your house looking out the window that faces or overlooks the garden room.

When you do this exercise, try not to let the existing plants influence your thinking. They can always be moved to a different spot in the garden room or even be removed entirely. Pretend you are composing a picture. As you stand in the three locations, notice where your eye naturally falls. What seems to be the focal point of each of the views? A focal point might be a nice trunk of a sycamore tree, a specimen spruce tree, or a flowering crabapple. Do you like what you see? When you think about each view, what element do you wish to avoid covering up because it is attractive in its own right?

Charles uses a term he calls "borrowed scenery." By that he means taking advantage of an exciting visual feature from the yard next door or one that happens to fall within the view and incorporating it into the view of your own garden. Examples might include a rustic, weathered old barn, an outstanding-looking tree, an attractive rock formation, or some other natural element that enhances the view.

On the other hand, there might be some background clutter you wish to cover up because it will detract from your flower garden. Perhaps you want to block off the driveway so you can't see the parked car when you are admiring the flowers from a certain position. Maybe you'd like to conceal the view of an unsightly air conditioning unit or a group of gas or water meters on the outside of the house. There are no rules here, but after you have completed this exercise, you should have a clearer idea of the best site for your 60-Minute Flower Garden.

A Closer Look at the Room

An important piece of information that you need to determine right at the start concerns the climatic factors that will affect your garden room. To understand these, you need to know in which climatic zone, or hardiness zone, you live. As you travel from the north of Canada and the United States to the south, the growing seasons become longer and the winters less damaging to plants. The boundaries of these zones are set up from northern Canada to the southernmost tip of the United States. Each zone is assigned a number. The zones are based on the average annual lowest winter temperature. The lower numbers designate colder zones, the higher numbers warmer zones. We live in southeastern Pennsylvania on the northern edge of Zone 7, which indicates that we have a slightly warmer climate than most of the rest of the state, which lies in Zones 5 and 6.

While a vegetable gardener is very concerned about frost dates (last frost in the spring and first frost in the fall), the flower gardener's interest in climatic zones is primarily centered on the minimum winter temperature that will be experienced in the garden each year. That will be the determining factor for which plants will survive in your garden and which will not. Winter soil temperatures are also important for perennials and bulbs (we'll talk more about the significance of soil temperatures in Chapter 6). Find your climatic zone designation on the Hardiness Zone Map in the Appendix. You'll need to keep this zone in mind when you begin your garden plan and plant selection.

Microclimates

From the "big picture" of your climatic zone you need to shift to the smaller picture of the microclimates within your garden room. Whether your garden room is large or small, you can usually identify a variation in the conditions that make up the microclimate in different sections of the room. For example, plants located in front of a brick wall or along a foundation are going to have more heat available than plants located out in the middle of the room, because the wall will collect and store heat from the sun. Plants located at the bottom of a slope may suffer more from the cold than those at the top, since cold air settles in low places. Plants in a flat, exposed area will feel the effects of the wind more than those sheltered by buildings or surrounded by taller plants. Learn how to observe the different microclimates within the room you have selected so you can keep their side effects in mind as you situate the garden.

Microclimates can affect the zone designation of your garden. For example, although the zone map shows that you're in Zone 5, the favorable microclimate in your yard or garden room may make it possible to grow plants suited to the milder conditions in Zone 6. A favorable microclimate can expand your choice of plants by expanding your zone. An unfavorable microclimate might have just the opposite effect, though, by making the conditions in your yard harsher than your zone designation would suggest.

You can influence the microclimate within your garden site to a certain extent, which may make it possible for a questionable plant to survive in your climate zone. Protecting the flower garden with a fence or a row of evergreen trees, establishing it next to a stone wall exposed to the sun, and covering the garden with heavy mulch are methods for improving the microclimatic conditions of your flower garden.

Orientation

The next thing to check is how your garden room is oriented in terms of the compass headings. Does your garden room face or have its long side oriented toward the south, north, east, or west? Knowing this orientation helps you understand how exposure to wind and sun will influence a garden in that room. This in turn will affect how you position your flower garden.

For example, in the northern part of the country where even the summers tend to be cool, you might try to find a site that is up against the house and facing south. That way the full benefits of sunny days can be gained from the reflection and heat storage provided by the wall. In southern parts of the country where the summer sun gets terribly hot, a more easterly or even northerly orientation may be desirable to protect the flower garden from burning up in the dead of summer.

Wind Exposure

Wind has the potential to either gently brush or buffet plants. You need to determine the direction and usual force of the prevailing winds in your area so you can take them into consideration as you locate the garden site and design the garden. Don't underestimate the power of the wind to undermine all your best efforts in the flower garden. In the summer, strong winds can blow over tall or newly planted specimens, turning a neat perennial bed into a mess. And winter winds can dehydrate and cause other physical damage to woody shrubs and evergreens. If the strength and direction of the prevailing winds seem like they'll wreak havoc with your flower garden, you must plan for some kind of protection in the form of a wall, a fence, or a row of shrubs.

Northern gardeners in particular need to be concerned about winter winds and keep their effects in mind as they locate the garden. As we just mentioned, north winds are drying and cause dehydration that will lead to windburn on evergreen leaves and needles. Plants cannot recover from dehydration as quickly during very cold weather as they can during warmer spells. Then there are the mechanical problems that winter brings. The cold makes the stems of woody shrubs brittle and vulnerable to strong winds. Heavy gusts on a bone-chilling day can break the limbs and blow the evergreen leaves off a rhododendron. You must be aware of the potential harm in a garden located on the north side of your home with no protection from prevailing north winds in the winter.

You might be wondering how you go about determining prevailing winds. There are ways to figure this out on your own, but the most reliable source of information is the local office of the National Weather Service (listed under U.S. Government Offices in the Blue Pages of your phone book). In most parts of the country, prevailing winds will come from different directions in the summer and the winter, so you should check with the weather service once each season.

Available Light

How much sun or shade is found in your garden room during the various seasons of the year? Don't overlook the fact that light can change with the seasons; observe these fluctuations carefully. In the early spring, before the leaves come out fully on the trees, you might have nearly full sun for your crocuses and early tulips. Later, that same flower bed could be shaded most of the day, requiring shade-loving plants such as impatiens and ferns. Shadows from the house or from trees may fall on the garden in different places in that same area as summer wanes, because the sun sinks lower in the sky as the season progresses. Don't assume the same light that shines on your spring garden will be there for your late summer garden; remember this seasonal aspect of light when you are looking at the different potential sites for your flower garden in the room.

The available light in your garden room is perhaps the greatest determining factor for which plants you will eventually choose. How is your garden located in relation to sources of shade like trees, the house, or other structures? How does the sun/shade pattern shift over the course of a day? The only way to find out is to go and see for yourself in early morning, at midday, and again in later afternoon.

While horticulturists use a more sophisticated set of definitions for the variations in light conditions, we suggest that the home flower gardener can do fine using "full sun," "partial sun," "partial shade," and "full shade." The box Light Terminology for the Flower Gardener on the next page gives the definitions for each of these terms so you can become familiar with them. We use these throughout the rest of the book whenever we discuss light conditions.

Same Garden, Two Seasons: *Light changes with the seasons, and that can influence what kinds of flowers you can grow at different times of the year in the same garden. In this garden, before the tree leafs out, the bulbs bask in full sun. As soon as the leaves appear on the branches, the garden is in partial shade. The summer-blooming garden includes such shade-tolerant flowers as astilbes, columbines, lobelias, sweet alyssums, forget-me-nots, and impatiens.*

LIGHT TERMINOLOGY FOR THE FLOWER GARDENER

Full sun: Unfiltered, uninterrupted sunlight all day.

Partial sun: Five or 6 hours of open sunlight a day, with shade or filtered sun the rest of the day.

Partial shade: Dappled sun, either all day long or interrupted for up to 4 hours by either direct sun or full shade. This can also be "high shade," where there is little direct sunlight but the source of the shade is quite high above the plants (such as a towering oak tree). This lofty canopy still allows considerable light into the garden area. Some people refer to this as indirect or reflected light.

Full shade: Solid, sunless shade such as that provided by a building or a dense overhang of foliage.

Checking below the Garden Room's Surface

You wouldn't consider buying a new car without first looking under the hood. Well, before you pick your garden site you need to look under the garden room's surface to see what lies below. Just as with a car, you don't want any hidden surprises.

If the potential site is next to large trees, you may have lots of roots to contend with as you build and maintain the garden. Small, shallow roots are more of an aggravation and tend to take more nutrients and moisture away from your plants than do deeper root systems. Some of the trees that are special troublemakers in this way include sycamores and Norway and red maples. You can dig these shallow roots out of a modest-sized garden without hurting the tree, but they will be back. Every couple of years you

will have to dig them out again—making the maintenance of a perennial garden somewhat more difficult. The ultimate solution, if the tree isn't valuable, is to cut it down. If the tree is valuable or is one that you'd rather not cut down, then you should plan a garden with plants that can tolerate drier soil and more shade and can survive the root competition they'll encounter from the tree. Examples of these sorts of resilient plants include barrenwort, fringed bleeding heart, and pachysandra.

If your soil is filled with rocks, you may want to find ways to avoid having to dig them up, such as building raised beds on top. (There may even be a way to incorporate the rocks into the garden design.) Problems with tree roots and rocks don't automatically eliminate a site within the room for a flower garden, but they are considerations you'll need to be aware of and be prepared to deal with.

While we will talk about soil in much more detail in Chapter 6, at this stage you need to get a general sense of the soil's condition in the garden room so you can pick the best location for the 60-Minute Flower Garden. Soil conditions can vary considerably within the same garden room. A low-lying section might be wet with bad drainage and a more elevated area might be dry but heavy with clay. Many of the most commonly grown flowers will do well in almost any soil, but for the best results the soil should be reasonably easy to work and well drained. If it doesn't quite measure up, it can always be improved. All you need to do now is determine what type of soil you have in each section of the garden room and make sure there aren't any major drainage problems, which can be caused by poor soil conditions.

It doesn't matter a great deal in the long run whether the garden site you select has a clay soil or a sandy soil, as long as your soil conditions are not in the extremes. As you'll see in Chapter 6, you can change the nature of your soil over time without too much trouble. Jeff feels that extremely sandy soil is easier to remedy than extremely clayey soil, although either problem can be solved. The issue in the beginning is simply how much work it is going to take right off to get your garden site in condition to plant.

The simplest technique for making a rough identification of soil type is to take a trowel or a shovel and dig a small hole 2 feet deep in soil that is moist but not soaking wet. This will give you an idea of how deep your topsoil is and how many rocks you are going to have to deal with. If the soil is hard and caked, you probably have a clay problem and will need to add some organic matter before you plant. If the soil appears to be loose and gritty and falls apart easily even when wet, your soil probably has too much sand in it. In this case, too, you'll have to add organic matter before you start your garden.

You may wonder at this point whether it's necessary to test the soil. We think a soil test can provide some very useful information that can help you later as you manage your garden, but it's not critical for making a decision on a garden site. Select the spot for your garden, then get the soil test as described in Chapter 6.

It's important to know about the drainage situation in the various parts of your garden room. Just like soil types, drainage conditions can vary throughout the relatively small area of a garden room. The simplest test for determining whether there's a drainage problem is to dig a hole about the size of a gallon pail and fill it with a gallon or so of water. Let the water drain out overnight and fill the hole with water again the next morning. The time it takes for this second addition of water to drain out will tell you what you want to know. If the water takes more than 8 to 10 hours to drain out of the hole the second time, you may have to take some steps to improve the drainage of the soil. If the problem isn't too severe, the addition of 1 to 2 inches of compost a year to the top 12 inches of soil can improve drainage.

However, if you are faced with a serious drainage problem on your prospective garden site, you have three choices. Putting the flower garden in that spot in the room anyway is not one of them. You can build a raised bed over the poorly draining soil; you can solve the drainage problem (which is potentially expensive, not to mention hard work); or you can find another site for your flower garden. Most flowers simply do not grow well in poorly draining soil, so it's not worth the effort to even try.

At this point you should have a pretty clear understanding of all the features, good and bad, in your garden room. This information will not only come in handy when you select a flower garden site, it will also be a big help when you plan that garden and pick the plants to go in it. However, before you get to the point where you're bringing in new plants, you need to look at the plants that are already in place in the garden room.

Checking the Existing Plants

Few people are going to start their flower gardens in a garden room that is currently devoid of plant life, unless they've just moved into a brand new house sitting on a bulldozed and barren site and surrounded by mud. Having existing trees, shrubs, and flowering plants on your flower garden site offers several possible advantages. Your flower gardening project will be much less expensive if you can incorporate plants already found on your property into the garden design. Also, your project is going to take less time when some of the garden is already in place.

If you have a flower garden site in mind that already contains some plants, you need to make some decisions. You have essentially four choices: leave a plant in its current position and build your garden around it; shift the plant to another spot in the garden room; move the plant to another location on your property; or dispose of it or give it away.

You may be wondering how feasible it is to move established plants around the yard. It's really quite impressive how easy it is to relocate them without causing any ill effects. In fact, when Charles was helping Liz and Jeff build their 60-Minute Flower Garden, Jeff accused Charles of being like the housewife in the cartoons who needed to move the sofa five different times to find the right spot in the living room. Jeff moved one azalea bush three times in two days before Charles was satisfied with the location. The bush survived nicely. (In Chapter 9 we'll give you pointers on how to transplant perennials, shrubs, and ground covers.)

At this point in assessing your room, don't be too concerned with the small plants such as the perennial and annual flowers, bulbs, and compact shrubs. Those can be moved easily and don't involve the time and energy that a large shrub like a rhododendron requires to be relocated even a few feet. We speak from experience when we say this. Last September we all spent the better part of an afternoon transferring a large rhododendron to a more desirable place on Jeff and Liz's property. Charles assured us that rhododendrons are easy to move because they have shallow root systems, but his definition of what was easy when you move a shrub that is 5 feet high and 4 feet wide was definitely not the same as Jeff's. The shrub did get moved, it has survived all the rough treatment and bad language, and it looks wonderful in its new home at the side of the house.

If the existing plants are mature trees and shrubs, don't decide to move them or get rid of them until you have fully explored their potential right where they are. Remember, you don't have to make all of these decisions in the first year. If you have a particularly large shrub that you aren't sure about, work around it for the first year and see what you think the next year.

Taking an Inventory

Your first task is to identify by common name all the plants (trees, shrubs, perennials, bulbs, and ground covers) you do have, both in your garden room and around the rest of your property, since you might use them in your flower garden. At this stage in your gardening experience, it isn't really necessary that you learn the scientific or botanical name (in Latin) of each plant, but it is important to know what it is and find out something about its characteristics.

If you are a complete neophyte in the plant identification business, one way to solve your inventory problem is to ask your gardening friends or neighbors. The previous owners of the house may also be a good source to ask. Be sure to confirm their identification in some good reference books, such as HP Books' *Annuals* and *Perennials* and, for trees and shrubs, *Know It and Grow It* (these and other books are listed under Recommended Reading in the Appendix). This way you can avoid some of the inadvertent mistakes people sometimes make in identifying plants. If you are really stumped by the identity of a particular plant, take a leaf or a twig to a local nursery; someone there may be willing to help you identify it and tell you about its growing habits. You might also want to try a local public garden or arboretum or the local garden club. In some areas agents from the Cooperative Extension Service (CES) will make house calls to answer gardeners' questions. (The CES is listed in the phone book under state or local government offices.)

Once all your plants have names, you need to take stock of their characteristics—especially those that pertain to your flower garden design. Since color is, after all, what the flower garden is all about, you want to find out as much as you can (from your own observations, from books, or from fellow gardeners) about the colors associated with the plants you already have on your property. Besides the obvious pastels of flowers, the yard's palette includes shades of green, brown, and gray that are found on perennial foliage plants, tree trunks, and dried grasses. To become familiar with the range of colors in your yard, find the answers to questions like these: What color are the perennial flowers and bulbs? When are they in bloom? Does the ground cover flower? What shade is its foliage? Are there any interesting markings? Does a particular shrub have blossoms and, if so, what color are they? Is the plant an evergreen or does it shed its leaves in the fall? Does the shrub have berries? What is their color? Do the tree's leaves change color in the fall?

You should also try to estimate an existing plant's stage of growth. Is it full grown or is it going to grow another 3 feet taller? You will need this information when you begin to plan your garden. Unless you can find out when it was planted, you'll have to settle for an educated guess. If a woody plant grew more than 6 inches this year, you can be fairly sure it is still growing its way to maturity. You'll need to take that fact into consideration if you decide to use that plant in your 60-Minute Flower Garden. (We give the sizes of mature flowering plants in the Appendix in the chart The Best Plants for the 60-Minute Flower Garden.)

Health Checkup

Confirming the good health of these existing plants is also very important. It makes no sense to plan a garden around a sick tree or shrub or to count on the presence of some perennials that are not growing well in that location. There are some simple clues that you can spot even though you're not a trained horticulturist. Of course, doing this health checkup in the summer when the leaves are out is easier than in the winter when most plants look bleak.

If you think a tree, shrub, or perennial flower is sick, get confirmation from someone who is more knowledgeable. Don't cut down the horse chestnut tree just because its leaves get brown around the edges in late summer—that is a common occurrence and doesn't hurt the tree at all. The set of criteria we provide here is simply to help you get started in reviewing the health of your plants.

Trees: Is the trunk solid or does it have wounds or rotten areas? Does it have a lot of dead branches in the top (dead branches in the middle are not so critical—they could just be the result of shading)? Unless the tree is defoliated, problems with the leaves are not generally lethal, but they still might need some attention.

Shrubs: Does the shrub have a lot of dead stems or stems that have been hacked back and don't look healthy? One good test is to see what you have left after removing all the dead stems; many shrubs rejuvenate from the base once the dead wood is removed. You can test a stem to determine whether it's living or dead by nicking the bark with a knife to see the layer of material directly under the bark. If it is green, the stem is alive; if it looks brown, the stem is dead. Foliage problems don't usually mean the plant is terminally ill. They can generally be treated and controlled once you've learned the cause of the problem.

Perennials: Do the plants seem to lack vigor? Have they died out in the center of the clump? These are signs of overcrowded perennials in need of division and rejuvenation. Leggy and straggly perennials aren't getting all the sun they need. They may have once been in the sun but with the growth of surrounding plants now languish in the shade. These need to be moved.

Do the Plants Fit into Your Plans?

Once you've identified the existing plants, learned about their color properties, and examined their overall health and vigor, you're ready to give them closer scrutiny to see how or even whether they'll fit into your garden plans. As you inventory the existing plants in your garden room, keep the following issues in mind.

Trees

A wrenching possibility is that a gorgeous tree may have to be sacrificed to permit the sun to shine on your garden room. While you can occasionally have flowers in a very shady area, most flowers prefer at least some sun. In a situation where you can't have both the flowers and the tree, you must decide whether you want the benefits of a sunny flower garden or the benefits of a tree and a shady garden.

If a tree is full grown and healthy, it is a very difficult decision to cut it down. There are certainly strong reasons to keep it. A tree makes a valuable addition to your property if it gives cooling shade next to the house, provides wind protection for the house, or screens out unpleasant street noise.

Trees that are still young are potentially valuable elements in a flower garden, especially if they don't create too much shade yet. Their flowers, foliage, and even the bark can be attractive features that complement the colors and textures in the garden. You might be able to keep an attractive young tree in the garden, at least for a few years, until other plants have time to grow and give scale and balance to the total view. At that point you have a choice: either move the tree to another site in the yard or cut it down.

Moving a tree or shrub that is more than 6 feet tall is a challenging and difficult task. It can be done if you have the proper tools, pick the correct season, and have a strong back. If you don't feel up to the task, you might be able to find a nursery that will move the tree for a reasonable fee. If the sole reason you're moving the tree is to put it in a more attractive spot in the garden, consider this: You can buy another tree and plant it in the desired location much more easily than you can move an existing one that is over 6 feet tall. In most cases, a tree that is not suitable for your flower garden is probably best cut down.

You should be aware that there are some trees that make bad neighbors for flower gardens. Earlier in the chapter we talked about the shallow-rooted sycamores and maples that can hinder the growth of neighboring plants. The black walnut is another tree to watch out for. The roots give off a powerful toxin that can stunt or wilt flowering plants like azaleas, lilacs, mountain laurel, and rhododendrons. You're probably better off giving black walnut trees a wide berth when locating your garden. Even if you cut down the tree, the roots will still remain and can potentially harm the plants in your garden.

Shrubs

Many people will want to put a flower garden along the front of the house, the same spot that is likely to be occupied by an assortment of shrubs. Shrubs, especially those that bloom, can become an asset in the flower garden design. But how can you tell which to keep and which to clear out to make way for the flowers?

The first thing to do is take a long, hard, objective look at them. Are they providing an attractive accent to the front of the home or do they block the view from the windows and overpower the balance of your home's design? If your shrubs don't measure up, there are two likely reasons: They've gotten too large or their natural shape may have been destroyed by pruning and crowding.

After a period of 15 to 20 years, shrubs planted close to a house, while still healthy, often have seriously overgrown the available space and need to be removed. At that age it is often best to replace a shrub rather than try to move it. However, any young, small, healthy shrub can be moved quite easily if you want to situate it in some other part of the garden room or garden site.

Years of pruning cause most shrubs to lose many of their natural characteristics and take on a uniform, somewhat unnatural, rounded shape. As we'll discuss in Chapter 9, hedge shears are not a very good tool

for pruning foundation plants in a flower garden. That type of drastic pruning usually suppresses some of the desirable aesthetic features of the shrub, including its colorful flowers and berries. A shrub like an azalea, flowering quince, honeysuckle, or forsythia that is used in a flower garden looks better if it has a more natural shape with some variety in its form.

As a rule of thumb, anytime you have to resort to heavy pruning to keep a shrub small enough to fit the available space, it's probably in the wrong spot. A shrub like that should be removed from the site of the flower garden. You can reduce the need for pruning by putting the right plant in the garden, one that will grow just tall enough and just wide enough and then continue to grow only very slowly. A shrub like this can be kept in the proper scale with light pruning with a hand pruning tool. Look at the shrubs included in the Gallery of Flower Garden Designs in Chapter 5 for examples of well-behaved shrubs for flower gardens.

If the shrub next to the house is so tall that it fully covers a window, remember

Inappropriate Shrubs:
These shrubs are prime examples of ones that have grown too large and as a result overpower the house. It's best to remove overgrown shrubs like these and replace them with smaller, more compact varieties that can be integrated into a flower garden design.

that it will block your view of the flower garden from the inside. Your first inclination may be to cut it back to clear the window. But few overgrown shrubs will look decent when severely pruned back to a more acceptable scale. They will take two to three years to begin to look good again. You're much better off replacing the shrub with a more compact one.

Flowers

What if your garden room already contains some flowers, but they're not in the spot you're favoring for your 60-Minute Flower Garden? Or perhaps they're already growing in the site you're considering, but you're afraid that in their present location they might not fit into the garden design. Don't worry; most flowers can be moved with no harm to their blooming ability.

Annual flowers in a garden site aren't a serious concern in this initial inventory. Since they're good for only one season, these "temporary" garden plants can be easily replaced or transplanted during the current year. Perennials are generally easy to transplant, so don't worry too much about them either, although you should keep track of what you have. Jeff and Liz have some very common daylilies that are perfectly healthy but are not the most beautiful lilies around. However, they have been in the family for five generations, so those lilies will always have a spot in the Ball flower garden.

If a perennial such as a daylily or iris is more than three or four years old, it can start to lose its vigor and bloom less prolifically. That doesn't mean you should discard it and plant a new one. Rejuvenation is as simple as dividing the root mass and replanting. (Chapter 9 will give you more pointers on how to do this.) Liz has been keeping the neighborhood supplied with irises for years. A short-lived perennial like a delphinium,

on the other hand, needs to be replaced every two or three years.

Most of us are real softies when it comes to throwing a plant away, but sometimes it may be necessary. If you have inherited an existing garden, the chances are good that there are some plants there that aren't really suited for that site's soil or light conditions. Or maybe there are some varieties that you simply don't like. Those are the plants that should go. In that same garden there may be others that are particularly suited for that spot and have thrived there for many years. If they look pretty and you like them, then for goodness sake keep them to use in your new 60-Minute Flower Garden.

Ground Covers

If there is some ground cover on your site already, you'll probably have to move all or some of it in the course of preparing the garden. Don't discard the ground cover, since it can provide some valuable (and free) material to use elsewhere in the garden room. Except for ivy, most ground covers, such as pachysandra, periwinkle, and hosta, are easy to transplant.

Selecting the Final Flower Garden Site

By now you should be able to locate your 60-Minute Flower Garden within your garden room. Our advice is to select a site that is between 100 and 200 square feet in total area. Using that range of dimensions, you can identify the rough boundaries of your flower garden.

While we want to give you these dimensions as a guideline to get started, you should be aware that there are some factors that may make your garden larger or smaller than 100 to 200 square feet. The size of the

SIZING UP THE GARDEN SITE

When you're house-hunting, there are certain features you look for that you know will make your life easier. For instance, you look at very practical things like the number of electrical outlets, how many closets there are, and how close the house is to work and school.

Searching a garden room for a good garden site calls for the same very practical attitude. You can have the prettiest flower garden on the block, but if it is inconvenient to take care of, your garden will probably be seeded back to lawn by next year. Here are a few features to consider when sizing up a garden site.

• Is there ready access to a water source? This is especially important if you'll be using a drip irrigation system.

• How close is the room to the compost pile? Or, in other words, how far do you have to travel to bring the compost to the flower garden?

• Is there enough room to bring wheelbarrows and garden carts of compost and mulch right to the garden? If space is tight, be prepared to make frequent trips with smaller conveyances like buckets, plastic bags, and bushel baskets.

• Will you need a border to keep the garden in bounds? Many people prefer to use an edging of bricks or stones to cleanly separate garden from lawn. When laid flush with the ground, these edgings eliminate the need for hand trimming, since the lawn mower can come all the way to the edge of the bed. Charles likes to keep his border stones about ¼ to ½ inch above the soil level to help keep the grass off the stones yet still allow the mower to ride over them. If you decide you want to provide some sort of edging, don't forget to include that treatment in the planning and developing of your garden. The same goes for sidewalks and patios. We have listed under Recommended Reading a number of excellent references for lots of creative and easily constructed features.

site and the type of garden you plan are interrelated. The space available in the garden room will have some influence on the type of flower garden you can plan. Some flower gardens need more space than others. If you have only 100 square feet for a garden, you can't realistically expect to create a Woodland Garden, which takes 200 to 300 square feet.

However, if there are no space limitations, the type of garden you have in mind will determine how much room to allow for the garden site. In Chapter 3 we will tell you how much space each type of flower garden requires. Most of them will fit within a 100- to 200-square-foot area.

This is the point in the garden planning process where the landscape architects and the horticulturists we discussed in the Introduction part company. Up to this point in the book we've been in the landscape architect's domain, where you view your yard as a whole and then analyze specific features in it. Now we'll adopt the horticulturist's point of view, so the site for your flower garden will be the focus of attention for the rest of the book. The other elements of your garden room, the ones that make up the "big picture" (lawn, trees, other shrubs, sidewalks, and so on), are left for the landscape architect. In the Recommended Reading list at the end of the book we give you several references for landscaping. You might wish to review these if you're interested in remodeling the whole garden room in which you're building your 60-Minute Flower Garden.

Making a Sketch of the Garden Site

A sketch or map of your site, while it isn't absolutely essential to planning an attractive flower garden, is still extremely helpful for a number of reasons. A sketch allows you to play with different arrangements or ideas without having to lift a single shovelful of dirt. Best of all, mistakes are easy to erase. A map also helps you keep track of what you have in your garden and where it is located.

Graph paper is handy for the map of your site, but make sure you use the kind that can be copied on a copy machine. By assigning a set number of squares to equal the length of 1 foot of garden, you can keep the sketch pretty much in scale. Make your sketch as large as the paper will allow so you have room to work. The scale of either two or four squares per foot is usually about right.

The sketch is easier to make if you have done a good job of measuring your site with a tape measure or yardstick. Your drawing doesn't have to look like it was done by a landscape architect, but if it is to be of any value to you later, it should be as accurate as you can make it. First draw a thick outline of the site without any of the plants in place and make some copies to work with. Then sketch in the existing plants, the northerly orientation, and any shady areas of which you're aware. Now you're ready to make copies of this master sketch and use them to play around with design ideas that we discuss in Chapters 4 and 5. Having extra copies is important because, if your experience is anything like ours, you'll be adding information as you are actually planting, and it is impossible to keep water, mud, or coffee from splattering all over your working sketch.

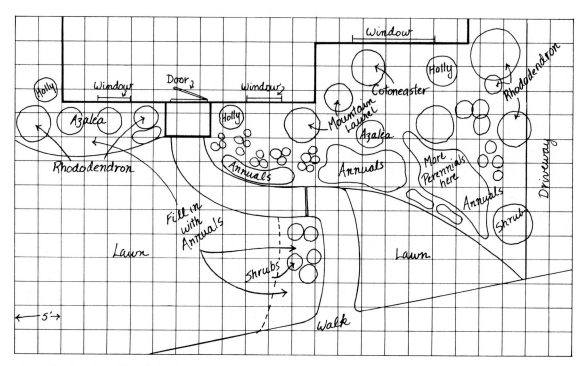

Sample Garden Sketch: *Refine your garden design on paper before you dig and plant, and you'll save yourself from some potentially costly and time-consuming mistakes. Your garden sketch doesn't have to be a work of art; it just has to be clear enough to keep track of what you're going to plant and where it will be located.*

Chapter 3

Choosing a Garden Model

Now that you've selected your garden site, we know you're probably itching to turn to those gorgeous flower catalogs and start the delightful process of choosing among pink-blushed peonies, bronzed-gold daylilies, and all the other wonderful flowers that beckon to you. We urge you to be patient and spend just a few minutes more doing some preliminary planning for your flower garden. Between the crucial steps of choosing the garden location and drawing up a detailed garden plan there is a very basic decision you must make: What type of flower garden do you want?

In this chapter we present five different basic "models" to give you some inspiration, such as a Woodland Garden, a Bank or Rock Garden, or a Decorative Home Garden. Each of these basic garden types has a set of characteristics that give it an identity and influence how you'll plan your garden and which plants you'll select for it. If all this sounds like you'll have no opportunity to exercise your creativity, don't worry. Through your choice of specific flowers and colors and their placement, you personalize these models and make a flower garden design that is truly your own.

Your choice of a garden model will affect how much time you spend keeping the finished garden in good shape. Some types of gardens take less time than others—and remember, none of the gardens in our book needs more than 60 minutes of maintenance a week. This chapter gives you a breakdown of all the tasks that need to be done in a flower garden and how much time you can expect to spend on them. We've also tried to give you a way to make some cost estimates so you'll have an idea of how much you'll spend on your garden.

Basic 60-Minute Flower Garden Models

Because we're working on the assumption that you have limited time and limited space to devote to a garden, the specific type of flower garden you choose should be adaptable to its environment and surroundings in order to minimize the time and effort it takes to prepare it. You must also consider the style and scale of your house so you can select a flower garden that will enhance your home's overall look. Do you want to create a formal impression or are you inclined toward an informal look for your property? A "formal" yard is one with lots of neat, straight lines and a balanced, symmetical layout. Most of the yards in front of American suburban homes have an informal design, with curved lines and assymetrical layouts. The way you decorate the interior of your home can also give you a clue. If your taste in decor is informal, then it's likely that you'll favor the same informal look outside. Once you've determined the style that suits your taste, browse through the next few pages to get an idea of the types of flower gardens that are available to fill in that site you have selected in the garden room.

We think that flower gardens can be grouped into three broad categories— decorative gardens, natural or wild gardens, and specialty gardens. Within these categories we've identified five different flower garden models you can consider as the starting point for your own particular plan. Some are easier than others to develop and maintain. We'll point out those differences as we take you for a tour of these flower gardens.

The chart Matching Flower Garden Models with Garden Rooms shows the relationship among the four functions garden rooms can serve (which were discussed in Chapter 2) and the five garden models we are about to describe. As you can see, some garden models aren't really appropriate for some of the garden rooms. For example, a Decorative Home Garden is probably not an appropriate choice for a garden room intended to be a strolling area. You would need to create such a large Decorative Home Garden to effectively fill the space in the garden room that you would easily exceed the 60-minute-a-week time limit on upkeep. Of course, if you have unlimited time, unlimited space, and a fair amount of money to spend, you can have almost any type of garden you want, tailored to fit any of the garden rooms. Our point here is that when you begin to limit the time and space you have available for a flower garden, some garden models are not going to be appropriate for certain garden rooms.

MATCHING FLOWER GARDEN MODELS WITH GARDEN ROOMS

	FUNCTION OF GARDEN ROOM			
GARDEN MODEL	Attractive View	Outside Living Area	Strolling Area	Attractive to Wildlife
Decorative Home Garden	Yes	Yes	No	Yes
Herbaceous Flower Border	Yes	Yes	No	Yes
Woodland Garden	Yes	No	Yes	Yes
Meadow Garden	Yes	No	Yes	Yes
Bank Garden	Yes	Yes	Yes	No

Decorative Home Garden

As we said in the Introduction, American homes, especially those in the suburbs, often have broad expanses of lawn with shrubbery and trees located in groups around the property. We have designed a 60-Minute Flower Garden to fit comfortably into that uniquely American landscape style, and we're calling it the Decorative Home Garden. This informal garden utilizes a mixture of shrubs and foliage plants and a pleasing assortment of flowers to give it color. As we see it, the Decorative Home Garden is the natural extension of the English "mixed border" flower garden, which focuses on the flowers but includes some shrubs and other plants. We believe that this Americanized version will fit quite nicely into the landscapes of over half the homes in this country.

The beauty of the Decorative Home Garden isn't measured simply by the number of different flower blossoms it displays but rather by the appealing combination of all the colors and textures of the shrubs, perennials, and annuals within its borders. Properly planned, the Decorative Home Garden gives the illusion of a profusion of flowers without the time-demanding requirements that come with keeping many flowers constantly in bloom. The Decorative Home Garden *is* a flower garden, but one with some special features that add to its good looks and subtract from its maintenance time. These special features are the shrubs and foliage plants that complement and enhance the flowers.

The collective colors, shapes, and textures presented by leaves, grasses, ground covers, bark, and berries have an ornamental value equal to that of the flowers. The color illustrations of sample Decorative Home Gardens on pages 86 through 89 give an example of how it's possible to achieve a rich mixture of colors and textures without relying entirely on flowers. Notice the variation in foliage colors from shades of yellow-

Springtime Decorative Home Garden: *Early-blooming bulbs adorn this flower garden in spring. As the tree leafs out and the sunlight that reaches the garden bed is reduced, shade-tolerant perennials will take over from the fading bulbs and provide attractive flowers and foliage. This garden is a season old and hasn't yet taken on the look of a mature, finished Decorative Home Garden.*

green to muted, pale green to deep emerald green. Look beyond the color to see the variety of pleasing shapes and textures, from smooth, broad leaves to spiky, grasslike foliage to soft, fluffy mounds of delicate leaves.

This diversity of plant material gives aesthetic interest to the Decorative Home Garden all year long, even in the middle of winter, a time when most flower gardens cease to look attractive. We feel very strongly that the mixtures of these colors, shapes, and textures, produced as much by foliage as by flowers, are especially valuable when you're limited by time and space in the flower garden.

We're certain that this flower garden will fit the amounts of space and time most people have available. Our Decorative Home Garden is planned for the normal-sized suburban or urban lot. For this garden we recommend an area of 100 to 200 square feet to stay within the 60-minute work limit each week. This garden model has definite limits in terms of size, scale, numbers of plants that can be used, and the time the gardener has to spend on maintenance. One nice feature is that you can incorporate shrubs already on the site into the design (that means fewer plants to buy and less time spent planting to fill the area). Another pleasant benefit is that this garden will reduce the size of the lawn (good news for the family member in charge of cutting the grass).

There are actually two types of Decorative Home Gardens—a sunny one and a shady one. In a sunny garden you can rely more on flowers to supply the bright color. There are more colorful flowering plants that need sun than there are colorful plants that tolerate shade. In a shady garden you'll need to call upon other plants in addition to flowers to create a colorful and striking effect. A shady garden can be just as interesting as any sunny garden you've ever seen; it is just a matter of selecting those plants that thrive in the shade.

We suspect that most people just getting started in flower gardening will choose to plan a 60-Minute Decorative Home Garden for the front of their house because that's the spot where the garden can be admired the most—by you and by other people. No matter where you decide to put it, this is a flower garden that adapts well to different garden rooms, as you can see in the chart at the beginning of the chapter. You can design a Decorative Home Garden to create an attractive view, to complement an outdoor living space, and even to attract some wildlife (at least birds). It isn't really appropriate for enhancing a strolling area, as we said earlier, because of its size limitations. However, before you agree with us and decide to build a Decorative Home Garden, let's look at your other options for garden models just to be sure you've made the right decision.

Herbaceous Flower Border

To understand the main characteristic of this flower garden you need to know that herbaceous means having no woody tissue. A daisy is a herbaceous plant; an azalea is not. A herbaceous border will be limited to perennial and annual foliage and flowering plants (including bulbs). It will not have any shrubs. This Herbaceous Flower Border is a classic flower garden that might contain airy sprays of baby's breath and coral bells, solid masses of snapdragons, bee balm, and salvia, bold single blossoms of daylilies and dahlias, and spikes of foxglove in all color combinations imaginable. (Take a look at the color illustrations of three sample borders on pages 90 through 94.)

There are several reasons why you might consider developing a Herbaceous Flower Border. If you're a bit pressed for space in your garden room and can only accommodate a garden that is 4 feet wide or smaller, then it is probably best not to include shrubs in your plan, since they would take up too much space in that situation. Herbaceous plants would be much better suited to your confined space. Or you may wish to split the 60-Minute Flower Garden into two different spots in the garden room, which might preclude the effective use of shrubs.

Unlike the Decorative Home Garden, you are more concerned here with planning your flower groups so there are blossoms during each month of the growing season, giving you color in your garden at all times. While the border can be as narrow as 3 feet, we recommend a 4- to 6-foot width so that a more interesting range of plants can be included, with higher plants in the back of the border and lower varieties in the front. If you do opt for a 6-foot border, remember to incorporate strategically placed stepping stones in your garden design. These will allow you to get into the flower bed to work without compacting the soil or crushing plants underfoot.

The Herbaceous Flower Border usually has some kind of physical background such as a fence, a wall, or some taller shrubs. Unlike the Decorative Home Garden, in this case the background shrubs will not be integrated into the garden design but will serve simply as a backdrop to the flower garden. You plan your Herbaceous Flower Border as if the shrubs aren't even there. This type of garden, like the Decorative Home Garden, lends itself well to the front of the house, where many people already have shrubs planted.

The traditional Herbaceous Flower Border filled with lots of flowers generally needs full sun, and for the full effect you will need at least a half day of good sun. But it is also possible to have a very nice herbaceous border, with blossoms throughout the season, in a shady spot—the key is to select the right types of plants. In Chapter 5 we'll show you how to select the proper plants for the amount of sun you actually have, so you can create a glorious border.

The flowers are, of course, the most important part of the herbaceous border, but the multiseason success of this type of flower garden depends upon a good array of attractive foliage to set off the blossoms. Some perennials, such as peonies, have good foliage that lasts long after their flowers have faded, and this enhances adjacent flowers later in the season. We'll show you how to achieve this balance between flowers and foliage in Chapter 5.

Natural Flower Gardens

If you prefer a more informal, naturalistic setting for your home, you might consider one of the three types of natural gardens. A natural flower garden is one where the plants grow in a relatively unstructured design, much the way you find flowers growing in the woods or in a field. This does *not* mean the garden is ignored and allowed to grow into an unkempt tangle. And it doesn't necessarily mean that your selection of plants is limited to what are referred to as native plants (a native plant is one that has originated in this country, like the foam flower or lady fern). What we do mean by a natural flower garden is one with a natural theme such as a woodland garden, a meadow garden, or a wildlife habitat garden. A natural flower garden can be designed to create an attractive view, it can become a strolling area, and of course it can be planned to attract wildlife. Its large size, its layout, and the kinds of plants that grow in it make it less suitable as an outside living area.

The natural flower garden is usually not built close to the house, as this is where most people prefer a little more formal appearance. Depending on the size of your project, you can develop a large natural flower garden in steps over a four- or five-year period, setting aside 60 minutes a week to slowly develop this larger project.

While natural flower gardens tend to be larger than Decorative Home Gardens, their basic planning principles are similar; you'll have the taller plants in the back of the garden and lower-growing mixed shrubs and perennials toward the front.

Woodland Garden

This is the type of natural flower garden you would consider if you had to contend with a great deal of shade, since many of the plants in it are tolerant of low light. Adding a Woodland Garden to your yard is also a good way to reduce the amount of lawn you must mow. This garden model can help you deal with "difficult" areas on your property that have dips, surface roots from trees, embedded rocks, tree stumps, and other less-than-perfect features. A Woodland Garden creates a pleasing scene that turns these "problems" into elements that have a positive value in the garden design. (See page 95 for a color illustration of a Woodland Garden.)

What sorts of plants would you find in this natural flower garden? A small Woodland Garden would use massed shrubs such as rhododendrons, lots of ground covers like vinca or pachysandra, and various woodland flowers for accents and color, such as trilliums, columbines, Virginia bluebells, and bloodroot. Most of the flower color in this garden will appear in the spring, but the handsome foliage of many shade plants, such as hostas, astilbes, lilies-of-the-valley, and ferns, will keep the garden attractive through the summer. You can add color accents through the season with some flowering annuals like impatiens and wishbone flowers.

The Woodland Garden is a very low-maintenance garden that is kept neat rather than manicured to stay attractive. A 60-Minute Woodland Garden would probably be from 200 to 300 square feet, at least in the beginning. As you grow more familiar with the woodland plants and give more thought to what you want to do with the area, you could eventually expand your small patch to cover 1,000 square feet. A Wood-

Woodland Garden in the Making: This bed in a Woodland Garden is still in its early, formative stage. The gardener has edged the area with Belgian block and is in the process of adding small shrubs, ground covers, and woodland flowers.

Mature Woodland Garden: *A Woodland Garden that's had a chance to become established has a delightfully natural, "unplanned" look. This type of garden is a perfect way to fill a shady spot or deal with a problem area that has rocks, tree stumps, or other less-than-perfect features.*

land Garden can be integrated smoothly into a lawn area by bordering it with natural stones or a ground cover such as pachysandra.

Meadow Garden

A meadow or wildflower garden is a relatively new form of flower garden and is sometimes called a prairie garden or a wild-flower lawn. This form of natural flower garden is best described as a fairly large, open area where flowers are allowed to grow naturally in among tall grasses, giving a country look to your property. Some favorite flowers for the Meadow Garden include black-eyed Susans, Mexican hats, lupines, goldenrod, and asters. Even spring bulbs like daffodils and crocuses can be tucked in to create a burst of color during that difficult time when we are not sure winter is really over yet. The mass effect of meadow garden plant-

ings can be quite striking, but not everyone appreciates the somewhat wild appearance.

Charles and his family have a fairly large Meadow Garden across the entire back line of their property, which runs along a little creek. The backyards of four neighbors abut the length of the garden, so Charles was mindful of their opinions when he began meadow gardening there some years ago. In the beginning, the neighbors weren't opposed to the idea but took a wait-and-see attitude. Over time they have become enamoured of the shifting effects of the Meadow Garden through the seasons.

A 60-Minute Meadow Garden can be as large as 1,000 to 2,000 square feet and still be maintained within the 1-hour-a-week limit. This size is possible because once the soil is prepared and the seeds are planted, weeding is seldom necessary, maintenance is modest, and little watering is required. It is possible to have an attractive Meadow Garden that is smaller, but if you have much less than 500 square feet, it will be difficult to achieve the complete meadow effect. No matter what the size, the Meadow Garden needs full or at least partial sun.

This Meadow Garden is similar to the gardens that have received some national attention—but with an important difference. In a few communities residents have let their front lawns grow wild and have been arrested for disobeying local lawn-mowing ordinances. The 60-Minute Meadow Garden is not a haphazard and potentially unsightly project where you simply stop mowing your lawn. It requires planning and preparation just as the other types of flower gardens do. You should have little problem with the neighbors and the local government if you develop the Meadow Garden as suggested in this book. At the same time, it is important to check with your local government to ensure that there are no ordinances prohibiting such a garden.

People who aren't sure whether the meadow effect is for them can start out with a small area (more of a wildflower border) to see how they like the idea and later expand that area to achieve the full effect. One option is to stop mowing the outer edges of parts or all of your property and develop a Meadow Garden using the techniques described in Chapter 9 under Planting and Managing a Meadow Garden. When properly planned, a Meadow Garden can be a very attractive adjunct to a suburban home, adding just a bit of wildness to its very tame setting.

Bank Garden

A bank or rock garden, as we define it, is a specialty garden located on a sharp hill or bank that is not conducive to a more traditional garden design. We are talking here about a bank or hill that is so steep it's nearly impossible to mow the grass. Trying to cover it with regular garden flowers won't work either, because of erosion problems. Many people blanket these banks with a ground cover such as ivy or pachysandra. We suggest a new approach—a revised version of the traditional rock garden that we're calling a Bank Garden.

Rock gardens try to imitate a high mountain environment with its stunted and smaller plants growing in well-drained soil full of granulated stone and organic matter. This soil is found in crevices between large rocks. True rock garden enthusiasts spend a great deal of their time locating special plants that are either miniatures or smaller versions of more common plants that will fit into the small scale of a traditional rock garden. The rocks in the garden are there to simulate the general appearance of the terrain of the higher mountain elevations. Traditional rock gardens often contain a large number of alpine plants that are generally difficult to grow at the lower elevations in which most of us garden.

We designed the Bank Garden to solve some of the problems that come with a steeply sloping piece of property; it will hold the soil in place and take very little time and effort to maintain. We also wanted this garden to give you the charming effect of a rock garden. With the pointers we provide in Chapter 5 you'll be able to create a natural-looking rock outcropping on your slope that will serve as the foundation for an eye-catching garden filled with an interesting mix of pastel and bolder-colored plants.

What we have done with our Bank Garden is to take some of the plants commonly grown in rock gardens, add some plants popular in other flower gardens, and combine them in such a way that they'll grow in that problem area where it is generally very difficult to cultivate a "normal" flower garden or a lawn. In the sample Bank Garden plan in the Gallery of Flower Garden Designs in Chapter 5 you'll see that we've taken such traditional rock garden plants as hen-and-chickens and added Michaelmas daisies, which are not normally found in the traditional rock garden. These new additions are easy to grow, easy to locate at the local nursery, and work well with the more modest scale and size of the traditional rock garden specimens.

The 60-Minute Bank Garden will tend to be somewhat smaller than the Decorative Home Garden or the Herbaceous Flower Border. A Bank Garden will probably be anywhere from 50 to 100 square feet in area. In the sample design in Chapter 5, roughly half the garden area is taken up by large stones that are embedded into the bank.

Taking Time to Garden

The time it takes to tend a flower garden is often the concern that keeps many of us from getting into gardening in the first place. While many devotees spend many hours every week in their flower gardens and enjoy the puttering that gives them splendid results, we are stating firmly that you too can have a beautiful flower garden in your yard that will be the envy of the neighborhood and will take you no more than 60 minutes a week to maintain. It is the development time or the construction time that is difficult to predict, since there are so many variables to consider. If major grading changes are necessary, if some large shrubs need to be moved, and if you intend to build a stone wall in the front of the garden, you can expect to spend more than one weekend building your 60-Minute Flower Garden.

Time to Develop the Garden

Every gardener is going to have a different situation in terms of how much effort he must spend in developing his 60-Minute

Flower Garden. But there is a basic set of tasks that most gardeners face when building a flower garden from scratch. Here is a list of the eight general steps, broken down by season.

Tasks Best Done in the Fall

- Design the garden and draw up a plan.
- Grade the garden room.
- Prepare the soil in the garden site.
- Transplant existing plants within the garden site or relocate them outside the site.
- Collect and lay down the initial mulch.

Tasks Best Done in the Spring

- Acquire and lay out the drip irrigation system.
- Acquire new plants.
- Add new plants to the garden.

This development process can be spread out over a period of months or even a year to avoid a back-breaking, all-or-nothing six days of hard labor in the fall. For instance, if the grading of the garden room is going to be a demanding 3- or 4-hour job, break it down into smaller chunks of time and work on it over a period of weeks. If you do adopt this slow and steady routine of garden preparation, then you must be patient about how soon you will be picking your first flowers. In our opinion, it's better to spread the garden development process over a whole year if that's what it takes to develop a garden that you'll be able to enjoy for years to come. There's no point in working like a maniac for three straight weekends only to give up before you complete the job because you can't afford to spend that kind of time.

Time for Garden Maintenance

The secret to managing a low-maintenance garden is built into each garden model's basic plan. If you have a flower garden that has a drip irrigation system, receives lots of compost each spring, and is protected by sufficient mulch, your maintenance tasks are minimized. This kind of garden doesn't need constant fertilizing because of the spring application of nutrient-rich compost. It doesn't take any time to water, since the drip irrigation system can be set to run automatically. It has very few weeds, if any, because of the mulch. And finally, if you follow our suggestions and select plants with low-maintenance qualities, the flowers in your garden will need little attention.

Tending an established flower garden involves about ten tasks that take variable amounts of time during the growing sea-son. Remember, we are talking here about a garden that has been properly planned and developed, probably during the previous year.

Basic Garden Maintenance

Soil preparation: This might take you about 1 to 2 hours in the early spring, spread over two weekends.

Planting: This task will vary with the type of garden you build. If you have a standard 60-Minute Decorative Home Garden, you will spend 4 or 5 hours a year putting in annuals and maybe transplanting a few plants. This will be spread throughout the spring and summer seasons.

Weeding: If you've mulched your garden properly, you shouldn't spend much more than an hour a year with this boring task. The odd weed that beats the mulch can

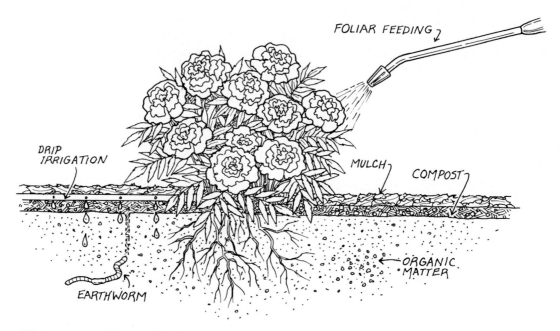

Low-Maintenance Flower Garden: A flower garden that needs only 1 hour of care a week is possible when you incorporate these features: a drip irrigation system; mulch; compost and a seasonal soil care plan that adds lots of organic matter; earthworms; foliar feedings; and flowers with low-maintenance qualities.

be pulled in a jiffy as you pass by.

Watering and feeding: Assuming you have a drip irrigation system with a timer built in, watering will take about an hour for the whole year—just turn it on and walk away. If you feel you need to fertilize your flowers over and above the compost and rock powders you apply in the spring, this should not take you more than 1 or 2 additional hours during the growing season.

Staking: While we recommend that you keep the number of plants that need staking to a minimum in your 60-Minute Flower Garden, there are bound to be a few that need support. This task won't take more than 1 or 2 hours a year at most.

Dividing perennials: This is a task that occurs only every two to five years, depending on the type of plant. If we prorate that time over the years, it will take you about 2 to 3 hours a year on the average.

Mulching: You will spend 1 or 2 hours laying out your mulch in the late spring or early summer and then you may wish to supplement that layer with another for winter protection in the late fall. Total time: about 3 to 4 hours.

Dead-heading: This task involves picking off the wilted remains of blossoms (which contributes to having more blossoms for a longer time throughout the season). It's difficult to set any kind of time estimate on this task, since it depends entirely on what kinds of flowers you have in your garden. Most gardeners find they do this as they walk by or when they are showing their garden to guests. Maybe you'll spend a whole hour throughout the growing season. It is an important task but not terribly time-consuming.

Pest and disease control: If you follow good preventive gardening practices as described in Chapter 8, your pest and disease problems should be minimal. Even if you have some problems, you should be able to manage them in 2 or 3 hours throughout the growing season.

Fall cleanup and sanitation: This is an important job for two reasons. It contributes greatly to the general good health of your garden (by reducing disease and pest potential), and it saves you time in the spring. If you spend 2 to 3 hours in the late fall cleaning up the garden, adding the winter mulch, pruning dead branches, and generally getting your plants ready for winter, you will have fewer problems and less work next year.

Grand total for the year: If you add up all the time we estimated for each maintenance task, you will be spending an average of 19 to 26 hours a year. Most people in the United States live in climates where they can work in their gardens at least 25 weeks of the year, and 30 to 35 weeks of gardening time is common. In southeastern Pennsylvania, Charles and Jeff begin puttering around the first week in March and put their gardens to bed for the winter sometime in early November, giving them about 35 weeks of gardening time. If it takes 20 hours to maintain a 60-Minute Flower Garden in southeastern Pennsylvania, then we are talking about taking care of our garden with only 40 minutes a week on the average. You really can do it all in 60 minutes a week!

To give you an example, we contend that a 200-square-foot Decorative Home Garden, planned as we suggest in Chapter 5, should not take more than 25 to 40 minutes a week to maintain in good shape in most parts of the country, once it has been built and become established. In the first year you'll take more time to do things because you're just learning the ropes. So during that first year we suspect it will take you 60 minutes a week on the average. Even in later years there may be a few weeks in the spring and in the fall that will require 60 minutes or so, but generally a properly planned 60-Minute Flower Garden should take less time, not more time, each year to manage.

TIME ESTIMATES FOR TENDING THE BASIC GARDEN MODELS*

GARDEN MODEL	HOURS A YEAR FOR MAINTENANCE
Decorative Home Garden	30 hours
Herbaceous Flower Border	40 hours
Woodland Garden	10 hours
Meadow Garden	8 hours
Bank Garden	40-50 hours

*Using sizes given for sample gardens in Chapter 5.

Cost of the 60-Minute Flower Garden

It is impossible to give a firm estimate of the costs for any of the 60-Minute Flower Garden models. The best we can do is to give you some ballpark figures and some general guidelines to help you estimate the sort of expenses you can expect.

If you use shrubs and other foundation plants that are already available on your property and buy only a few perennials and annuals to fill in the empty spots, you might be able to build a 200-square-foot Decorative Home Garden for under $100. On the other hand, if you start from scratch and purchase prime, full-grown shrubs and exotic flowers and foliage plants, you can spend $1,000 for just 100 square feet of Decorative Home Garden.

The cost of the garden goes up with the age of the plants you buy. Shrubs will cost more than perennials and perennials tend to cost more than annuals. A quick method for calculating the approximate cost of your plants is to use the going price of a common indicator shrub, perennial, annual, and bulb at your local nursery or in a quality catalog. These indicator plants could be a small aza-lea, an astilbe, an ageratum, and a tulip bulb. After checking the price of each of these plants, multiply the price by the number of shrubs, perennials, annuals, and bulbs you have planned for the garden. Total the four numbers and you have a rough idea of how much the bill for the whole garden will be.

FREE PLANTS FOR THE TAKING

In this book we tell you lots of ways to save time in the garden. Here are some helpful suggestions on how to save money as well. The best way to cut costs is to find sources of healthy plants that are free for the taking.

Tell fellow gardeners you're willing to take any perennials or bulbs they're dividing or separating in their gardens. These plants will be available in early spring or fall.

Charles always tries to root extra cuttings of plants like fuchsias so he is assured of getting at least one good specimen for himself. Of course, this means he must then find homes for his extras. This ultimately leads to his receiving gifts of new plants in return for those he's placing in foster gardens. This custom generates a very pleasant circle of bartering.

Chapter 4

Starting Your Flower Garden Design

Now you're at the point in planning the 60-Minute Flower Garden that is similar to the stage in remodeling the living room where you have refinished the floors and replastered the ceiling and are now ready to select wallpaper, carpet, and furniture. This is the time when you begin to wonder: "Where do I start? Are there any rules to guide me? How will I know which plants to select and how to arrange them in the garden?"

The best way to answer those questions is to follow the lead of professional garden designers. As a starting point, they use a few simple design principles for laying out the garden. Then within that basic garden layout they select the appropriate plants that will create the right effect and color scheme. Everyone who goes through the planning process will come up with a slightly different collection of plants, because we all have slightly different preferences and styles. There are principles or guidelines to help you, but no hard-and-fast rules for planning a flower garden.

Organizing the Flower Garden

In this chapter we are going to give you a summary of these garden structure principles. Try not to make your final plant selection until you've had a chance to read this chapter. We've simplified these flower garden planning principles as much as we can. Our intent is to have them serve as guidelines, without becoming intrusive or overpowering, as you make your final plant selections with the help of our suggestions in Chapter 5. First we'll give you some general principles for the overall design of the garden and then we'll provide some guidelines for selecting the perennials, bulbs, annuals, and shrubs for your 60-Minute Flower Garden. We should note here that most of these guidelines apply primarily to the Decorative Home Garden and the Herbaceous Flower Border that we described in the last chapter. These are the most common types of flower gardens, and they have very similar planning principles. While many of the

37

principles outlined in this chapter also apply to the Woodland, Meadow, and Bank gardens, these specialized gardens often have specialized planning principles. It's beyond the scope of our book to go into detail on the design requirements for these gardens. Instead, we suggest that you consult the Recommended Reading list in the Appendix, where you'll find books that focus on those types of gardens.

We believe that you can follow the principles presented in this chapter fairly closely and be confident that your garden will be attractive and easy to manage. At the same time, if you have an idea that seems to detour from one of these planning guidelines, by all means try it out—it might be fantastic. It is very difficult to plan a flower garden that is ugly! Some gardens are just prettier than others, and you must keep reminding yourself that if you don't like something this year, you can always change it next year. So here are some ideas for you to consider before you put the final decisions down on paper, based on our guidelines in Chapter 5.

Tall to Short, Background to Foreground

You'll have a much more attractive flower garden if you use tall plants in the back, fill in the middle ground with medium-sized plants, and then use shorter plants in the front. This approach creates an effect of depth and a sense of three dimensions that a garden with plants all of equal height doesn't have. This approach will also show off your smaller plants to their greatest advantage since they aren't buried out of sight among taller plants.

We do not mean that you should line up all your tall plants along the back like soldiers, with strict, even, military lines. As you will see in the sample plans in the Gallery of Flower Garden Designs at the end of

Chapter 5, you can vary the height of plants in gradual stages throughout the garden, avoiding what is called a step profile. This unattractive profile looks like the uniform, even, three levels of steps leading up to a porch. If you're new at flower gardening, it might be a little tricky to create a pleasing integration of heights on your first attempt. As you gain experience and become more familiar with plants' growing habits, you'll be able to develop a more subtle blending of heights. Just remember that you will not go wrong if your garden gives the general impression of being tall in the back, medium in the middle, and short up front.

Draw and Plant from Back to Front

We suggest you draw your plan on paper from back to front. Put your larger plants into the sketch and then add your medium-sized and small plants. Make sure you're satisfied with the placement of the bigger plants. It's a lot easier to move a large rhododendron around on your sketch than it is to move it around in your garden.

For almost all types of gardens, it is wise to plant your garden in the same direction you sketched it—from the back toward the front of the space. In the first place, as we pointed out, your larger plants are usually situated along the back and should be established first. In the second place, if you plant from the back to the front you will not have to stomp all over the tender, newly planted flowers to finish preparing the garden.

Jeff and Liz discovered that there can be a great difference in plant size between what's sketched on the piece of paper and what is actually planted in the garden. The background of their garden includes a holly bush that shows up on paper as being 5 feet wide. However, the holly plant that got placed in the garden is only 1 foot tall and maybe 10 inches across. In their garden plan they wanted to be sure to accommodate the full-grown size of the bush. In reality this holly has a few years to grow before it reaches its mature dimensions. In the meantime, the open spaces will be filled with some tall perennials and annuals until the holly can fill the background of the garden on its own.

Vary the Heights from Side to Side

There are no hard-and-fast rules for the height of the flower garden as you face it and look from side to side. If you wish, you can group the tallest plants on the left, then let your eyes shift up and down as you look to the right, where there are lower plants. Or you can collect the taller plants toward the center and have plants of gradually decreasing heights fan out on both sides. The only guideline you might follow here is to vary the line in some fashion as you look from side to side. Don't let the plants form a monotonous straight line, like the sheared-off top of a newly clipped hedge.

If your 60-Minute Flower Garden is going to be in the front of your home in two beds flanking the front door, you might want to consider this common rule of thumb. Use plants that are short and colorful near the entrance of the home and gradually change to ones that are taller and less colorful as

Planning Principles: The garden on the left is an example of good design elements at work. There's a pleasing variation of heights from the tallest plants in the back to the shortest in the front. The garden's profile (as you look from left to right) has dips and peaks and isn't a boring straight line. The garden on the right shows what can happen when planning principles are ignored. There is a rigid "step profile" on the left of the bed, where no attempt has been made to integrate the plant heights. On the right of the bed, tall flowers have been allowed to crowd the foreground, an area better suited to small or medium-sized plants.

you move away from the entrance. This movement from high to low creates a very welcoming effect as you scan the flower beds to focus on the door.

Use a Mix of Foliage Textures and Shapes

In the interest of creating a low-maintenance flower garden, we've included in the garden plans in this book some shrubs and foliage plants that are particularly easy to care for. But low maintenance isn't their only asset; we chose these plants primarily for the beauty of their foliage. Flowers aren't the only things that make a garden attractive. In all the gardens we've designed, we've made sure foliage shapes and textures contribute to the overall aesthetic appeal. When you design your own garden, be sure to have a pleasing variety of foliage throughout the bed. This guideline is especially important in a shady garden, which will generally have fewer flowers than a sunny garden. The foliage then becomes an even more important visual feature.

One of the tricks you can use here is to visualize your final garden while pretending that you are color-blind and can see only shades of green and brown. Look at some of the color photographs in this book and try to pretend that all you can see are variations of the color green. That will allow you to focus on the different shapes of foliage or the actual outline of the leaves. When you really examine the shapes, you'll see that some are broad with wavy margins, others are narrow and grasslike, and still others look like plumes. Leaves can be shaped like kidneys, hearts, diamonds, arrows, or swords. Also look at the surface of the leaves. Are they glossy, puckery, feathery, fuzzy, ribbed, or smooth? Those are examples of foliage textures. In the garden, texture isn't only a

tactile sensation, it's something you respond to visually. Light will hit a fuzzy leaf differently than it will hit a smooth, glossy leaf. So texture can also become an interesting element to play with as you design your garden.

We don't want to overly complicate your plant selection and garden design. But if you do remember to vary the shapes and textures of the leaves of the plants you place next to each other, you'll be adding some exciting visual interest to the flower garden.

Groups Look Better Than Individual Plants

Your garden will look better if you follow this general guideline: Always plant in groups of two or more plants of the same type rather than scattering individual specimens throughout the garden. This is especially important with perennials, bulbs, and annuals. The reason for grouping is that your garden's appearance from a distance will be more pleasing if there are small masses of color instead of a polka-dotted collection of individual blossoms. Grouping plants also makes it easy to take care of the particular needs of each variety. One exception to this point would be the case of a very large perennial like a peony or a shrub. There simply won't be space for more than one of these plants and its mass will balance any of the other groupings. Another exception may be a Meadow Garden that has five or six varieties of wildflowers sprinkled over the entire garden.

It is a general rule in flower gardening that any smallish group should have an odd number of plants rather than an even number. Even numbers of plants tend to create a boxy look that is not as natural as a group made up of an odd number. Once you have more than six or seven plants in a grouping, then the even-versus-odd guideline isn't as

Textures to Use in the Garden: *Flower color isn't the only tool you can use to create an interesting garden display. Don't underestimate the ability of foliage textures to add some excitement. Feathery ferns (above) contribute a nice, light, delicate touch. Ribbed leaves, like those on the* Hosta plantaginea, *(below), catch the light and create intriguing patterns. Even interesting tree bark, like stewartia (right), can add year-round visual interest to the garden.*

Poor Spacing: *Here's an example of what
not to do as you design and plant your
flower garden. In this garden, individual
plants have been scattered too far apart.
To avoid an empty, half-finished look, use
groupings of plants and space them close
enough together to avoid gaps but not so
close that they hinder each other's growth.*

important as the actual arrangement of the
plants. When you lay out larger numbers of
plants, remember to avoid a squarish look.

You can make any shape you feel will
be attractive with your groups of flowers,
but be sure to keep the size of the groups
within the scale of your total garden. That
means that no group of a single type of plant
should be so large that it overwhelms all the
other features in the garden. You will see
some examples of groupings in the sample

plans in the Gallery of Flower Garden Designs
in Chapter 5. Notice how many individual
plants compose a cluster that stays within
the scale of the overall garden.

Garden Shapes

Our bias is that a garden with a curved
shape is more appealing than one with
straight lines. One exception to this bias
would be a garden that accompanies a house
with ultramodern contemporary architec-
ture. In that case a garden with straight
lines would be more in keeping with the
linear emphasis of the house design. Another
exception would be a small site that can
only be rectangular because of the other
features around it.

It's highly unlikely that home gardeners will be designing a formal, 1-acre, Ital-
ian classical garden for a large estate (a
situation that calls for lots of straight lines).
We feel that in the settings in which most
gardeners will be developing a flower garden, curved lines create a more natural effect.
There happen to be few straight lines found
in nature. Curves are particularly pleasing
if the garden is on the small side. The best
guide to follow is to build a curve or sweep
into your garden outline to conform with
a natural curve in the topography of your
yard. Thus, for example, a garden next to
a sidewalk can gracefully hug the curve
of the walkway. Or the curve of a slope in
the lawn can help establish the sweep of the
flower bed. A garden that is wider on one
end and narrower on the other can be particularly striking.

One of the major reasons for planning a
flower garden with curves is that it is easier
to mow the adjacent lawn if there are no
corners to turn. As a timesaving tip, try to
eliminate as many corners on your lawn as
you can and you'll greatly reduce your mow-

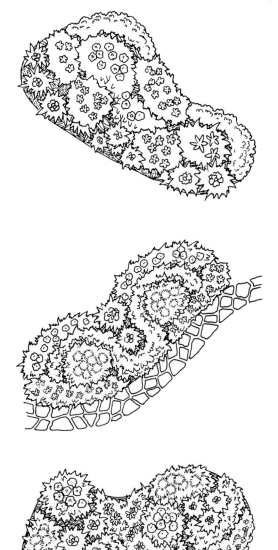

ing time. If you can plan your flower garden so that it not only reduces the amount of grass you need to mow but also makes the mowing of what is left easier, then there's a double bonus.

Of course, you will be the one who ultimately decides what shape your garden takes. If the flower garden of your dreams is rectangular, then that's the best choice for you. You'll see in Chapter 5 that we do give one rectangular garden plan to suggest ways to work with that garden shape. We're only offering guidelines in a process that should be guided more by your personal preferences than by what we say.

Color in the Garden

Color is one of the main attractions of a flower garden. Whole books have been written about this very complex subject of choosing flower colors. In this book we want to avoid all the intricate and overwhelming details of creating a color scheme with flowers. We believe that with just a few simple guidelines you should be able to create a gorgeous, colorful flower garden (and avoid any color combinations that you don't like). In this section we give you five color principles. These aren't "rules," but they should give you enough confidence to be able to combine colors attractively in your flower beds.

If you want to explore in more detail the fascinating but somewhat technical concepts of color relationships in a flower garden, look in the Recommended Reading list for a number of excellent books.

Relate Color to the Garden's Surroundings

Your flower garden does not sit in a vacuum. It is surrounded by the textures and colors of the materials used in your

Variations on Curved Beds: Here are just a few examples of the shapes you can create when you use curving lines instead of straight ones to outline your flower beds. Use some natural feature in the yard, such as the walkway shown in the center, to help determine the shape of the bed.

house and in your walkways. The leaves, bark, and berries of the trees and shrubs in the nearby landscape will also have an impact on your flower garden. While we believe that most colors go well together, it is helpful to think about the colors that surround this new flower garden. A moment's thought will let you make a complementary selection of plants and colors. For example, a predominantly pink flower garden would look better with a gray stone house than it would with a bright red brick house.

Three to Five Colors Are Easier Than One

In your first few flower garden designs we suggest you plan to use at least three to five different-colored groups of flowers. In the beginning that is easier than designing a flower garden to show subtle variations of a single color throughout the season. A garden with pinks, whites, purples, reds, and greens is simpler to plan than one that tries to have five different variations of pink exclusively through the season. A garden featuring a single hue is certainly very eye-catching, and its subtleties in color can look quite sophisticated, but selecting and locating the plants in this kind of garden can be quite challenging for the beginner.

Provide for Continuous Color All Season

Experienced flower gardeners with a lot of space and a number of different gardens in their care will often plan to have one entire flower bed in complete and breathtaking bloom during a particular two- or three-week period in the season. Such a garden might contain delphiniums, campanulas, foxgloves, astilbes, carnations, coral bells, and Siberian irises, all strategically

combined to explode into glorious color in June. A garden like this will have little to show during the rest of the season, but during that two or three weeks of glory it can be spectacular. Orchestrating the timing so that the blooms of a large number of perennials, annuals, and shrubs come to their peak at about the same time is a difficult task. We suggest you save that challenge for the second or third year of your flower gardening adventures.

For the smaller scale of the 60-Minute Flower Garden, we recommend that you take the broader approach, at least in the beginning. We believe it is easier to plan a flower garden in which the plants flower in sequence in various parts of your garden throughout the whole growing season. At no time is your entire garden ablaze with flowers, but over the course of the season your garden will always have some attractive and colorful features. For example, in the spring you can have white pansies and white daffodils sitting beside blue Siberian squills and grape hyacinths. Then in the early summer the pink coral bells and pink bearded irises can contrast nicely with the blue delphiniums and bellflowers. Later in the summer yellow coreopsis and black-eyed Susans can join the red dahlias and verbena in bloom. And finally, in the fall you can have the purple-colored mealy-cup sage and orange chrysanthemums and marigolds as the last act in your season-long show of continuous color.

Color Schemes

In a small garden like the 60-Minute Flower Garden, there are three possibilities for creating color schemes. One is to avoid a fixed color plan altogether and have a general mixture of colors. Another option is to plan for contrasting colors. A third possibility is to plan the colors to be harmonious with each other.

The first option, having no color scheme at all, is probably the easiest approach for the beginner. A garden with a broad mix of colors looks like a bright, multicolored patchwork quilt set down in your yard. It can have more visual impact than a garden with a harmonious color scheme, which seems subdued and subtle in contrast to the riot of colors in a mixed-color garden. It's difficult to make any serious mistakes with color. If you're not pleased with one season's color combination, you can always change things the next year.

How do you know if colors are contrasting or harmonious? The simplest method is to use the classic color wheel with the

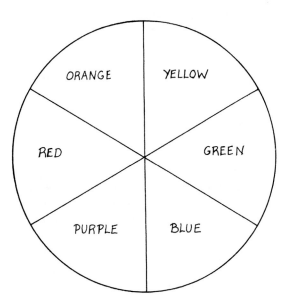

Color Wheel: To find out which colors are contrasting and which are harmonious, pick one color along the wheel. Those colors not touching your color are contrasting; the colors adjacent to your color are harmonious.

three primary colors (red, yellow, and blue) and the three complementary colors (orange, green, and purple).

To determine which are in contrast and which are in harmony, do this simple exercise. Pick a color on the wheel. Any other colors that are not touching your color on the wheel are contrasting colors. The two colors on either side of your color are harmonious colors. For example, we'll pick the color yellow. By looking at the wheel we can see that red, purple, and blue are contrasting colors and orange and green are harmonious colors. Charles, the professional, rightfully argues that this approach is oversimplified. Jeff, the beginning flower gardener, argues that it serves as a start in understanding how colors work in the garden and is helpful even if oversimplified.

If you plan your garden so that some or all of its flower colors are contrasting, you can create a striking and eye-catching effect. An example of this approach is to have intense red flowers such as zinnias and deep mustard-yellow flowers like gloriosa daisies in bloom at the same time. This sharp contrast of colors draws immediate attention to the garden, especially from a distance. Sometimes, though, the contrast may be more than you want. A mauve-colored phlox next to a bright orange zinnia may create more of a clash than a pleasing contrast. If you're concerned about clashes between contrasting colors, remember this tip: Use a buffer of white flowers, gray foliage, or green foliage between two potentially conflicting colors. Dusty miller is a common soft gray foliage plant that would make a nice buffer. A perennial not simultaneously in bloom can provide the green buffer. In the example of the phlox and zinnia, Siberian irises would be a suitable choice.

You can also have some fun playing around with the harmony effect. As we said earlier, color harmonies are more subtle than the bolder color mixtures and color contrasts. Referring to the color wheel, you could combine red bee balm and purple delphiniums to create a very harmonious and pleasant effect. In this example the purple also serves to quiet down the brightness of the red, which can, by itself, be a bit jarring.

Given the relatively small size of the 60-Minute Flower Garden, we think you should keep the color scheme simple and not try to work with both contrasting and harmonious color combinations in the same garden.

Color Is More Than the Flowers

This last color principle is certainly not the least, for most gardeners will not be able to count on flowers to supply year-round color. During the flowerless periods you'll need to rely on other attractive plant features to provide the color interest in the garden. Even when there are flowers blooming, you'll want to have some of these interesting plants in the garden to complement the flower colors.

Don't underestimate the visual power of foliage. There are many plants with few or no blossoms that have strikingly colored leaves that add significant value to the overall aesthetic effect of your flower garden. One of the most popular perennial foliage plants today is the hosta, which is available in many exciting varieties with leaves that are bluish, bright yellow-green, or even striped and splashed with white. Another example of stylish foliage is the cool gray of the annual dusty miller, which, as we mentioned earlier, can serve as a mediator between two colors that might clash. Begonias have beautiful burnished red foliage, and some tulip varieties feature delightful vertical reddish stripes along the inside of each of the leaves, giving an attractive mottled effect.

Examples of Foliage Colors

Blue-green: Hosta 'Krossa Regal'
Dark green: Pachysandra
Gray: Dusty miller; lamb's-ears; wormwood
Reddish: Begonia; perilla
Speckled silver and gray: Lungwort
Yellow-green: Hosta 'Golden Sunburst'
Variegated colors: Coleus; hosta

Planning Principles for Perennials

Perennials are long-term performers in the flower garden. In the winter their annual topgrowth dies back, but the root system remains alive and ready to begin new growth in the spring. There are some perennials that never die back and remain evergreen in southern parts of the country (such as lily-turf, barrenwort, Christmas rose, and evergreen daylilies), but these are in a minority. At the other extreme are perennials that are simply short-lived and normally last only two or three years and then need replacing. These include delphiniums, columbines, and lupines. Hardy perennials are those that are comfortable with the climate and soil conditions in your area.

Perennials are some of the easiest-care plants you can put in your garden. Every five to seven years you may need to divide certain types of perennials like astilbe, iris, and daylily to keep them healthy and vigorous. Other hardy perennials will grow for decades, needing little attention other than an annual feeding and sufficient watering. These long-lived, extra-low-care varieties include gas plant, blue wild indigo, and peony.

There are a few plants for the flower garden that fall midway between perennials and annuals. These are called biennials. Some common examples include foxglove and cup and saucers. These are plants that live for only two years and then die. They usually don't blossom until the second year. Some biennials, such as foxglove, will reseed themselves and act much like a perennial in that they come up every year. For our purposes in this book we are treating biennials like perennials as far as the design process is concerned.

Using Perennial Height in the Design

There are many perennial plants that will grow tall enough to serve as foundation or background plants along with shrubs in a Decorative Home Garden. In the Herbaceous Flower Border, tall perennials are all you need to make up the background or foundation layer. Perennials like purple loosestrife, meadow rue, and globe thistle will grow from 4 to 6 feet tall and can stand alone or make a nice addition to the shrub background. As a handy rule of thumb, the height of tall perennials shouldn't exceed two-thirds of the width of your flower bed.

Many perennials fall into the mid-sized category of between 15 and 36 inches tall

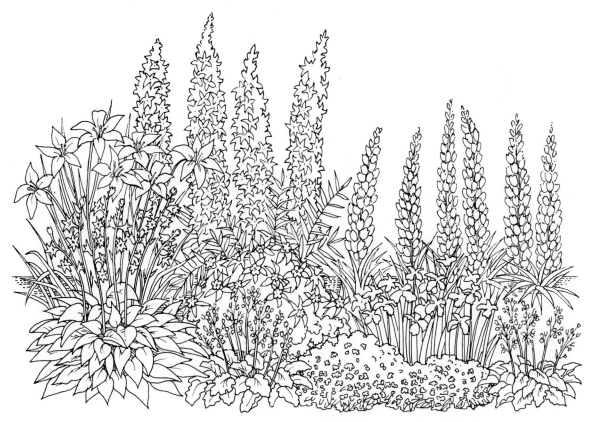

Perennial Heights: *On the left of this grouping of perennials are daylilies and hostas. The important thing to remember about these is that their flowers extend quite a bit above their foliage. In planning your garden design, count the height of the foliage as the significant measurement. The other perennials in the bed give you an idea of the wonderful range of sizes that are available, from 5-foot-tall spikes to ground-hugging clumps.*

and are generally used to fill in the middle sections of the border or bed. Common examples include bee balm, baby's breath, Siberian iris, and columbine. Many gardeners forget that there are also lots of very low-growing perennials (under 15 inches) that can be used in the front edge of a flower bed along with the annuals. Perennials such as basket-of-gold, coral bells, and low varieties of sedum make fine additions to the front of the flower garden.

One of the things to remember with perennials is that there is often a great difference in the height of the flowers and the height of the plant's foliage. In planning your garden, consider the height of the foliage as the more important of the two. The flowers are in view for only about three weeks, while the foliage is there all season long. Perennials like daylilies and hostas are good examples of plants with very tall blossoms (36 to 48 inches), but with medium or even low foliage (18 to 24 inches). You should place plants like these in your plan according to their foliage heights.

How Many Perennials to Include

While the number of different kinds of perennials you include in the plan will vary with the type and size of the garden, we can offer a few helpful guidelines. If this is your first garden, it is better to work with only a few kinds than to plunge in right away with a vast number of different varieties. While browsing through flower garden catalogs, it is tempting to order one of everything because they all look so beautiful, but you should resist. You're better off starting out with a few varieties that will do well in the type of garden you have and then expanding the number over the next few years as you learn more about your own preferences. In the beginning you can always fill in the gaps with annuals, which are not permanent.

Our rule of thumb is to plan the succession of perennial blossoms to cover three periods—late spring, summer, and early fall (early spring is filled with blooms from flowering shrubs and early bulbs). If you have three different kinds of perennials in blossom in each of those three periods, you'll have a very well balanced flower garden with a changing array of seasonal beauty.

As you gain experience, you can begin to expand the size of your garden and the number of time periods to fill with flowering perennials. In the beginning, we suggest no more than nine different kinds of peren-

FOUR SEASONS OF BLOOM

SEASON	MONTHS	PLANTS IN BLOOM
Early spring to midspring	April to mid-May	Bulbs and flowering shrubs
Late spring through early summer	Mid-May through June	Early perennials
Midsummer	July through mid-August	Annuals and perennials
Late summer through early fall	Late August through September	Annuals and perennials

NOTE: The months that correspond to the seasons in this chart apply to the middle zones of the country. Gardeners in the South know that spring starts sooner and fall lasts longer in their climate, just as northern gardeners know that spring comes later and fall starts earlier than the months in our chart would indicate.

nials in any of the 60-Minute Flower Gardens. Most perennials will blossom for two to three weeks, so three blossoming periods will give you six to nine weeks of perennial flowers during your first season. When you remember that you will probably have some early-blossoming shrubs and bulbs and some annuals that will bloom all summer and fall, your first garden should be beautiful all season long following this guideline.

Planning Principles for Bulbs

Bulbs are divided into two distinct groups, hardy and tender. Hardy bulbs can stay in the garden for years and do not need to be dug up each season. All the bright and cheery spring-blooming bulbs like crocuses, hyacinths, tulips, and daffodils that tell us winter is over are hardy. The other category, tender bulbs, must be removed from the garden in the fall, dried, and stored indoors over the winter. Because they must be replanted every year, in this book we refer to these as annual bulbs. Some favorite tender annual bulbs are dahlias and gladiolus.

This may surprise you, but we strongly recommend that you do not plant hardy bulbs in the 60-Minute Flower Garden until its second year. The reason we say this is because we are assuming that you will be making a fair number of changes in your garden after its first year of display. You may decide to move some of the shrubs and perennials into new locations after having a year to see how the garden looks. Hardy bulbs are planted quite deep, but they'll still be disrupted if you uproot and transplant a perennial that had been growing right next to or on top of the bulbs. We appreciate that this approach requires considerable restraint, but in the long run we feel that you'll be happier with your garden design. Wait to sink the hardy bulbs into the ground until after you've had a chance to make your final adjustments of shrubs and perennials.

On the other hand, you can plant annual bulbs during your garden's first year, using them to fill gaps and add spots of color as needed. Plants like dahlias that are 15 to 36 inches tall are great space fillers in the middle areas of a garden. Charles didn't include any annual bulbs in his garden plans in Chapter 5 because they require more attention than hardy bulbs (the autumn digging, drying, and storing). However, that doesn't mean you can't include some in your own garden design. These flowering plants are very good summer color substitutes for perennials that have faded away.

Working Hardy Bulbs into the Design

When you do plant your hardy bulbs, you should place them between perennials that are slow to come up and therefore won't compete directly with the blossom period of the bulbs. Asters, phlox, and coneflowers make good perennial companions for hardy bulbs. You should plan to have hardy bulbs and annuals share the same space in the garden. After the bulbs have put on their spring show, you'll be setting out your annual transplants or starting your annual seeds in the same general location. Your goal is to have a summer-blooming perennial or annual in flower to hide the spot where the bulbs were blooming earlier in the spring.

In the Decorative Home Garden for a sunny spot we suggest you can have as many as 12 different varieties of hardy bulbs. In general, for the larger varieties (tulips and daffodils) you would plant groups of about 12 bulbs; for the smaller ones (crocuses and Siberian squills) you would use 25 bulbs in a group. In the narrower Herbaceous Flower Border you might use only 6 to 12 varieties, with the same groupings of bulbs recom-

Using Bulbs and Annuals in the Design:
After the flowers of spring bulbs have faded, add spots of color to the garden by setting annual transplants in among the bulb foliage. You can place the annuals right in among the foliage without harming the bulbs.

mended for the Decorative Home Garden. One good strategy is to go slowly and plant only 2 to 3 varieties of large bulbs and 2 to 3 varieties of small bulbs in the first year to see what happens. The next year you'll know where you need to fill in some holes or accent a flowering shrub, and then you can go ahead and add some more varieties for special effects.

Planning Principles for Annuals

Annual flowering and foliage plants are very satisfying for the beginning gardener

because they are very easy to handle. They have shallow root systems, so they require only about 4 to 6 inches of good soil. Many are simple to start from seed, which makes it easy to take advantage of the broad selection offered in seed catalogs. If you don't want to start your own seedlings, most nurseries offer an adequate assortment of annuals ready for transplanting.

There are some very hardy early annuals such as pansies that can be used to supplement the bulbs and flowering shrubs in the earliest part of the season. However, once the heat of summer appears, these cool-loving early annuals won't hold up. Most annuals will flower from early summer all the way to first frost, giving your garden continuous color while perennials and shrub blossoms come and go.

Annuals are the last plants you will fit into your garden plan. They're generally used to fill in the gaps after the shrubs and perennials have been located. In the early stages of a garden's development, you'll rely on annuals to fill in spaces that in a few years' time will be occupied by mature shrubs and perennials.

How Many Annuals to Include

Four to six different varieties of annuals should be sufficient for your first 60-Minute Flower Garden. Remember, annuals are used as color accents, so for maximum impact you'll want to mass these plants rather than spot them individually all over the garden. As you gain experience and begin to develop your own preferences for how your garden should look, you can expand the number and types of annuals you use.

Using a Succession of Annuals

Because annuals are not permanent residents of your garden, they are particularly flexible and adaptable. You can use them in creative ways to provide maximum color in your display. For instance, borrow the idea of succession planting from the vegetable garden and consider a succession of annuals through the season. (This requires being a bit ruthless, because you must be willing to pull them before they are totally finished to make room for the next variety.)

Start the season off with frost-tolerant annuals such as pansies and forget-me-nots. They'll give the early spring garden some quick color at a time when the perennials are just coming out of the ground. Then in May or June you can replace those early annuals (which will soon be flagging from the heat) with summer annuals like petunias, ageratums, geraniums, and dusty miller. Use these to fill in the spaces left between your perennials. Finally, in the fall, replace the summer annuals with some potted chrysanthemums, which can create some new color combinations for the autumn garden. By sinking the pots into the ground for later removal you are using chrysanthemums as annuals instead of perennials. This allows you to take advantage of the range of color options they offer without committing any permanent space to them in your garden earlier in the year. Succession planting with annuals is a relatively inexpensive and time-saving way to supplement the color in your garden and get three very different color effects over the growing season.

Planning Principles for Shrubs

For the sake of simplicity, we divide the large family of shrubs that are available to gardeners today into two broad categories—shrubs for landscaping and shrubs for flower gardens. Some shrubs, such as rhododendrons, have some characteristics that apply to both categories. The distinction is important to understand as you plan the garden, especially if you are intending to build a

Decorative Home Garden using the shrubs already in place in front of your house as integral parts of the design. This section will give you some guidelines to follow as you select shrubs and incorporate them into the plans for your flower garden.

Landscaping Shrubs

In this book we define landscaping shrubs as those that usually have very dense growth and never flower. This category would include such common shrubs as yews and junipers. These are the shrubs that developers use as a windbreak along a property line or as a foundation planting across the front of a new house.

These landscaping shrubs, especially if they are in good condition and stretch across the front of the house, can be used as the background for a very colorful Herbaceous Flower Border. On the other hand, you should avoid using these kinds of shrubs in the middle of a Decorative Home Garden.

Flower Garden Shrubs

The shrubs that deserve a special place in the flower garden are those with outstanding blooms and interesting growth habits. Their ornamental attributes allow them to blend in with the colors and textures of the other flowers in the garden. This group of shrubs includes such familiar examples as rhododendrons, forsythias, azaleas, astilbes, lilacs, and buddleias. (Look at the plant lists in the Gallery of Flower Garden Designs for some more examples of good flower garden shrubs.)

If you're designing a Decorative Home Garden for the front of your house and the site contains mature landscaping shrubs, there's a way you can take advantage of those shrubs while introducing new flower garden shrubs. Let's say you purchase one or more flower garden shrubs while they are still quite small (and less expensive). If you remove all the older landscaping shrubs and put the newer, smaller shrubs in their place, the garden site might look a little off-balance and even a little sparse in spots. A way around this is to leave one or more fully grown landscaping shrubs in the flower garden plan for a few years. This gives the flower garden shrubs time to fill out until they can take over and make their full contribution to the overall look of the garden.

Shrub Size

As a general guide, you should not have any shrub in your 60-Minute Flower Garden that when full grown will be higher than your flower bed is wide. Many professional garden designers prefer to limit the height of the background to no more than two-thirds of the width of the bed. Following these standards, if you have a flower bed that is 6 feet wide, you should avoid shrubs that will exceed 4 to 6 feet in height when full grown. This means, of course, that you must find out what the mature size of a shrub will be *before* you plant that innocent-looking 12-inch seedling. If you're fore-warned, it could surprise you by soaring to 15 feet tall in the next six or seven years—and completely outgrow the flower garden. Be sure to ask the nursery where you purchase the shrubs about their mature size and their maturation time in years.

Some people have trouble visualizing how a little 18-inch-tall rhododendron is going to look when it reaches the 6 feet high and 5 feet wide promised on its nursery tag. Here is where having a sketch of the garden is important, because you can draw in the mature size of a shrub and get a feel for whether it will overwhelm your garden when it is full grown.

If you're designing a garden site that already contains some nice flower garden shrubs, don't forget to take their mature size into consideration. For example, if you have a young rhododendron already in place that you realize will eventually outgrow the flower garden, don't assume you must remove it right away. If it will take five years for the rhododendron to grow too large, you can accommodate it in the garden plan for a year or two and then transplant it outside the flower garden. At that point you can replace it with a more suitably sized flowering shrub.

The size of shrubs is also important in keeping your flower garden's overall appearance in scale with its background, especially if that background is your house. If you live in a low, ranch-style home, you certainly don't want towering shrubs in your flower bed that will overpower the house. At the same time, if you have a three-story Victorian home with a sweeping front porch, you can afford to have shrubs that might reach to the top of the porch roof without upsetting the scale of the overall scene.

How Many Shrubs to Include

A large shrub or a large number of shrubs can overwhelm a small garden, so you must take care not to let these plants dominate your plan. In the gardens that Charles created for the Gallery of Flower Garden Designs in Chapter 5, you'll see that he includes no more than two or three large shrubs and no more than five smaller shrubs in any of the plans. In the end, the number of shrubs you can use depends a great deal on the size and shape of your garden site and on how large a shrub you wish to use.

Create an Attractive Winter View

For most gardeners, winter is the most challenging season for creating an attractive display in the garden. All of the annual and perennial flowers will have disappeared after the first serious frost. In the absence of their bright colors, evergreen shrubs will become the mainstay in the garden's winter palette. In addition to the different shades of green foliage, they offer interesting bark colors and patterns and sometimes eye-catching berries that last through most of the winter to add pleasant accents to the garden view. To give you some examples of plants with special "off-season" features, holly provides red berries and evergreen leaves, viburnum also contributes colorful red berries, Red Osier dogwood has striking red stems, and P.J.M. rhododendron provides purple leaves.

In the Gallery of Flower Garden Designs, the Decorative Home Garden, Woodland Garden, and Bank Garden have been designed to include shrubs for year-round good looks. Check the plant lists that accompany the plans for some ideas on what kinds of shrubs you can include in your garden for 12 months of beauty.

Getting Set for the Next Step

At this point you have reviewed all of the major issues that will affect which plants you are going to select for your final 60-Minute Flower Garden plan. We want to take a moment to caution any beginning gardeners to be very conservative and to avoid going into the plant selection process with overly ambitious visions of their first flower garden. We believe you'll have more success during your first year of flower gardening if you keep your design fairly simple. We certainly don't want to discourage the more adventurous among our readers, but we do want everyone who constructs a 60-Minute Flower Garden to be so successful that they're hooked on the pleasures of flower gardening, no matter how modest, for the rest of their lives.

In the next chapter, we'll take you by the hand and lead you through the process of selecting and locating the plants in your very own flower garden. Now, at last, you're ready to open the flower catalogs!

Chapter 5

Selecting the Plants and Finishing the Design

For many of us just beginning to get into flower gardening, the enormous number of different plants can be terribly intimidating. There seem to be too many choices for us to feel confident that we won't make a mistake. This chapter is designed to cut through all that confusion and give you some easy guides to follow to make your flower selection process a painless one. Up to this point, you've been thinking in terms of general design issues for the flower garden. Now you can get more specific and select the actual plants that will fit into those basic design decisions you made in the last chapter. Here is where you begin to put the finishing touches on the flower garden design you began creating back in Chapter 1.

In this book we provide you with three handy "tools" to help you pick the best plants for your garden and figure out the best place to put them in the design. The first of these tools are the lists that accompany each of the discussions under Making Your Selections later in this chapter. Each list contains plants we recommend highly. The second tool comes at the end of this chapter and it's called A Gallery of Flower Garden

Designs. This section contains nine sample 60-Minute Flower Gardens designed by Charles. Each of these features a garden layout and a list of his suggestions for easy-to-find and easy-to-grow plants. And finally, at the end of the book, is the third plant selection tool. This comes in the form of a detailed chart, The Best Plants for the 60-Minute Flower Garden. In this chart you'll find useful information on 173 of the most popular and easy-to-grow garden plants. We feel confident in saying that with the use of these three tools you should have no trouble working out your own 60-Minute Flower Garden design.

How to Pick the Best Plants for Your Garden

When you select anything, from a new car to a brand of detergent to the flowers for your garden, you use the same basic approach: You want to find ways to narrow all the many options available until you arrive at the best choice for you. There are literally thousands of plants available in this country, either through your local nursery or through the many mail-order companies from all over the world. As we compiled the names of plants to feature in this chapter's lists and garden designs and in The Best Plants chart, Charles applied certain criteria that only a horticultural professional would know. He used his professional judgment to sort out from the thousands of possibilities only those plants that are easy to obtain and easy to grow and represent the very best variety of each type of plant. Charles has grown most of these plants himself, so he can vouch for their good qualities. Now that you know how we chose the plants to feature in this book, let's see what criteria you can use to make your own selections. The accompanying Checklist for Selecting Plants gives you nine issues to consider, in order from highest priority to lowest priority.

Checklist for Selecting Plants

- What type of garden model are you planting?
- What are your favorite flower garden plants?
- Have you selected plants that qualify as "better plants"?
- Are the plants hardy in your area?
- Have you considered the mature height of the plants?
- Have you planned for a sequence of blooming times?
- Have you selected a garden color scheme?
- Do the plants have a pleasing fragrance?
- Have you created a pleasant mix of plant textures, colors, and shapes?

Type of Garden

Just by selecting a specific 60-Minute Flower Garden model, you narrow the choice of plants for your plan. If you're planting a

Herbaceous Flower Border in the shade, then any of the plants suited for that design that require full sun, such as yarrow and plumed cock's-comb, are no longer contenders. As you can see in the plant lists that accompany each of the sample garden plans at the end of this chapter, we have tried to help you identify those plants that are best suited for each basic garden model. Among those nine garden plans with their common sun-versus-shade situations, you should be able to get some good ideas for your own garden.

Favorite Plants

Even if you feel that you're just a rank beginner and don't know anything about flowers, you probably still have a number of favorite plants. You may not even know their names, but over the years you have come across certain plants that have always seemed particularly attractive to you. Maybe it was a flower in your grandmother's garden or a shrub in a neighbor's yard. In any case, before you make the final plant selections for your 60-Minute Flower Garden, make a list of all your favorite plants to see if they can be used in your design. Why try something you've never seen before when you may have a favorite that will grow and do well in your particular area? There are no "right" plants for your garden. If your favorite plant is one like the petunia, which has the reputation of being awfully common, use it anyway. This flower garden is being built first and foremost for *you* to enjoy, and you shouldn't worry about what the neighbors think.

Concept of "Better Plants"

Professionals in the horticulture business are familiar with the concept of "better plants." It is an idea that we nonprofessionals should also try to understand, especially as we design a new flower garden. A "better plant" is one that, when compared with other plants or even with other varieties of the same plant, has greater value to the home gardener. It is a plant that is adaptable to a wide range of climates and soils and thus can be grown successfully in many parts of the country. It blooms longer than other varieties and has attractive foliage throughout most of the season. The "better plant" will likely be quite disease resistant and will have a rather neat growth habit, eliminating the need for staking. Any plant that satisfies all those criteria qualifies as a "better plant." Some examples of these outstanding plants, in Charles's opinion, are Moonbeam coreopsis, Goldsturm black-eyed Susan, and mealy-cup sage.

You will find that the "better plants" tend to be a bit more expensive than other plants, although that is not always the case. The relatively modest higher cost is well worth the security of knowing that your plants are less susceptible to disease and have other highly desirable qualities.

One of the easiest ways to identify a "better plant" is to get a list of all the varieties of flowers that have received an All-America Selection award in the last 25 years. The All-America Selection organization has been testing new flowers and vegetables grown from seed all around the country since 1933. The organization is constantly looking for varieties with greater disease resistance, earlier bloom, and new and improved flower colors—in other words, "better plants." (For more information and a list of trial grounds and display gardens around the country, write: All-America Selections, 628 Executive Drive, Willowbrook, IL 60521.)

Some plants may not be considered "better plants" across most of the nation but may be terrific in your particular area. Your local nursery's staff can help identify varieties of certain flowers that might be especially successful in your area—in other words, a *local* "better plant."

Hardiness

It doesn't make any sense to include a plant in your garden that might not survive the winter because you overlooked its hardiness rating. Most of the plants listed in this book will grow well in Zones 3 through 8 (see the Hardiness Zone Map in the Appendix). At the same time, we feature a number of plants that are only hardy to Zone 5. It's wise to check the hardiness rating for each of your plant selections in The Best Plants chart in the Appendix to be sure you've made a proper choice.

The zone map and the chart will help you with your choice of perennials and shrubs. Annuals, although they don't survive the winter, have varying degrees of hardiness just the same. When we use the term *hardy* to describe annual plants, we mean that they will withstand some frost. Hardy annuals will usually perpetuate themselves with self-sown seed each spring. The hardiness of the seed is as important as the hardiness of the plant itself. *Half-hardy* is a term we use for annuals that will stand some cold but won't survive a heavy frost. The seed doesn't survive outside over the winter, so you must step in and plant seed in the spring after all danger of frost is past. A *tender* annual will not stand any frost whatsoever, and that applies to both the plant and the seed. Start tender annuals either indoors or outside when the soil has warmed—probably four to six weeks after the last frost.

Mature Plant Height

Shrubs and perennials may not reach their mature height for a few years. The cute little shrub you see in the nursery could easily grow to be 6 feet tall in five years and completely overwhelm a small flower garden. It is possible for different varieties of the same plant to have significantly different heights when they're full grown. Perennial asters, for example, include some varieties that grow to only 12 inches, while cousins can shoot higher than 48 inches. We've been careful to note the expected mature height of all the varieties included in The Best Plants chart. As you go through this chapter and refer to the plant lists, you'll see that we also give sizes here; the first measurement refers to the height and the second to the width or breadth of the plant. (You'll also notice that in some cases we've included the Latin name of the plant or shrub so that you'll know exactly which variety we're recommending.) In a case where you wish to use the same plant but a different variety from the one we have listed, be sure to check the mature height of your substitute before you include it in your plan.

Blooming Times

In the last chapter we emphasized how nice it is to have some blooms in your flower garden throughout the entire growing season. To achieve that kind of floral display, you should find out when each flower in your plan is expected to bloom. Perennials will usually flower for only two to three weeks, while annuals, once they begin blooming, will often flower throughout much of the season. Flowering shrubs, such as azaleas, often bloom early in the season, although some varieties like certain late-blooming azaleas, butterfly bush, and rose-of-Sharon can be found that will bloom in the summer. Flower catalogs will always tell you when to expect a certain variety to bloom, plus or minus a week or two. It is the plant you get from a friend or on sale at a nursery that

might not be marked with such information. Remember that the information from the companies that develop and sell flowers comes from trials in almost-perfect growing conditions; your own experience may fall somewhat short of their close-to-ideal descriptions.

To refresh your memory, the four major bloom periods we talked about in Chapter 4 are early spring to midspring, late spring through early summer, midsummer, and late summer through early fall. A good approach is to fill each period with three to five kinds of plants that will be in bloom. For an eye-catching display, group these plants in twos or threes throughout the garden. (See the sample plans at the end of the chapter for examples of how Charles groups plants for an attractive effect.)

Many gardeners plan the major bloom period of their flower gardens for June through August because that's when they spend the most time outdoors. Others will want the most spectacular flower show early in the season because they spend July or August away on vacation. Think about your own habits and schedules to figure out how you want to plan the various bloom periods in your 60-Minute Flower Garden.

Flowering can occur in sequence even within one of the major bloom periods. Liz discovered that the tulips Charles had given her all blossomed at slightly different times. Plaisir, with its pink candy stripes, blossomed first, a week later Apricot Beauty came out, and then two weeks later President Kennedy opened. There was at least a week's overlap between varieties, so the garden was filled with some vivid-colored tulips for four or five weeks in early spring. This fine-tuning of the bloom periods is one of the things you can enjoy as you gain in experience.

One way to make planning for blooming times easier is to make five or six photocopies of your final flower garden plan. Then, using one copy for each month of the growing season, color in those circles of flowers that are expected to be in bloom that month, using the appropriate colors. (This is a fun way to get young children involved in the flower garden.) When you're done you'll have a handy, easy-to-read check on how well you have planned for blooming color throughout the season in your 60-Minute Flower Garden.

Color Scheme

In the last chapter we gave you some ideas about the different effects you can create by combining colors in the garden. Now is the time to pick the specific flowers that will carry out the color scheme you've decided on. Flowers come in so many pleasing shades that you should be able to create whatever look you want. Remember that one type of plant can come in a whole range of colors. To see what we mean, just open up a flower catalog and take a look at all the color choices you have among zinnias, columbines, gladiolus, and daylilies.

Fragrance

It's unfortunate, but having lots of flowers in the garden doesn't automatically guarantee that you'll have lots of wonderful scents wafting through the evening air. Plant breeding over the past 25 years has caused many flowers to lose most of their original scents. As new hybrids have been developed, the visual appeal of flowers has outweighed fragrance. If you want a delightfully fragrant flower, in most cases you'll have to look for an old-fashioned cultivar of a species. The list of Delightfully Fragrant Plants gives you some names to look for in catalogs or nurseries. There are several good books available that deal especially with using scented flowers and foliage in your garden. We've listed two under Recommended Reading in the Appendix.

Delightfully Fragrant Plants

Fragrant Flowers

Lilac
Lilies
Lily-of-the-valley
Peony
Pink, allwood
Tobacco, flowering (fragrance is released at night)

Fragrant Foliage

Bee balm
Gas plant
Lavender
Thyme
Wormwood

Patterns in Textures, Colors, and Shapes

By now you know that when you are selecting plants for the flower garden, you need to consider more than the flower colors, the time of bloom, and the height of the plants. Throughout the book we've been reminding you of the amazing variation that exists among foliage colors and textures and how plants can provide other interesting features like seed pods and berries. Now is the time for you to put that idea to work in the garden. Create variety in the foliage display by putting a broad, smooth hosta beside a feathery astilbe. Set a plant with yellow and green variegated leaves next to one with deep emerald foliage. Place a plant with grasslike leaves next to one with broad, flat, rounded leaves. When you think along those lines, the subtle variations you create will contribute to the overall visual interest of the garden. These patterns have a lower priority than hardiness and type of garden in guiding your plant selection, but they are still worth keeping in mind as you fill in the blanks in your garden sketch.

Making Your Selections

Now let's get to the best part—selecting the plants for your 60-Minute Flower Garden. Remember the guideline we provided in Chapter 4: Select plants for the back of the garden first and for the front last. Keep in mind the three basic areas of the garden you'll be filling with flowers. The first is the sculptural area at the back, where you form the garden's basic framework or background. The second area is the functional or filler section in the middle space, where the bulk of the plants will be established. Along the front edge you have the foreground area, which provides the finishing touches to the overall garden design.

The Background

Here you select the framework plants that will serve as a background to your 60-Minute Flower Garden. When you design this part of the garden, think first about shapes and textures and then give some attention to seasons of bloom. Your main con-

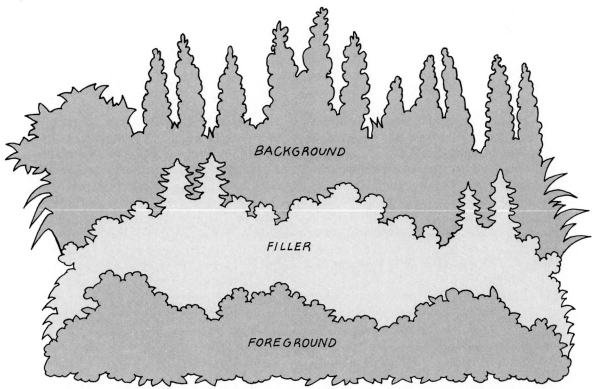

Basic Design Areas in the Garden: These are the three areas you'll be filling with flowers. In the back is the background section, in the middle is the filler area, and in the front is the foreground section.

cern is to build an appealing backdrop against which your main flower sections in the middle and the front will be viewed. One example of a pleasing background is the combination of eulalia grass, with its tall, grassy texture, and queen-of-the prairie, with its coarser, bold leaves. The background section might take up one-third of the width of the garden, unless your garden is particularly deep (more than 6 to 8 feet). In that case, your background can take up a bit more room, if you wish.

This background or framework section of the flower garden can include shrubs (in Decorative Home Gardens or Woodland Gardens) and/or some tall perennials. In certain situations, a climbing vine might be an appropriate addition. Liz and Jeff have used a climbing hydrangea to dress up the corner of the house behind their Decorative Home Garden. This vine serves as a focal point in the background while simultaneously hiding their electric meter from view.

Selecting Shrubs

In our sample garden designs at the end of the chapter, you'll find some good examples of shrubs for backgrounds. In Chapter 4 we gave you some general planning principles. Here we'll give you a few basic criteria to use in making your final selection of shrubs, if you decide to include them in your flower garden.

If you're bringing new shrubs into the garden, an important issue to check is their hardiness. It makes no sense to plant a shrub that will not survive winter in your climate. We assume that local nurseries take care of such concerns, but if you order your shrub through the mail, make sure you check the hardiness rating first. You'll also want to be aware of the shrub's preference for acidic or more neutral soil. Rhododendrons,

Shrubs for Flower Gardens

Sun

Butterfly bush *(Buddleia davidii);* 72 × 60 in.
Rose-of-Sharon *(Hibiscus syriacus* 'Diana'); 96 × 60 in.
Weigela; 72 × 72 in.
Shrubby cinquefoil *(Potentilla fruticosa);* 18 × 18 in.
Spirea 'Gold Flame'; 18 × 24 in.

Shade

Azalea; 24-72 × 48-72 in.
Rhododendron 'P.J.M.'; 60 × 48 in.
Drooping leucothoe *(Leucothoe fontenesiana);* 36 × 48 in.
Cherry cotoneaster *(Cotoneaster apiculata);* 36 × 36 in.
Mountain laurel *(Kalmia latifolia);* 60 × 60 in.

azaleas, and mountain laurel must start out in acid soil. You can adjust your soil for either preference, but you need to know the plant's needs on this score ahead of time so you can prepare.

Selecting Tall Perennials

The "perfect" perennial is one that looks good all season, needs dividing only every three years or more, is hardy without protection, has no special soil requirements, needs little or no staking, and is hardly ever bothered by pests and diseases. That sounds like a pretty tall order! All the perennials we feature in the book come very close to this picture of perfection. The tall perennials we recommend for the background of the 60-Minute Flower Garden may need some staking, but otherwise they should be nearly perfect.

When you're selecting these tall perennials, don't think about what plants might be going into the middle section or foreground of the garden. Try to make a nice arrangement of the perennials and the shrubs by themselves — think about how the flower colors, the bloom times, and the foliage shapes and textures can create a nice effect.

Tall Perennials

Sun

Anemone, Japanese; 60 × 24 in.
Eulalia grass; 72 × 24-36 in.
Gay-feather; 60 × 12 in.
Globe thistle; 48-60 × 24 in.
Queen-of-the-prairie; 48-72 × 36 in.

Shade

Anemone, Japanese; 60 × 24 in.
Bugbane; 72 × 24 in.
Goat's-beard; 72 × 36 in.
Meadow rue; 60 × 24 in.
Monk's-hood; 48 × 12 in.

Selecting Vines

While not common, a climbing vine can be used quite effectively in the background section of a Decorative Home Garden or even a Herbaceous Flower Border. A flowering vine is an exciting way to gain an additional source of color in the season.

Vines need support for their climbing growth. Most people automatically think of trellises, but you can actually grow a vine right on a shrub. Charles has an azalea with a clematis planted right underneath. The vine grows up through the azalea branches and emerges on the top. Charles makes sure to prune the clematis every year in early spring to avoid shading the shrub. In this spring pruning he clips away all vine growth

on top of the azalea. The effect that's created is two bloom periods from the same plant; first the azalea bursts into color and then one month later the clematis follows.

If you decide to go the more traditional route, make a place for a trellis or other vertical support in the garden design. On surfaces like wood and stucco, avoid vines that cling directly to the wall, such as climbing hydrangea and Virginia creeper. These vines will leave a residue that is difficult to remove.

Flowering Vines

Clematis hybrids
Climbing hydrangea
Honeysuckle 'Gold Flame'
Hyacinth bean
Morning glory

The Middle Section

This is the main body of your flower garden. The background level may establish some broad shapes and forms, but this is the level where the character of the garden will be set. This middle ground should be attractive, but it shouldn't steal the show from the rest of the garden. You want it to relate to the background area behind it as well as serve as a backdrop for the finishing touches in the foreground.

The garden's middle section may have some small shrubs in it, but it will definitely have a good share of perennials, supported by some annuals. Any bulbs you put in this area will be the larger types, such as tall tulips and daffodils, planted among the larger perennials.

Here is where you group flowers as we discussed in the last chapter. Locate your groupings from the edge of the background section up to within 1 to 3 feet of the front edge of the garden. Select and position one group of plants at a time. As you can see in the sample garden plans in the Gallery of Flower Garden Designs at the end of the chapter, varying the number of plants in each group creates lots of visual interest. Using the same number of plants in a group throughout the garden can lead to a dull display. A cluster of three daylilies right beside five shasta daisies will create more excitement than if you used the same number of each.

When you select plants for this section, think carefully about color, texture, and blooming time. It can be a bit tricky, but try to distribute all three evenly throughout the garden and throughout the season. This will give your garden a nicely balanced visual effect. For example, you don't want all the plants to bloom in May so there's nothing left to flower in July or August. Don't group all the red flowers on one side of the garden; disperse them evenly throughout. Likewise, don't put all the grassy textures in one end of the garden and all the ferny textures in the other. Over the first few years you can work with different ideas and different combinations until the garden begins to look like the one you've been carrying around in your head all this time.

Selecting Perennials

The wider the plant, the fewer there will be in any one grouping. Individual clumps of peonies can even stand by themselves. Create some variation from group to group in height, texture, and color (both blossoms and foliage). Be sure to leave enough space for plant growth in this dense middle section (look at Calculating Spacing in the Flower Garden later in this chapter). As you select and locate the perennials, don't forget to leave some space for annuals and tender

bulbs. The hardy spring bulbs can be planted right between the perennials, so you really don't need to set aside separate space for them.

Mid-Sized Perennials

Sun

Baby's breath; 36 × 24 in.
Bee balm; 36 × 12 in.
Daylily; 12-48 × 24 in.
Foxglove; 48-72 × 18 in.
Iris, Siberian; 24-48 × 18 in.
Sneezeweed; 24-72 × 18 in.

Shade

Geranium, hardy (*Geranium maculatum*); 24 × 18 in.
Hosta; 24 × 24 in.
Solomon's seal; 24-36 × 12 in.
Turtlehead; 36 × 18 in.

Selecting Annuals

Annuals can help you achieve the desired balance of color, texture, and size in the garden. Tuck them in as needed to complement or contrast with the perennials you've chosen for this middle section. You can think of annuals as "problem solvers," especially when you want to balance blooming time and color. An annual's blooming period is usually much longer than a perennial's. Wherever an early-blooming perennial has faded away, leaving a drab spot, pop in a fresh annual to perk up the color in the middle section.

Selecting Bulbs

We're going to point out some common mistakes with bulbs so you can avoid making them. These frequent mistakes include

Mid-Sized Annuals

Sun

Cock's-comb, plumed; 18-24 × 12 in.
Cosmos; 48 × 12 in.
Daisy, gloriosa; 36 × 12 in.
Sage, mealy-cup; 24 × 12 in.
Spider flower; 36-60 × 15 in.

Shade

Coleus; 24 × 18 in.
Perilla; 30 × 12 in.
Sage, mealy-cup; 24 × 12 in.
Sage, scarlet; 12 × 8 in.
Spider flower; 36-60 × 15 in.

planting too few in a group; planting single bulbs; arranging them in straight, "soldier" rows; and not planting enough throughout the garden. Group bulbs into masses of anywhere from 12 to 25, depending on the size of your garden. The hardy spring bulbs are going to be the main source of early color in a garden where little else will be blooming. Since they'll be in the "spotlight," make sure you arrange them attractively. On the other hand, as you plant tender bulbs like dahlias and gladiolus, remember that they will be blooming in the summer with all the other perennials and annuals.

Don't be hesitant about having bulbs and perennials share tight quarters in the garden. Liz was nervous about planting her new purple coneflowers on top of the tulip bulbs last fall as Charles encouraged her to do, but this arrangement has worked out beautifully. When the tulips died back, the coneflowers were just filling in and preparing to blossom. All the plants are healthy and vigorous and doing fine.

There are two approaches to adding lilies, the hardy summer bulbs, to your garden. You can plant them together in a tight group, which means you have to leave a space for them in your plan. Or, if you work with groups of two or three or even with singles, you can set them in among low perennials. The second approach is preferable, since many lily varieties die down in late summer. The surrounding perennials can keep the area filled into the fall. Also, since lilies are tall and narrow, they offer a nice accent to a group of low perennials and don't take up much space.

Mid-Sized Hardy Bulbs

Sun

Daffodil; 15 × 8 in.
Hyacinth, grape; 12 × 3 in.
Hyacinth, wood; 20 × 8 in.
Onion, flowering (*Allium aflatunense*);
     30 × 8 in.
Tulip; 6-30 × 8 in.

Shade

Amaryllis, hardy; 24 × 8 in.
Colchicum; 8 × 8 in.
Daffodil; 15 × 8 in.
Hyacinth, wood; 20 × 8 in.

Mid-Sized Annual Bulbs

Sun

Canna; 36-60 × 36 in.
Dahlia; 24-72 × 24 in.
Gladiolus; 36-48 × 8 in.

Shade

Begonia, tuberous; 12-18 × 12 in.
Caladium; 12 × 12 in.

The Foreground

Here you'll use a combination of low perennials, annuals, and bulbs, either in groupings or as an edging. Many people like to have more annuals in this front section to take advantage of their longer blooming season. For instance, impatiens and marigolds will bloom steadily all summer and into the fall. Attractive, nonflowering annuals like dusty miller are nice in this area to add contrast to the bright and colorful blossoms.

It is in this foreground section that you should be thinking about adding the final elements that will tie the garden design together. Look for any deficiencies in color, texture, or size in the middle area and try to balance them with your choice of plants in the front. If one part of the middle section has broad, deep green foliage, then the front decorative area might include some delicate, light green, fernlike foliage. Or, if the color in the middle section is looking a bit drab, compensate by adding some bright-colored flowers in the foreground. To a degree, you select foreground plants with more concern for how they relate to the plants in the middle section than for how they relate to other foreground plants.

Selecting Low Perennials

Some low-growing perennials, like creeping sedums, lamb's-ears, and creeping phlox, tend to have a matlike growth habit instead of forming individual clumps. This means that they will merge together naturally, which gives a sense of cohesion to the front of the garden. Spacing is not so critical here. If you plant these spreading perennials a little too close, they will not be harmed by the competition and will simply fill in sooner. To position other low-growing but non-creeping perennials, use the guidelines we gave you earlier for perennials under The Middle Section.

Low Perennials

Sun

Bergenia; 12 × 12 in.
Daisy, dwarf Michaelmas; 12 × 12 in.
Geranium, hardy (*Geranium sanguineum*); 12 × 12 in.
Lamb's-ears; 10 × 12 in.
Pink, allwood; 12 × 8 in.

Shade

Barrenwort; 12 × 12 in.
Bleeding heart, fringed; 12 × 12 in.
Fern, Japanese painted; 12 × 12 in.
Lily-turf; 12 × 12 in.
Phlox, creeping; 6 × 8 in.

Selecting Annuals

The approach to using annuals in the foreground is much the same as for using annuals in the middle section. They are still problem solvers and space fillers. In addition to the annuals you choose first thing in the season, you can always pick some up later to solve a problem or replace a plant that isn't living up to your expectations.

Low Annuals

Sun

Alyssum, sweet; 4 × 6 in.
Dusty miller; 12 × 12 in.
Globe amaranth 'Buddy'; 8 × 8 in.
Moss rose; 4 × 8 in.
Nasturtium; 12 × 12 in.

Shade

Begonia, bedding; 12 × 12 in.
Browallia; 12 × 12 in.
Caladium; 12 × 12 in.
Impatiens; 12 × 12 in.
Lobelia; 8 × 6 in.

Selecting Bulbs

Here you use bulbs that will grow to only 15 inches or so. You can plant lots of them in among the low perennials just as you set higher bulbs among the taller perennials. Follow the same rules for grouping bulbs rather than sprinkling individual ones around the garden.

Small Bulbs

Sun

Crocus, Dutch; 4 × 4 in.
Glory-of-the-snow; 6 × 3 in.
Iris, netted; 4 × 4 in.
Narcissus; 4-15 × 4-8 in.
Onion, flowering *(Allium ostrowskianum)*;
    6 × 4 in.

Shade

Crocus, Dutch; 4 × 4 in.
Hyacinth, grape; 12 × 3 in.
Snowdrop; 6 × 4 in.
Squill, Siberian; 6 × 4 in.
Winter aconite; 3 × 3 in.

Some Special Features

By now you should have a pretty solid idea of how to make the final selections of plants for your 60-Minute Flower Garden. In addition to the more practical, basic steps we've been discussing, there are some other factors you might want to consider. Do you want to attract birds and butterflies to your garden? Do you want to have lots of flowers for cutting so you can bring the beauty of the garden inside? This section is full of ideas to inspire you to create some special features in your flower garden.

Working Wildlife into the Plan

All the different types of flower gardens described in this book can include plants that will attract some favored wildlife such as songbirds, hummingbirds, and butterflies. There are perennials, annuals, and shrubs that provide food for some of nature's most beautiful creatures while at the same time bringing beauty to the garden. We feel that if you can accomplish both objectives simultaneously, the enjoyment of your flower garden increases correspondingly.

Songbirds bring joy to any garden with their bright colors and their happy songs. They can also help the gardener control pests by eating insects. Here is a list of attractive shrubs that provide a source of food and shelter for songbirds. Since our modest-sized 60-Minute Flower Gardens have a limited number of plants, you may want to focus attention on those shrubs that provide some food for your birds in the winter.

Plants to Attract Songbirds

Shrubs

Autumn olive
Bayberry
Butterfly bush
Holly
Pyracantha
Spice bush
Viburnum

Flowers

Aster
Cosmos
Forget-me-not
Marigold
Portulaca
Zinnia

There is something very special about hummingbirds. Whether it's their dazzling colors, their diminutive size, or their amazing flying skills, their appearance excites us for a tantalizing moment as they dart through our flower garden. Their constant state of motion requires a large quantity of nectar each day, but they are choosy about the kind of flower they frequent. They prefer red blossoms and a long, narrow flower shape to use that toothpick of a beak they have.

If you are really interested in attracting some hummingbirds to your garden, we suggest a dual approach. Set up an artificial hummingbird feeder right in your garden and keep it filled with sugar water that's colored red. In addition, choose two or three flowers for the garden that will bloom at different times in the season to keep these little hummers interested in your yard. This two-pronged approach should work if you live in an area where hummingbirds can be found.

Flowers to Attract Hummingbirds

Azalea
Bee balm*
Beauty bush
Cotoneaster
Delphinium
Fuchsia
Impatiens
Morning glory
Petunia*
Phlox
Salvia*
Trumpet creeper*
Weigela

*These have red, trumpet-shaped flowers that are special favorites.

Brightly colored butterflies almost seem like flying flower blossoms as they flit and dodge around your flower beds. These delightful creatures live on flower nectar. Since certain flowers have more nectar than others, those are the ones you want to plant to attract butterflies. The very best lure for butterflies is the aptly named butterfly bush, which is a shrub that will grow from 3 to 10 feet tall. It is a good candidate for a sunny Decorative Home Garden. From early summer until frost, the butterfly bush bears abundant fragrant flowers that resemble lilacs. Various varieties have lilac, purple, red, or white blossoms. It's easy to grow and just one plant is sure to attract dozens of pretty butterflies. Butterfly weed and certain sedums are supreme among perennials for attracting hordes of butterflies.

Flowers to Attract Butterflies

Alyssum, sweet
Aster
Butterfly bush
Butterfly weed
Candytuft
Cardinal flower
Coreopsis
Daisy, shasta
Mignonette
Phlox
Scabiosa
Sedums (*Sedum spectabile* and S. 'Autumn Joy')
Verbena
Viper's bugloss

Having Flowers for Display in Your Home

Most people would agree that if you have a flower garden, you'll want to be able to bring some flowers inside to add color and warmth to your living areas. There are two ways you can do this. You can grow flowers that are good for cutting fresh and flowers that are particularly attractive for drying. Many experienced flower gardeners will have a separate flower bed that is devoted exclusively to cutting flowers. Likewise, a serious dried flower artist will have a whole garden planted only with grasses, foliage plants, and flowers that are best suited to drying. (In Chapter 9 we'll give you some ideas on how to handle freshly cut flowers and flowers for drying to get the best results.)

Because the 60-Minute Flower Garden is considered a relatively small garden, you won't have the space for a wide variety of cutting or drying flowers. Nevertheless, you can select some plants for these purposes. There is no reason why you can't plan your 60-Minute Flower Garden so that you'll have at least one fresh bouquet almost every week. Some varieties of flowers, such as zinnias and dahlias, will flourish and produce even more blooms if they are routinely picked.

Liz begins the season with little snips of azalea, a few stems of pussy willow, and the ubiquitous forsythia arranged in a bright bouquet on the coffee table. As the season develops, vases with lilacs and tulips appear, then pansies and lilies of-the-valley take over, followed by breathtaking splashes of peonies. Later she switches to bunches of zinnias and dahlias, and finally closes the season with fall chrysanthemums.

Outstanding Flowers for Cutting

Aster, China
Black-eyed Susan
Cock's-comb
Columbine
Cosmos
Dahlia
Gladiolus
Indigo, false
Marigold
Peony
Sage, mealy-cup
Snapdragon
Yarrow, fernleaf
Zinnia

Outstanding Flowers for Drying

Baby's breath
Cock's-comb, crested
Cock's-comb, plumed
Globe amaranth
Globe thistle
Lavender, Hidcote
Lavender, Mitcham gray
Sage, mealy-cup
Statice
Strawflower
Tansy
Wormwood, Silver King
Yarrow, fernleaf
Xeranthemum

Evaluating the Final Design

As you select plants to fill the areas in your garden, you should be drawing them into your plan. This is where having a few extra copies of your garden sketch will come in handy. You can make a few different versions before you do the fine-tuning to arrive at your final design.

Use circles to represent the plants as you sketch them in their places in the garden. There's no need to get fancy and do an artistic version showing leaves, flowers, and actual plant shapes. Simple circles will serve your purposes. As you place the plants in your "paper" garden, you also need to take into account the proper amount of growing space they need.

Calculating Spacing in the Flower Garden

One of the key tasks in designing your flower garden is to allow the right amount of space between the various plants so that when they are full grown their leaves will just barely touch each other, creating a natural canopy over the soil. This tightly spaced garden will look better, have fewer weeds, and lose less water to evaporation. You're probably wondering how you're supposed to plan the spacing between plants when each variety is a different size.

In The Best Plants chart in the Appendix, as well as in each of the lists in this chapter, we give you two numbers—the height and the width or breadth of each plant. It is the plant's width that is important in figuring out plant spacing. What we're calling the width is the same as the diameter of the plant. This also happens to be the same figure you find on most seed packets and in many garden books as the spacing to use between plants in the garden. You must remember, though, that this spacing refers only to the distance between plants of the *same* variety and doesn't apply to the spacing between one plant and another completely different plant. The seed packet may tell you to plant dwarf zinnias 12 inches apart, but that spacing guide isn't much help when you're planting zinnias next to peonies.

The best way to deal with the spacing between different-sized plants in the garden plan is to use the *radius* of all the plants in your calculations. The radius is one half the diameter, or width, of the plant. The accompanying illustration shows that when you use the radius of each of the plants as your guide, it's easy to determine the spacing between completely different-sized plants. This trick is also handy for figuring the proper spacing between plants of the same size.

As a general rule, it is better to leave too much space between plants than not enough. As you gain more experience with flowers you'll know when you can tighten up on the spacing. There is another guide you might need to remember, especially when working in the relatively small area of the 60-Minute Flower Garden. On occasions you may want to squeeze a few plants into a space that seems too small for them. The rule in this case is to fit plants of the same variety into a tight space rather than two very different types of plants. It has been Charles's experience that plants of the same variety are better able to compete in tight quarters than two completely different plants.

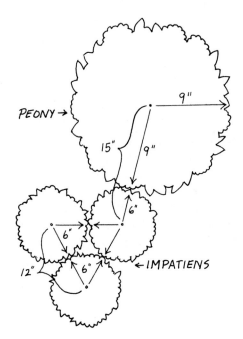

Plant Spacing: *Use the radius, or half the diameter (width), of each plant as your guide. When you set two of the same plants side by side, add their radius measurements together to get the distance to allow between the centers of the plants. In this example, impatiens with a 6-inch radius are planted 12 inches apart. When you set two different plants next to each other, add their radius measurements in the same way. Here the peony, with a 9-inch radius, is planted 15 inches away from the neighboring impatiens.*

While we're on the subject of spacing, most flower garden plants should be at least 1 foot (3 to 4 feet if you can spare the space) away from the house or any other building to provide access for checking electric meters, painting, and washing windows. This buffer zone also provides better ventilation to the plants, which reduces disease possibilities.

A Final Review

Some gardeners will point out that the design for a flower garden is never finished, and they're quite right. The garden plan is adjusted every year, maybe only slightly, but still it changes steadily over time. Even though a garden design is never permanent, at this point you might want to give your 60-Minute Flower Garden design the once-over to make sure you haven't forgotten something. This final review can be especially helpful for those gardeners who are designing their first flower garden. What follow are a few questions to ask yourself as you review the garden design. These questions are simply meant as a useful checklist, so don't feel there's something wrong with your garden if you don't have an answer for every single one.

First of all, is your design appropriate for the garden room you selected? Is it too formal or does it create an access problem you didn't spot before? Is your flower garden design simple? A simple plan will work better than a complex plan, at least for the beginning gardener. Are the height transitions from front to back and from side to side gradual as opposed to extreme? Extreme changes can be very effective but usually take some experience to pull off well. Have you filled in blank spaces with annuals rather than with perennials, which will have to be transplanted later as they mature and take up more space?

Does your garden have some kind of interesting feature throughout every season of the year? Are you taking advantage of existing evergreen shrubs to form a backdrop for your flowers? Do you know what color the leaves of each plant turn in the fall and winter? There are shrubs that change to a nice yellow or even orange. Any kind of variation throughout the season will have some value. While not a top priority, is there anything in your design that provides winter interest, such as berries or seed pods?

Now that your design is complete, go back and try to visualize the different views your garden will offer. Does it look as nice from inside the house as it will from across the street? Do a final check of the scale of the plants in the design and how that will change over time. Remember that some flowers, particularly perennials, take a year or two to settle in and become established. Often another critical look the following year will demonstrate that you did better than you thought. If there are any empty spaces, you can always add some bulbs or annuals.

After reviewing these questions, you should have in hand a design for a 60-Minute Flower Garden that will be easy to build and even easier to maintain. Now that you're done with the "mental" stage of flower gardening, in the next three chapters we'll talk about the "physical" parts—soil care, watering, feeding, and controlling pests. Then, finally, in Chapter 9 we'll put all the pieces together and show you how to plant and maintain the garden. We're sure that a few years from now you'll find that you have one of the finest flower gardens in the neighborhood, not because you spend huge amounts of time caring for it but because initially you took the necessary time to properly plan and design it. This initial planning is one of the secrets that make the 60-Minute Flower Garden such a success.

A Gallery of Flower Garden Designs

With these garden designs we want to inspire you and give you a starting point for creating your own flower garden. In theory, if you take one of these garden plans and the accompanying list of plants to a local nursery, you should be able to get almost everything you need right there (or appropriate local substitutes) and be able to come home and put in a stunning 60-Minute Flower Garden. But we don't expect that everyone will want to copy these plans precisely as they are offered. Every gardener has favorite plants that aren't necessarily included in these plans. Plus, there are certain plants we feature that might not grow as well in your area as some local substitutes. Nevertheless, these plans can act as guidelines. Pick the one that excites you the most and comes closest to the vision of the flower garden you carry in your head. Take it to the nursery, discuss it with a knowledgeable nursery staff person, and use it to help you select plants.

We should explain here that you won't find every plant in these lists covered in The Best Plants chart at the back of the book.

For instance, some of the lists give names of flowering shrubs. Because we had to limit the size of the chart, there was no room to include shrubs along with perennial and annual flowers. Some of the flowers suggested in these lists aren't in the chart, either. We view the chart as featuring the best of the best. The plants included in this section's lists that aren't in the chart are still outstanding choices. If you have questions on how to grow them or you want to know more about them, consult one of the general flower gardening books listed under Recommended Reading.

There are nine plans offered here that have been developed by Charles. They are designed to be maintained within the 60-minute-a-week time frame. The plants in the designs are generally easy to grow in most parts of the country. Obviously, you can easily change the shape of the garden to fit your own needs, but we hope that the way Charles has laid out each plan will be helpful in illustrating the techniques and principles we have discussed in the past five chapters.

70

To make the garden plans easy to follow, the plant shapes are numbered to correspond to the accompanying plant lists. The gray-shaded areas with numbers in boxes hold bulbs and spring-blooming annuals. The jagged circles represent shrubs. Perennials are shown as groups of individual circles connected by straight lines or outlined by a boundary line. Annuals appear as irregular groupings with no individual circles inside boundary lines.

In addition to the plant list, each illustrated garden plan has some notes that you'll find helpful in carrying out that particular garden design. And to help you visualize how beautiful the finished garden will be, there are color illustrations of six of the nine gardens, beginning on page 86.

Decorative Home Garden for Sun

This garden is designed to be a spectacular mixed flower garden of shrubs and flowers. All of the shrubs (except the holly) bloom in summer to add to the riot of color provided by the other flowers. This garden could be located anywhere, but in our example it is situated in front of a house between the driveway and the front door.

The shrubs are an important part of this Decorative Home Garden since, when they mature, they will provide most of the height at the back of the bed. For the sake of the garden's proportions, don't let these shrubs become overgrown; it is essential to learn how to prune each type to maintain the proper effect. While the shrubs are small, use annuals to fill in the spaces around them. Don't allow the annuals to crowd and cause potential damage to the shrubs. We chose Diana rose-of-Sharon for this garden because it is a variety that doesn't produce seed, which eliminates an extra weeding chore.

Some space-saving techniques have been used to fit as much into the garden as possible. Early-blooming Oriental poppies have been placed under the butterfly bushes. Butterfly bushes need to be cut back in the spring, and this gives the poppies a chance to be out in the open while they're in bloom. As the poppies go dormant in midsummer, the butterfly bushes will overgrow the space. Larger bulbs such as tulips, daffodils, and flowering onions are normally planted between larger clumps of perennials. As the bulbs go dormant in early summer, the perennials cover the space that's left bare. You can also put tulips directly under shallow-rooted bee balm. (Different hybrid groups of tulips are used in this plan to provide a range of heights and bloom times.) Small, very early-blooming bulbs such as crocus and snowdrop can be planted under deciduous shrubs (those that shed their leaves in the fall) like rose-of-Sharon. They can also be planted along the front among the low perennials (remember that they may get in the way when you transplant and divide those perennials). Summer-flowering bulbs such as lilies are placed between lower perennials, which they will tower above.

A few patches of annuals have been regularly spaced in the plan to provide continous summer color. In the early spring, before it is warm enough to plant summer annuals, use early frost-tolerant annuals such as pansies. Or count on spring-blooming bulbs such as tulips that you planted the previous fall to provide early spots of color. Then, as the bulb leaves begin to die down in late spring, set young annual plants among them.

Decorative Home Garden for Light Shade

Spectacular color is difficult to achieve in the shade. You can't rely heavily on flow-

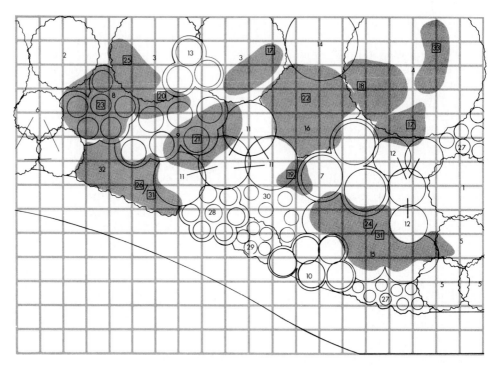

Decorative Home Garden for Sun (gray areas show additions for spring)

ers, so interesting foliage combinations and contrasts become especially important. Most shrubs for shade are spring blooming, but even after their flowers have faded they provide a nice background for the rest of the garden. Many are also evergreen, so they'll provide continuous foliage interest throughout the year. The shrubs are arranged first, since they are the largest elements in the design, and then the rest of the garden is planned around the shrubs. (For our purposes, we show you the mountain laurel in bloom; in a real garden it would not be in bloom at the same time as the other plants shown.)

When the shrubs are small you can plant perennials and annuals in among them, but watch carefully to be sure that they don't crowd and possibly damage the shrubs. This can also happen with smaller varieties of shrubs that are mixed in with larger flowers. For example, in this garden the bugbane could fall over onto the cherry cotoneaster and shade out a section of its branches.

The early-blooming small bulbs will do well planted under deciduous shrubs like hydrangea and under some perennials like hosta. Plant these diminutive bulbs in masses of 50 to 100 for the most impact. Tulips from different hybrid groups are featured

Decorative Home Garden for Sun

Small Shrubs

1. Bluebeard (*Caryopteris clandonensis*); 36 × 36 in.
2. Blue holly 'China Girl' (*Ilex* 'China Girl'); 96 × 60 in.
3. Butterfly bush (*Buddleia davidii*); 72 × 60 in.
4. Rose-of-Sharon (*Hibiscus syriacus* 'Diana'); 96 × 60 in.
5. Shrubby cinquefoil (*Potentilla fruticosa*); 18 × 18 in.
6. Spirea 'Gold Flame'; 18 × 24 in.

Other Suggestions

Deutzia gracilis; 36 × 36 in.
Rosa rugosa; 72 × 48 in.

Mid-Sized Perennials

7. Anemone, Japanese; 60 × 24 in.
8. Bee balm; 36 × 12 in.
9. Coneflower, purple; 36 × 18 in.
10. Coreopsis, thread-leaf 'Moonbeam'; 15-18 × 12 in.
11. Daylily; 36 × 24 in.
12. Iris, Siberian; 24-48 × 18 in.
13. Poppy, Oriental; 36 × 18 in.
14. Queen-of-the-prairie; 48-72 × 36 in.

Other Suggestions

Baby's breath; 36 × 24 in.
Bellflower, clustered; 12-36 × 24 in.

Mid-Sized Annuals

15. Sage, mealy-cup; 24 × 12 in.
16. Spider flower; 36-60 × 15 in.

Other Suggestions

Canna; 36-60 × 36 in.
Cock's-comb, plumed 'Century Mix'; 18-24 × 12 in.
Cosmos 'Sensation Mix'; 48 × 12 in.
Dahlia, bedding; 18 × 12 in.
Daisy, gloriosa; 36 × 12 in.
Larkspur; 24-48 × 10 in.
Sage, scarlet; 12-36 × 8-12 in.
Zinnia; 12-36 × 8-15 in.

Mid-Sized Bulbs

17. Daffodil; 15 × 8 in.
18. Hyacinth, wood; 20 × 8 in.
19. Lily, Asiatic hybrid; 24-60 × 8 in.
20. Lily, Aurelian hybrid; 48-72 × 24 in.
21. Onion, flowering (*Allium aflatunense*); 30 × 8 in.
22. Tulip, Darwin; 20-26 × 8 in.
23. Tulip, Fosteriana; 10-20 × 8 in.
24. Tulip, Greigii; 8-12 × 8 in.
25. Tulip, lily-flowered; 20-26 × 8 in.
26. Tulip, single early; 12-14 × 8 in.

Other Suggestion

Hyacinth, grape; 12 × 3 in.

Low Perennials

27. Coral bells; 18 × 12 in.
28. Daisy, dwarf Michaelmas; 12 × 12 in.
29. Lamb's-ears; 10 × 12 in.
30. Pink, allwood; 12 × 8 in.

Other Suggestions

Basket-of-gold; 10 × 12 in.
Bergenia; 12 × 12 in.
Geranium, hardy (*Geranium sanguineum*); 12 × 12 in.
Speedwell, spike; 15 × 12 in.
Speedwell, woolly; 12-18 × 12 in.
Yarrow, woolly; 12 × 10 in.

Low Annuals

31. Pansy; 8 × 8 in.
32. Periwinkle, rose; 12-18 × 12 in.

Other Suggestions

Ageratum; 15 × 15 in.
Alyssum, sweet; 4-8 × 6 in.
Dusty miller; 12 × 12 in.
Gazania; 8 × 8 in.
Globe amaranth 'Buddy'; 6-8 × 8 in.
Moss rose; 4 × 8 in.
Nasturtium; 12 × 12 in.
Petunia; 12-18 × 12 in.

Small Bulbs

33. Crocus, Dutch; 4 × 4 in.

Other Suggestions

Crocus, autumn; 3 × 3 in.
Crocus, snow; 3 × 3 in.
Daffodil, dwarf; 6 × 4 in.
Glory-of-the-snow; 6 × 3 in.
Iris, netted; 4 × 4 in.
Sternbergia; 6 × 4 in.

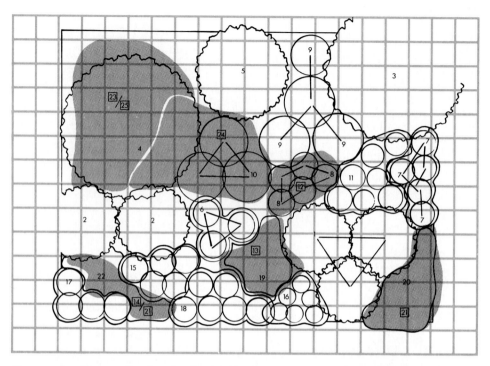

Decorative Home Garden for Light Shade (gray areas show additions for spring)

in this plan to provide a range of heights and bloom times.

Annuals have been used at regular intervals for continuous color. Although they primarily provide summer color, early annuals, such as pansies and forget-me-nots and spring bulbs, can be used in these areas for early infusions of color.

The foxgloves are biennials that will sow their own seed to give you new seedlings each year. Transplant these new little foxgloves in July. Pull the extras and be careful that the numerous seedlings don't crowd out your other flowers. You can prevent a population explosion of foxgloves by removing the flowering stalks before all the seed has fallen.

Herbaceous Flower Border for Sun

This border could be backed by either a building, a fence, or a solid background of existing shrubs as shown here. Since shrubs aren't an integral part of the design, tall perennials must be used at the back for height. The tall eulalia grass was chosen for its dramatic textural contrast and for its contemporary appearance. Its fall-blooming, plumelike flower stalks will provide interest all winter. (Although eulalia grass is not

Decorative Home Garden for Light Shade

Small Shrubs

1. Cherry cotoneaster *(Cotoneaster apiculata)*; 36 × 36 in.
2. Drooping leucothoe *(Leucothoe fontanesiana)*; 36 × 48 in.
3. Mountain laurel *(Kalmia latifolia)*; 60 × 60 in.
4. Oakleaf hydrangea *(Hydrangea quercifolia)*; 72 × 72 in.
5. Rhododendron 'P.J.M.'; 60 × 48 in.

Other Suggestion

Azalea; 24-72 × 48-72 in.

Mid-Sized Perennials

6. Anemone, Japanese; 60 × 24 in.
7. Astilbe; 24-48 × 24-36 in.
8. Bugbane; 72 × 24 in.
9. Goat's-beard; 72 × 36 in.
10. Hosta *(Hosta sieboldiana)*; 24 × 36 in.

Other Suggestions

Bleeding heart, common; 30 × 24 in.
Columbine 'McKana Hybrids'; 24-36 × 18 in.
Geranium, hardy *(Geranium maculatum)*; 24 × 18 in.
Hosta 'Aureo-marginata'; 24-36 × 36 in.
Meadow rue; 60 × 24 in.
Solomon's seal; 36 × 12 in.

Mid-Sized Biennials

11. Foxglove; 24-60 × 18 in.

Mid-Sized Annuals

Suggestions

Coleus; 24 × 18 in.
Perilla; 30 × 12 in.
Sage, mealy-cup 'Victoria'; 18-24 × 12 in.
Sage, scarlet; 12-36 × 8-12 in.
Spider flower; 36-60 × 15 in.

Mid-Sized Bulbs

12. Daffodil; 15 × 8 in.
13. Tulip, Darwin; 20-26 × 8 in.
14. Tulip, single early; 12-14 × 8 in.

Other Suggestions

Amaryllis, hardy; 24 × 8 in.
Colchicum; 8 × 8 in.
Hyacinth, wood; 20 × 8 in.

Low Perennials

15. Bleeding heart, fringed; 12 × 12 in.
16. Fern, Japanese painted; 12 × 12 in.
17. Lamium 'Beacon Silver'; 8 × 12 in.
18. Siberian bugloss; 15 × 18 in.

Other Suggestions

Ajuga; 6 × 8 in.
Barrenwort; 12 × 12 in.
Lenten rose; 12 × 18 in.
Lily-turf; 12 × 12 in.
Pachysandra; 8 × 8 in.
Phlox, creeping; 6 × 8 in.

Low Annuals

19. Begonia, bedding; 12 × 12 in.
20. Impatiens; 12 × 12 in.
21. Pansy; 8 × 8 in.
22. Wishbone flower; 8-14 × 6-8 in.

Other Suggestions

Begonia, tuberous; 12-18 × 12 in.
Browallia; 12 × 12 in.
Caladium; 12 × 12 in.
Forget-me-not; 9 × 6 in.
Lobelia; 8 × 6 in.
Periwinkle, rose; 12-18 × 12 in.

Small Bulbs

23. Crocus, snow; 3 × 3 in.
24. Snowdrop; 6 × 4 in.
25. Squill, Siberian; 6 × 4 in.

Other Suggestions

Crocus, autumn; 3 × 3 in.
Crocus, Dutch; 4 × 4 in.
Glory-of-the-snow; 6 × 3 in.
Hyacinth, grape; 12 × 3 in.
Iris, netted; 4 × 4 in.
Winter aconite; 3 × 3 in.

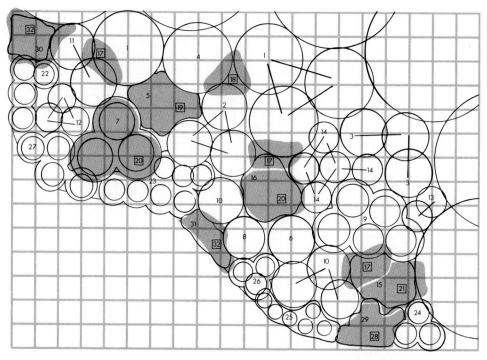

Herbaceous Flower Border for Sun (gray areas show additions for spring)

normally in bloom in midsummer, we have included the flowers in the color illustration to show you how dramatic this grass can be.) The eulalia grass was set in the garden first, then all the other plants were put in place, working from the back toward the front.

The Oriental poppies were strategically placed behind other perennials to camouflage the bare spot the poppies leave when they die down in early summer.

There are several tricks Charles has used to get the maximum color from the space available. As in the Decorative Home Garden, annuals have been included in the plan at regular intervals for continuous summer color. These spaces can be planted with tulips or early annuals such as pansies

for early bursts of spring color. Then, as the tulip foliage matures in late spring, you can set the young annual plants in the open spaces.

Plant spring-blooming bulbs between the clumps of larger perennials. As the perennials grow they cover the dying bulb foliage. You can even plant the taller varieties of daffodils and tulips directly under shallow-rooted perennials such as bee balm. (Different hybrid groups of tulips are included in the plan for a range of heights and bloom times.) Although they're not included in this plan, you can tuck small bulbs like crocus and sternbergia among low perennials at the front of the bed. Just keep in mind that they are likely to get in the way of future dividing and transplanting of the perennials.

Herbaceous Flower Border for Sun

Tall Perennials

1. Eulalia grass; 72 × 30 in.
2. Gay-feather; 60 × 12 in.
3. Globe thistle 'Taplow Blue'; 48-60 × 24 in.
4. Queen-of-the-prairie; 48-72 × 36 in.

Other Suggestion

Anemone, Japanese; 60 × 24 in.

Tall Annuals

5. Spider flower; 36-60 × 15 in.

Mid-Sized Perennials

6. Baby's breath; 36 × 24 in.
7. Bee balm; 36 × 12 in.
8. Bellflower, clustered; 12-36 × 24 in.
9. Coneflower, purple; 36 × 18 in.
10. Daylily; 36 × 24 in.
11. Heliopsis; 36-48 × 24 in.
12. Iris, Siberian; 24-48 × 18 in.
13. Poppy, Oriental; 36 × 18 in.
14. Sneezeweed; 48 × 18 in.

Other Suggestion

Coreopsis, thread-leaf 'Moonbeam';
    15-18 × 12 in.

Mid-Sized Annuals

15. Sage, mealy-cup 'Victoria'; 18-24 × 12 in.
16. Snapdragon 'Rocket' series; 30 × 12 in.

Other Suggestions

Canna; 36-60 × 36 in.
Cock's-comb, plumed 'Century Mix';
    18-24 × 12 in.
Cosmos 'Sensation Mix'; 48 × 12 in.
Dahlia, bedding, 18 × 12 in.
Daisy, gloriosa; 36 × 12 in.
Larkspur; 24-48 × 10 in.
Zinnia; 12-36 × 8-15 in.

Mid-Sized Bulbs

17. Daffodil; 15 × 8 in.
18. Hyacinth, wood; 20 × 8 in.
19. Tulip, Darwin; 20-26 × 8 in.
20. Tulip, Darwin hybrid; 20-26 × 8 in.
21. Tulip, Greigii; 8-12 × 8 in.

Other Suggestions

Hyacinth, grape; 12 × 3 in.
Lily, Asiatic hybrid; 24-60 × 8 in.
Lily, Aurelian hybrid; 48-72 × 24 in.
Onion, flowering *(Allium aflatunense)*;
    30 × 8 in.

Low Perennials

22. Bergenia; 12 × 12 in.
23. Daisy, dwarf Michaelmas; 12 × 12 in.
24. Geranium, hardy *(Geranium sanguineum)*;
    12 × 12 in.
25. Lamb's-ears; 10 × 12 in.
26. Pink, allwood; 12 × 8 in.
27. Wormwood, Silver Mound; 12 × 18 in.

Other Suggestions

Basket-of-gold; 10 × 12 in.
Coral bells; 18 × 12 in.
Speedwell, spike; 15 × 12 in.
Speedwell, woolly; 18 × 12 in.
Yarrow, woolly; 12 × 10 in.

Low Annuals

28. Forget-me-not; 9 × 6 in.
29. Gazania; 8 × 8 in.
30. Globe amaranth 'Buddy'; 6-8 × 8 in.
31. Moss rose; 4 × 8 in.
32. Pansy; 8 × 8 in.

Other Suggestions

Ageratum; 15 × 15 in.
Dusty miller; 12 × 12 in.
Nasturtium; 12 × 12 in.
Periwinkle, rose; 12-18 × 12 in.
Petunia; 12-18 × 12 in.

Small Bulbs

Suggestions

Crocus, autumn; 3 × 3 in.
Crocus, Dutch; 4 × 4 in.
Crocus, snow; 3 × 3 in.
Daffodil, dwarf; 6 × 4 in.
Glory-of-the-snow; 6 × 3 in.
Iris, netted; 4 × 4 in.
Sternbergia; 6 × 4 in.

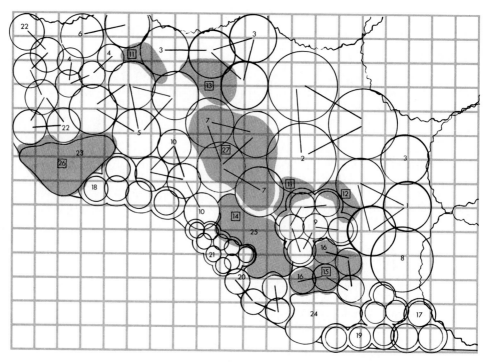

Herbaceous Flower Border for Light Shade (gray areas show additions for spring)

Herbaceous Flower Border for Light Shade

As in the Decorative Home Garden for light shade, flower color is less spectacular in this shady garden, so there must be a greater reliance on interesting foliage combinations and contrasts. Without tall flower garden shrubs in this Herbaceous Flower Border, tall perennials are used at the back for height. Arrange these first and then build the design forward, paying particular attention to interesting foliage combinations.

Here are a few pointers on placing plants in the plan so they'll be used to their fullest advantage. The common bleeding heart has been given a space at the back of the border so that it will be hidden when it goes dor-

mant in the summer. Annuals are included at regular intervals, since they provide more continuous color than perennials. We don't show any in the plan, but mid-sized annuals can be used in place of some mid-sized perennials (in the interest of an easy-maintenance garden, don't replace *all* the perennials with annuals). Since most shade-tolerant annuals are short, they must be used toward the front. Supplement these in the spring with bulbs and early annuals. The small, early-flowering spring bulbs such as Siberian squill, glory-of-the-snow, and snowdrop can be planted under perennials such as hostas. Plant larger bulbs between the more widely spaced perennials. Different tulip hybrids are featured in this garden to provide a range of heights and bloom times.

Herbaceous Flower Border for Light Shade

Tall Perennials

1. Bugbane; 72 × 24 in.
2. Goat's-beard; 72 × 36 in.
3. Meadow rue; 60 × 24 in.
4. Monk's-hood; 48 × 12 in.

Other Suggestion

Anemone, Japanese; 60 × 24 in.

Mid-Sized Perennials

5. Astilbe; 24-48 × 24-36 in.
6. Bleeding heart, common; 30 × 24 in.
7. Hosta *(Hosta sieboldiana);* 24 × 36 in.
8. Hosta 'Aureo-marginata'; 24-36 × 36 in.
9. Solomon's seal; 36 × 12 in.
10. Spiderwort; 24 × 18 in.

Other Suggestions

Columbine 'McKana Hybrids'; 24-36 × 18 in.
Geranium, hardy *(Geranium maculatum);*
    24 × 18 in.
Meadowsweet, Siberian; 48 × 18 in.
Turtlehead; 36 × 18 in.

Mid-Sized Annuals

Suggestions

Coleus; 24 × 18 in.
Perilla; 30 × 12 in.
Sage, mealy-cup 'Victoria'; 18-24 × 12 in.
Sage, scarlet; 12 × 8 in.
Spider flower; 36-60 × 15 in.

Mid-Sized Bulbs

11. Daffodil; 15 × 8 in.
12. Hyacinth, wood; 20 × 8 in.
13. Tulip, cottage; 20-26 × 8 in.
14. Tulip, Darwin; 20-26 × 8 in.
15. Tulip, Greigii; 8-12 × 8 in.

Other Suggestions

Amaryllis, hardy; 24 × 8 in.
Colchicum; 8 × 8 in.

Low Perennials

16. Barrenwort; 12 × 12 in.
17. Fern, Japanese painted; 12 × 12 in.

18. Lamium 'Beacon Silver'; 8 × 12 in.
19. Lily-turf; 12 × 12 in.
20. Lungwort; 12 × 12 in.
21. Phlox, creeping; 6 × 8 in.
22. Siberian bugloss; 15 × 18 in.

Other Suggestions

Ajuga; 6 × 8 in.
Bleeding heart, fringed; 12 × 12 in.
Pachysandra; 8 × 8 in.

Low Annuals

23. Begonia, bedding; 12 × 12 in.
24. Browallia; 12 × 12 in.
25. Impatiens; 12 × 12 in.
26. Pansy; 8 × 8 in.

Other Suggestions

Alyssum, sweet; 4-8 × 6 in.
Begonia, tuberous; 12-18 × 12 in.
Caladium; 12 × 12 in.
Forget-me-not; 9 × 6 in.
Lobelia; 8 × 6 in.
Periwinkle, rose; 12-18 × 12 in.

Small Bulbs

27. Snowdrop; 6 × 4 in.

Other Suggestions

Crocus, autumn; 3 × 3 in.
Crocus, Dutch; 4 × 4 in.
Crocus, snow; 3 × 3 in.
Glory-of-the-snow; 6 × 3 in.
Hyacinth, grape; 12 × 3 in.
Iris, netted; 4 × 4 in.
Squill, Siberian; 6 × 4 in.
Winter aconite; 3 × 3 in.

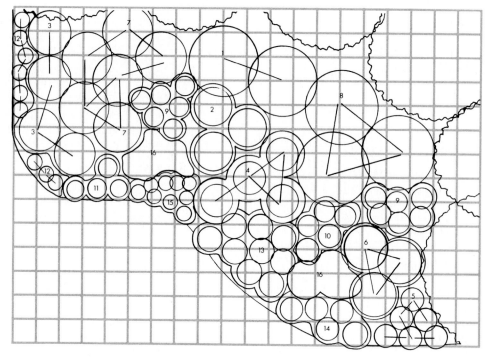

Herbaceous Flower Border for Full Shade

Herbaceous Flower Border for Full Shade

This is a garden designed for fairly heavy shade, a situation that causes many people to despair of ever having an attractive, thriving display of plants. The primary way to overcome the light limitation is to be creative and combine interesting foliage with attractive variations of size, shape, and color. Flower color is more incidental. Although many varieties used in this garden have pleasing flowers, the blossoms aren't usually as showy as those on plants that grow in brighter light. Impatiens is the only flowering annual that will perform adequately in heavy shade.

A patch of impatiens has been used in two places to brighten up the garden.

Although we aren't illustrating the use of bulbs in this plan, the accompanying plant list gives you some ideas of what kinds you can include if you so desire. As in the previous garden designs, you'll count on these for early spring color and tuck them in among perennials. These bulbs will be much more successful in a garden with deciduous shade rather than the year-round shade provided by evergreens. In early spring the leafless trees let in the sun when the bulbs are actively growing.

Herbaceous Flower Border for Full Shade

Tall Perennials

1. Goat's-beard; 72 × 36 in.

Mid-Sized Perennials

2. Bugbane; 72 × 24 in.
3. Fern, Christmas; 24 × 24 in.
4. Fern, lady; 24 × 24 in.
5. Fern, maidenhair; 18 × 12 in.
6. Hosta *(Hosta plantaginea);* 24 × 24 in.
7. Hosta 'Frances Williams'; 24 × 36 in.
8. Hosta 'Krossa Regal'; 60 × 36 in.
9. Solomon's seal; 36 × 12 in.

Other Suggestions

Fern, marginal shield; 18 × 18 in.
Hosta 'Albo-marginata'; 36 × 36 in.

Mid-Sized Bulbs

Suggestions

Amaryllis, hardy; 24 × 8 in.
Colchicum; 8 × 8 in.
Daffodil; 15 × 8 in.
Hyacinth, wood; 20 × 8 in.

Low Perennials

10. Barrenwort; 12 × 12 in.
11. European ginger; 6 × 12 in.
12. Foam flower; 12 × 8 in.
13. Hosta 'Ginko Craig'; 12 × 12 in.
14. Lamium 'Beacon Silver'; 8 × 12 in.
15. Phlox, creeping; 6 × 8 in.

Other Suggestions

Ajuga; 6 × 8 in.
Lily-of-the-valley; 8 × 12 in.
Sweet woodruff; 8 × 12 in.
Trillium; 15 × 12 in.

Low Annuals

16. Impatiens; 12 × 12 in.

Small Bulbs

Suggestions

Daffodil, dwarf; 6 × 4 in.
Glory-of-the-snow; 6 × 3 in.
Snowdrop; 6 × 4 in.
Squill, Siberian; 6 × 4 in.

Woodland Garden

The Woodland Garden doesn't need a lot of maintenance to stay neat and attractive, so it can cover a much larger area than the previous gardens that take a bit more attention (but never more than 60 minutes a week!). To enjoy the Woodland Garden to its fullest, it should be laid out so that you can stroll among and admire the plants.

You'll probably use many more shrubs here than in the other gardens of smaller proportions. The shrubs provide the skeleton of the design and a background for the herbaceous plants.

To begin designing a Woodland Garden, first decide where the path should be placed in relation to the tree trunks and any existing shrubs. Once the backbone of shrubs is planted, you can have fun filling in the spaces between and to the front of the shrubs with a variety of shade-loving perennials that will be attractive all summer long.

Many of the plants we're calling ground covers in this garden were used as low perennials in previous gardens. In this type of garden they can be used to fill in large areas with a carpet of growth, so we are recom-

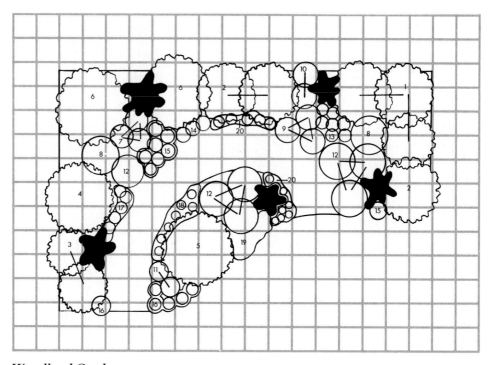

Woodland Garden

mending them for use as weed-suppressing ground covers to reduce maintenance.

If you find that your woodland setting is too dark to grow the attractive plants you want, there are two possible solutions. Where there are many trees crowded together, you can remove the less desirable ones. If you want to keep all the trees, then remove some of the lower branches to allow more light to enter from the sides. High shade is one of the best types of light for a shady garden.

In our list we suggest some plants that aren't shown in the illustrated garden plan.

We're offering these so you have some options to use as you design your own garden. The mid-sized annuals can be used to perk up an area that receives bright light. However, given the choice, we would encourage you to use perennials because of their lower maintenance requirements and because we feel they are more in keeping with the setting. Mid-sized bulbs can be set between low perennials for spots of spring color. Small, early-blooming bulbs planted in masses can be arranged under deciduous shrubs like hydrangea and under perennials like hostas.

Woodland Garden
Shrubs

1. Andromeda *(Pieris japonica)*; 72 × 60 in.
2. Azalea; 24-72 × 48-72 in.
3. Drooping leucothoe *(Leucothoe fontanesiana)*; 36 × 48 in.
4. Linden viburnum *(Viburnum dilatatum)*; 96 × 72 in.
5. Oakleaf hydrangea *(Hydrangea quercifolia)*; 72 × 72 in.
6. Rhododendron; 96 × 72 in.

Tall Perennials

7. Bugbane; 72 × 24 in.
8. Goat's-beard; 72 × 36 in.

Other Suggestions

Anemone, Japanese; 60 × 24 in.
Meadow rue; 60 × 24 in.
Monk's-hood; 48 × 12 in.

Mid-Sized Perennials

9. Astilbe; 24-48 × 24-36 in.
10. Bleeding heart, common; 30 × 24 in.
11. Columbine 'McKana Hybrids'; 24-36 × 18 in.
12. Hosta 'Aureo-marginata'; 24-36 × 36 in.
13. Solomon's seal; 36 × 12 in.

Other Suggestions

Fern, lady; 24 × 24 in.
Geranium, hardy *(Geranium maculatum)*; 24 × 18 in.
Spiderwort; 24 × 18 in.
Turtlehead; 36 × 18 in.
Virginia bluebell; 36 × 12 in.

Mid-Sized Annuals

Suggestions

Coleus; 24 × 18 in.
Foxglove; 48 × 18 in.
Honesty; 18-36 × 12 in.

Mid-Sized Bulbs

Suggestions

Amaryllis, hardy; 24 × 8 in.
Camassia; 36 × 10 in.
Daffodil; 15 × 8 in.
Hyacinth, wood; 20 × 8 in.
Summer snowflake; 15 × 6 in.

Low Perennials

14. Barrenwort; 12 × 12 in.
15. Bleeding heart, fringed; 12 × 12 in.
16. Fern, Japanese painted; 12 × 12 in.
17. Iris, crested; 5 × 8 in.
18. Primrose, polyanthus; 10 × 8 in.

Other Suggestions

Bloodroot; 6 × 8 in.
European ginger; 6 × 12 in.
Golden star; 8 × 12 in.
Lenten rose; 12 × 18 in.
Trillium; 15 × 12 in.

Low Annuals

19. Impatiens; 12 × 12 in.

Other Suggestions

Begonia, bedding; 12 × 12 in.
Coleus; 24 × 18 in.
Forget-me-not; 9 × 6 in.
Periwinkle, rose; 12-18 × 12 in.
Wishbone flower; 8 × 8 in.

Small Bulbs

Suggestions

Anemone, Greek; 4 × 3 in.
Crocus, Dutch; 4 × 4 in.
Crocus, snow; 3 × 3 in.
Glory-of-the-snow; 6 × 3 in.
Guinea flower; 12 × 4 in.
Hyacinth, grape; 12 × 3 in.
Iris, netted; 4 × 4 in.
Snowdrop; 6 × 4 in.
Squill, Siberian; 6 × 4 in.
Winter aconite; 3 × 3 in.

Ground Covers

20. Phlox, creeping; 6 × 8 in.

Other Suggestions

Ajuga; 6 × 8 in.
Foam flower; 12 × 8 in.
Lamium 'Beacon Silver'; 8 × 12 in.
Lily-of-the-valley; 8 × 12 in.
Lungwort; 12 × 12 in.
Pachysandra; 8 × 8 in.
Periwinkle; 6 × 12 in.
Siberian bugloss; 15 × 18 in.
Sweet woodruff; 8 × 12 in.

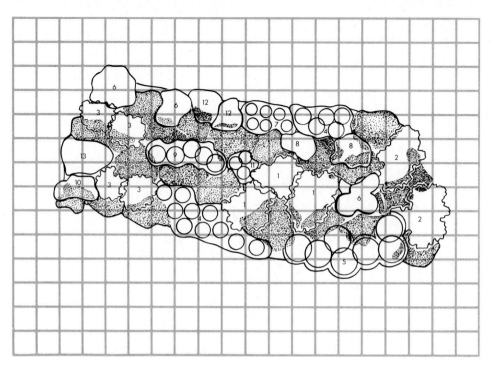

Bank Garden for Sun

Bank Garden for Sun

The Bank Garden takes its inspiration from the traditional rock garden. We are presenting it here as a way of dealing with a bank that is unsightly or difficult to mow. This is one of the few gardens where you actually welcome the rocks! The rocks help hold the soil and create a pleasantly varied terrain for planting. Look for stones that have a natural and somewhat uniform appearance. The stones should be as large as you can manage to work with and should have many shapes, angles, and facets to lend a lively look to the garden. Plain, flat stones are much less interesting. The largest stones should be placed at the bottom of the garden. Most of each rock must be buried for stability and for a natural appearance. Many bank garden plants, such as basket-of-gold, like to have their roots located in the nooks and crannies between two rocks. Fill the

spaces behind the rocks with gritty or sandy topsoil, since many of these plants need excellent drainage. The plants will eventually cover much of the rocks' surface, so that the garden will have 75 percent of its area covered with foliage and blossoms when it matures.

The first plants to be placed should be shrubs, since they provide structure and visual appeal (particularly in the winter). During the first year you'll probably use more annuals to fill space not yet occupied by full-grown perennials. In future years, once the perennials have expanded, you'll need fewer annuals. Seedlings may pop up in cracks and crevices and can be encouraged unless they are crowding other plants.

Although we don't show them in this illustrated garden plan, small or dwarf varieties of bulbs are best suited to the scale of the Bank Garden. Tuck them in among or between low perennials, where they'll thrive.

84

Bank Garden for Sun

Small Shrubs

1. Dwarf Japanese juniper (*Juniperus procumbens* 'Nana'); 18-24 × 24 in.
2. Mugo pine (*Pinus mugo*, dwarf varieties); 36 × 36 in.
3. Shrubby cinquefoil (*Potentilla fruticosa*); 18 × 18 in.

Other Suggestions

Creeping cotoneaster (*Cotoneaster adpressa*); 12-18 × 24 in.
Heller Japanese holly (*Ilex crenata* 'Helleri'); 24 × 24 in.

Mid-Sized Perennials

4. Iris, bearded; 12-36 × 8 in.
5. Geranium, hardy (*Geranium sanguineum*); 12 × 12 in.
6. Sedum 'Autumn Joy'; 24 × 15 in.
7. Woolly veronica; 18 × 12 in.

Other Suggestions

Beard-tongue; 18 × 12 in.
Coral bells; 18 × 12 in.
Spurge, cushion; 12 × 18 in.
Salvia 'East Friesland'; 18-24 × 18 in.
Wormwood, Silver Mound; 12 × 18 in.
Yarrow, moonshine; 24 × 18 in.

Low Perennials

8. Basket-of-gold; 10 × 12 in.
9. Carpathian harebell; 12 × 10 in.
10. Myrtle spurge; 6 × 12 in.
11. Pink, allwood; 12 × 8 in.
12. Pink, moss; 4 × 12 in.

Other Suggestions

Candytuft, hardy; 8 × 12 in.
Daisy, dwarf Michaelmas, 12 × 12 in.
Hen-and-chickens; 3 × 3 in.
Rock cress (*Arabis albida*); 6 × 10 in.
Thyme, lemon (*Thymus serpyllum*); 3 × 8 in.

Low Annuals

13. Moss rose; 4 × 8 in.

Other Suggestions

Ageratum; 15 × 15 in.
Alyssum, sweet; 4-8 × 6 in.
Globe amaranth 'Buddy'; 6-8 × 8 in.
Nasturtium; 12 × 12 in.
Pansy; 8 × 8 in.
Phlox, annual; 12 × 8 in.
Poppy, alpine; 8 × 8 in.
Verbena; 8 × 10 in.
Zinnia, creeping; 6 × 12 in.

Small Bulbs

Suggestions

Anemone, Greek; 4 × 3 in.
Anemone, poppy-flowered; 12 × 8 in.
Crocus, autumn; 3 × 3 in.
Crocus, snow; 3 × 3 in.
Daffodil, dwarf; 6 × 4 in.
Hyacinth, grape; 12 × 3 in.
Iris, netted; 4 × 4 in.
Onion, flowering (*Allium albo-pilosum*); 24 × 8 in.
Onion, flowering (*Allium ostrowskianum*); 6 × 4 in.
Tulip (smaller types); 6-15 in. × 4-8 in.

A Gallery of Flower Garden Designs continues on page 118

Decorative Home Garden for Sun (midsummer)

Decorative Home Garden for Shade (early summer)

Herbaceous Flower Border for Sun (midsummer)

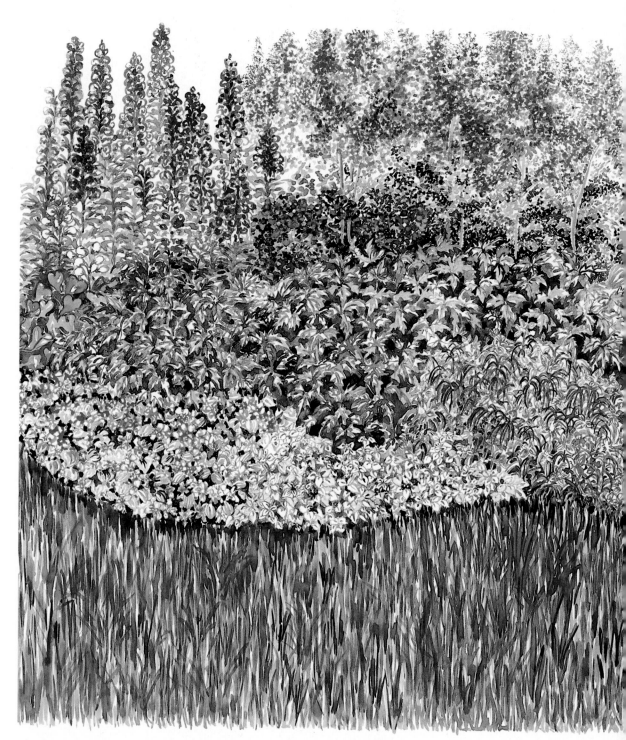

Herbaceous Flower Border for Light Shade (late summer)

Herbaceous Flower Border for Full Shade (late summer)

Decorative Home Garden for Sun: *A delightful mix of shrubs and flowers fills the space between the house and the pathway. As the spring-blooming bulbs fade, perennials and annuals take over to provide a progression of color.* **Decorative Home Garden for Shade:** *Annuals are the main source of bright color in this design. Plants in this garden are selected for their interesting foliage colors, shapes, and textures.* **Herbaceous Flower Border for Sun:** *Eulalia grass makes a dramatically effective background plant in a flower garden. Strategically placed groups of annuals and perennials create attractive pockets of color throughout this border.* **Herbaceous Flower Border for Light Shade:** *Light or partial shade doesn't rule out a colorful, attractive flower garden. Brightly colored flowers are interspersed among plants with interesting foliage shapes and markings to create a garden with pleasing features.* **Herbaceous Flower Border for Full Shade:** *The emphasis in this garden is on plants with striking foliage colorations and textures; impatiens and hosta flowers add the interesting touches of color.* **Woodland Garden:** *Shrubs form the foundation of this garden and the open spaces are filled with shade-loving perennials. A pathway is incorporated into the design to allow the gardener to stroll among the plants.*

Woodland Garden (midspring)

Photo 1

Photo 1: *A woodland garden illuminated by morning sun.* **Photo 2:** *This close-up of the shady flower garden shown in* **Photo 3** *reveals the wonderful interplay of foliage and flower colors and textures. This shaded flower garden in its midsummer splendor is proof that you can have a pleasant display of color in the shade.* **Photo 4:** *Fluffy cream-colored astilbes and two-tone pastel columbines share space in the partially shaded flower garden.*

Photo 2

Photo 3

Photo 4

Photo 5

Photo 6   *Photo 7*

Photo 8

Photo 9

Photo 5: *A sunny herbaceous border designed by Charles Cresson. He has incorporated a pleasing variation in plant heights and has added foxgloves for vertical accents.* **Photo 6:** *A glimpse of part of a sunny herbaceous border created by Charles, with a gold and orange color scheme.* **Photo 7:** *The gloriosa daisy is one of the best annuals for the summer garden.* **Photo 8:** *This sunny herbaceous border contains mostly annuals for a long display of color throughout the summer. The use of more perennials in a garden like this would reduce the amount of work that needs to be done in the spring.* **Photo 9:** *A sunny herbaceous border in which annuals are planted among perennials. This garden won't have the same color impact in summer as the garden in Photo 8, but there's less work to be done in the spring because there are fewer annuals to plant.*

Photo 10   Photo 11

Photo 10: *Snapdragons are traditional favorites in summer gardens. They are easy to start from seed right in the garden, or, if you prefer, you can start them indoors for an early show of color. You can even pick up a flat of snapdragons at the local garden center to tuck into empty spaces in your garden design as the season progresses. Snapdragons are available in practically any color you might desire, and they make excellent cut flowers.*
Photo 11: *The purple and blue flowers in this garden close-up are delphiniums. These perennials are most successfully grown in areas with cool summers. They make good vertical accents in the background of a flower bed.*

Photo 12

Photo 12: *A profusion of peonies and Oriental poppies adds midspring color to this flower bed. The pastel pink of the peony flowers and the delicate shading along the edges of the poppy blossoms make an attractive combination. Both of these plants are available in a wide range of colors in addition to the ones shown here, so you have lots of opportunities to create pleasing color combinations. Peonies and poppies are some of the most popular perennials for midspring displays. These plants share the same light and growing requirements, so they are highly compatible neighbors in the garden. Their size also suits them both for use in the background or middle of a bed. Peony and poppy flowers are excellent for cutting.*

Photo 13

Photo 13: *The informal look of this garden is created by the masses of annual flowers. The low-maintenance way to start a garden like this is to sow the seed directly in the garden soil. To provide some color in early spring, you might want to include some perennials that will be in bloom while the annuals are becoming established.* **Photo 14:** *Foliage textures and colors can create a dramatic effect. In Charles Cresson's shaded herbaceous border, a white-edged hosta is in bloom, flanked by a silvery Japanese painted fern (middle left), with a creeping, yellow-flowered sedum in the foreground. The bearded iris on the right has stopped blooming, but its foliage remains to provide a pleasing accent to the other leaf shapes and colors.*

Photo 14

Photo 15

Photo 16

Photo 15: *Fall and winter are considered the "off-season" in the flower garden, but you can still enjoy a bright, colorful view if you select trees and shrubs with attractive features like these red berries. A holly bush, with its deep green leaves and clusters of red berries, is another good example of a colorful plant.* **Photo 16:** *Charles Cresson designed this sunny herbaceous border at Meadowbrook Farm in Jenkintown, Pennsylvania. He incorporated the misty gray foliage of Silver King wormwood into the midst of Sensation Mix cosmos and the pink spikes of butterfly bush to make their flower colors appear brighter. Plants with gray foliage can also be used as a buffer between contrasting colors.*

Photo 17

Photo 17: *This neat, rock-bordered bed is filled with a mass planting of globe candytuft (Iberis umbellata), a hardy annual that prefers full sun but can tolerate light shade. Annuals like this that you can sow directly into the flower bed are an easy way to fill an area with a summer's worth of color. During your garden's first season, when there may still be some bare spots, you might want to sow patches of annuals to add bright touches to the garden scene. As you continue to refine your garden design over the seasons and as the perennials and shrubs fill out, you probably will cut back on the amount of space you devote to plantings of annuals.*

Photo 18

Photo 18: *This spring garden is in its prime. When the yellow and red tulips have finished blooming, perennials planted among the bulbs will start to flower, providing an uninterrupted, season-long display of color. As you design your garden, keep this idea of a succession of blooming flowers in mind so that there will always be color in some part of the garden at all times throughout the season. The inviting green pathway underscores this garden's intended use as a delightful place for strolling. Most people walk among their garden beds in the daytime; try visiting your flowers at dusk or even on a bright moonlit night. By seeing your garden in a different light you may discover a part of its "personality" that was hidden before.*

Photo 19

Photo 19: *Clusters of spring flowers add color to this garden. In this shaded border, maintenance is kept to a minimum by the combination of low-care plants like bulbs, perennials, and shrubs. This border helps make the transition between the very neat carpet of grass and the natural-looking wooded area beyond.* **Photo 20:** *Pink and orange tulips are surrounded by a carpet of blue forget-me-nots. As the spring bulbs fade, the annual forget-me-nots continue blooming for a while until they are replaced by summer annuals. This succession of flowers provides a continuous display of color. Although this garden isn't in a home setting, you can adapt the idea for your own garden and treat patches of annuals the same way.*

Photo 20

Photo 21

Photo 21: *Painted daisies (with yellow centers) and columbines are beautiful mainstays in the midspring garden. The flower forms and colors of these perennials complement each other nicely. When you're selecting plants for your garden, or even when you're selecting specific varieties of plants, keep the general color principles discussed in Chapter 5 in mind. Some gardeners may find they don't want to be constrained by an established color scheme and may decide to create an eye-catching display of mixed colors. Other gardeners prefer to choose a general color scheme and stick to it. Flower gardening gives us all a wonderful opportunity to express our own creativity.*

Photo 22

Photo 22: *Butterflies add a delightful accent of moving color to the flower garden. If you want to attract butterflies to your garden, include some of their favorite plants, like butterfly bush, China aster, sedum, and sweet alyssum.*

Photo 23: *In this shaded Bank Garden the spring-blooming wild blue phlox flowers have all but obscured the rocks. A pathway that winds through the garden makes this a pleasant place to stroll to get out of the hot sun.*

Photo 23

Photo 24

Photo 25

Photo 24: *Charles Cresson included roses in this herbaceous border. In this book we haven't discussed roses because we feel they require too much care and attention to qualify for a 60-Minute Flower Garden. Charles feels that roses are worth that extra effort, so he features them in what would otherwise be a 60-Minute Flower Garden.*
Photo 25: *In this sunny herbaceous border there is an attractive gradation of plant heights from back to front.* **Photo 26:** *The China asters, zinnias, and plumed cock's-comb in this garden make excellent cutting flowers.*

Photo 26

Photo 27

Photo 27: *A shaded bank like this might appear to be an unlikely place for a bright, cheery flower garden. But when the right plants are selected, even a potentially troublesome site can be transformed into a beautiful garden. In this garden, Charles Cresson overcame the limitations of the space by featuring yellow and orange primroses, purple ajuga, and moss pink. The closely spaced plants and the layer of mulch in the garden make weeding a pleasantly infrequent task.*

Photo 28

Photo 28: *This garden contains some of the easiest annuals to grow. The deep red flowers in the center are plumed cock's-comb; they are ringed by orange and yellow marigolds. In the foreground are pink petunias. All of these annuals will bloom reliably all summer long. Dead-heading will encourage continual flowering.* **Photo 29:** *This garden is an example of how annuals can be used to add color to replace perennials that bloomed earlier in the season. Annuals are also good for camouflaging perennial foliage that may have died back. In this colorful flower bed, the perennial shasta daisy that is no longer blooming is surrounded by petunias, zinnias, and geraniums.*

Photo 29

Photo 30

Photo 30: *Painted daisies (mass of pink in the foreground) and lupines (tall pink and white spikes) highlight this sunny herbaceous border. This garden is a good example of the sort of color display you can expect from perennials throughout the season. There will be a succession of plants in bloom, with some starting to flower as others are fading from the scene. There will not be a continuous mass of color for the whole time as there would be in a garden filled with mostly annuals. The advantage to the floral display provided by perennials is that you don't have to replant them every spring; once you've planted them they can stay in place for several years.*

Color Photography Credits

Liz Ball: photos 5, 15, 22

David Cavagnaro: photo 23

Charles O. Cresson: photos 2, 3, 6, 9, 14, 16, 24, 27

Jill Elliot: photo 7

Derek Fell: photos 1, 18

John P. Hamel: photo 4

J. Michael Kanouff: photo 13

Alison Miksch: photo 29

Gary Mottau: photo 8

Joanne Pavia: photos 11, 17, 20, 21, 30

Rodale Press Photography Department: photos 10, 19, 25, 26

Pat Seip: photos 12, 28

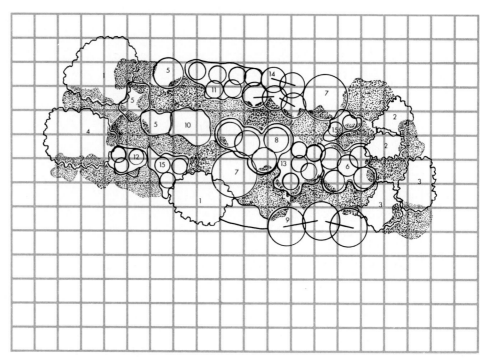

Bank Garden for Light Shade

Bank Garden for Light Shade

The shady Bank Garden is much like the sunny Bank Garden, with one essential difference: The plants are tolerant of low light conditions, just like the ones used in a shady Herbaceous Flower Border or Woodland Garden. The soil should contain leaf mold or peat, which is more to the liking of these plants than the sandy soil in a sunny Bank Garden. Be wary of nearby trees; their roots may rob the plants of water and nutrients and sap your garden of its vigor and beauty.

Although they're not shown in this plan, you can use the small annuals recommended in the list to tuck into the garden in places where the perennials haven't become established yet. The small bulbs given in the list are the right size to place among the low-growing perennials.

Bank Garden for Light Shade
Small Shrubs

1. Azalea (dwarf varieties); 24 × 36 in.
2. Creeping cotoneaster (*Cotoneaster adpressa*); 12-18 × 24 in.
3. Dwarf Japanese juniper (*Juniperus procumbens* 'Nana'); 18-24 × 24
4. Mugo pine (*Pinus mugo*, dwarf varieties); 36 × 36 in.

Other Suggestions

Heller Japanese holly (*Ilex crenata* 'Helleri'); 24 × 24 in.

Mid-Sized Perennials

5. Bleeding heart, fringed; 12 × 12 in.
6. Columbine, American; 24 × 12 in.
7. Fern, Christmas; 24 × 24 in.
8. Geranium, hardy (*Geranium sanguineum*); 12 × 12 in.
9. Hosta (*Hosta undulata*); 12 × 18 in.
10. Lady's mantle; 18 × 24 in.

Other Suggestions

Coral bells; 18 × 12 in.
Lily-turf; 12 × 12 in.
Phlox, wild blue; 15 × 12 in.
Trillium; 15 × 12 in.

Low Perennials

11. Carpathian harebell; 12 × 10 in.
12. Fern, Japanese painted; 12 × 12 in.
13. Golden star; 8 × 12 in.
14. Hosta 'Ginko Craig'; 12 × 12 in.
15. Phlox, creeping; 6 × 8 in.

Other Suggestions

European ginger; 6 × 12 in.
Foam flower; 12 × 8 in.
Hen-and-chickens; 3 × 3 in.
Iris, crested; 5 × 8 in.
Primrose, polyanthus; 10 × 8 in.

Low Annuals

Suggestions

Ageratum; 15 × 15 in.
Forget-me-not; 9 × 6 in.
Impatiens; 12 × 12 in.
Lobelia; 8 × 6 in.
Pansy; 8 × 8 in.
Alyssum, sweet; 4-8 × 6 in.
Wishbone flower; 8 × 8 in.

Small Bulbs

Suggestions

Anemone, Greek; 4 × 3 in.
Crocus, autumn; 3 × 3 in.
Crocus, snow; 3 × 3 in.
Daffodil, dwarf; 6 × 4 in.
Glory-of-the-snow; 6 × 3 in.
Guinea flower; 12 × 4 in.
Hyacinth, grape; 12 × 3 in.
Iris, netted; 4 × 4 in.
Snowdrop; 6 × 4 in.
Squill, Siberian; 6 × 4 in.
Winter aconite; 3 × 3 in.

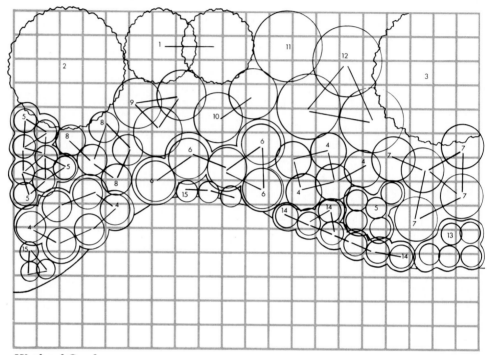

Wetland Garden

Wetland Garden

This plan uses plants that will tolerate growing in a poorly draining area. These exceptional plants can have "wet feet" for at least part of the year and still do well. This doesn't mean they are suited for a swamp, but rather for an area that usually stays moist, not waterlogged. You can plan a Wetland Garden as one end of a Herbaceous Flower Border or as one corner of a Decorative Home Garden. This type of garden gives you an attractive way to deal with a site where the soil drainage is less than ideal. Most of the plants we recommend are best

suited to partial sun. However, you'll find that plants that normally must have shade, such as astilbe, will often tolerate much more sun as long as they have adequate moisture. In this case a "drainage problem" has actually expanded your options for plants to use in the garden.

The principles for designing this garden are essentially the same as those for any of the other gardens where the plants are arranged to provide a distribution of bloom season, color, height, and foliage.

Wetland Garden

Shrubs

1. Inkberry (*Ilex glabra* 'Compacta'); 60 × 36
2. Red Osier dogwood (*Cornus alba* 'Sibirica'); 84 × 72 in.
3. Sweet pepper bush *(Clethra alnifolia)*; 108 × 72

Other Suggestions

Sweet shrub *(Calycanthus floridus)*; 96 × 96 in.
Winterberry *(Ilex verticillata)*; 108 × 96 in.

Mid-Sized Perennials

4. Astilbe; 24-48 × 24-36 in.
5. Cardinal flower; 36-60 × 24 in.
6. Daylily; 36 × 24 in.
7. Hosta *(Hosta ventricosa)*; 36 × 24 in.
8. Iris, Japanese; 36-48 × 12-18 in.
9. Ligularia; 48 × 24 in.
10. Loosestrife, purple; 36-60 × 24 in.
11. Queen-of-the-prairie; 48-72 × 36 in.
12. Rose mallow; 36-72 × 36 in.

Other Suggestion

Fern, lady; 24 × 24 in.

Mid-Sized Bulbs

Suggestions

Camassia; 36 × 10 in.
Guinea flower; 12 × 4 in.
Summer snowflake; 15 × 6 in.

Low Perennials

13. Fern, Japanese painted; 12 × 12 in.
14. Lungwort; 12 × 12 in.
15. Primrose, Japanese *(Primula japonica)*; 24 × 12 in.

Other Suggestion

Lamium 'Beacon Silver'; 8 × 12 in.

Low Annuals

Suggestions

Begonia, bedding; 12 × 12 in.
Impatiens; 12 × 12 in.
Lobelia; 8 × 6 in.

Chapter 6

Caring for Soil in the Flower Garden

If you don't properly prepare your flower garden's soil, if you don't use mulch, and if you routinely walk all over your established flower beds, then you are making it very tough for your flowers to grow well. They will manage to grow under those circumstances, but they will survive in spite of you. On the other hand, if you do use compost and mulch and encourage an earthworm population, then you can greatly reduce the need for fertilizers, forget about pH problems, and have the healthiest flower garden in town.

We think that most flower gardeners in this country don't follow a soil management scheme like the one we describe in this chapter. We think they should, though, and we recommend it for three simple reasons — it gives you better plants, it saves time, and it is cheaper. Those are pretty good reasons for trying our system.

Some Words about Soil

We cannot emphasize strongly enough the importance of having good soil in your flower garden. If they wish, vegetable gardeners can dig up their whole garden every year and work in soil-improving conditioners. But a flower gardener, especially one who uses lots of perennials and shrubs, really digs the entire garden only once, and that is when it is initially built. After that the flower gardener needs to use techniques other than digging to add amendments and nutrients to the soil and keep it loose and friable (crumbly).

We are convinced that the quality of your flower garden is directly related to the thoroughness with which you follow certain steps in initially preparing the garden's soil. (These steps are outlined in the accompanying list. Steps two through seven will be described in detail as you continue through the chapter; step one is discussed in Chapter 8.) After that, the few key tasks you perform each year in managing your garden should leave the soil in a more fertile condition, with a better structure, and with a healthier level of beneficial soil microbes than it had when you started the season. Concentrate on feeding your soil instead of feeding your plants; then, in turn, the healthy soil will feed the plants.

Seven Steps in Preparing Flower Garden Soil

1. Deal with any perennial weed infestations.
2. Add significant amounts of organic material.
3. Double-dig or rotary-till the soil.
4. Add rock powders.
5. Add compost or an equivalent.
6. Establish stepping stones to avoid compaction.
7. Apply mulch.

You should approach your garden soil in much the same way that you deal with your plants. Soil needs tending just as much as plants do. We look at soil management as having four components. A gardener needs to care for the soil's structure and nutrient content, moisture level, temperature, and general health. The 60-Minute Flower Garden system of soil care addresses all four of these concerns, without taking much time.

To give you a quick preview of this system, the structure and nutrient needs of the soil are satisfied by adding enough compost and/or manure and rock powders so that regular fertilizing in the traditional manner of applying side-dressings isn't needed. Moisture level and temperature are managed with the drip irrigation system discussed in Chapter 7 and by a combination of seasonal mulches. The soil's health is maintained by good garden hygiene.

What Is Good Soil?

Your garden's soil is much more than merely a means of support for your plants. While it is the primary vehicle for transmitting food and water to plants for healthy growth, it is also the source of that food and the storage area for that water.

The ideal flower garden soil is fertile, loose, friable, well drained and high in organic matter. Soil containing 5 percent humus (organic material) is considered to be in excellent shape for growing flowers (and anything else, for that matter). In the 60-Minute Flower Garden, soil fertility is increased by adding compost and mulch, which can be transformed into nutrients for the plants. With the addition of 1 inch of compost or 3 inches of chopped leaves to your garden each year, the soil will reach the desirable 5 percent humus level. Following our system, the soil is initially loosened by double-digging and is kept crumbly and light by a large earthworm population and the yearly addition of organic material. These regular infusions of humus help to keep the soil well drained. Once you've gotten the soil into great shape, it never becomes compacted because walking in the beds is kept to a minimum.

An ideal soil also has a very active population of microorganisms (mostly fungi and bacteria). The number and activity of these microbes determine the amount of nutrients that is available each day for your flowers. Soil temperatures between 65° and 80°F are about the ideal range for the microlife in a flower garden, including earthworms. So the challenge to the flower gardener is to develop a soil that has all these wonderful characteristics without breaking your back or taking up too much time.

Soil Types

As we mentioned in Chapter 2, you shouldn't have to worry too much about what type of soil you have for the 60-Minute Flower Garden. Whether it is very clayey, loamy, or sandy, we recommend that you treat it the same way—add as much organic material to it each year as is practical. It is impossible, absolutely impossible, to add too much organic material to your soil. You will be a very unusual gardener if you can ever say that you have more compost than you can use. You will also be an unusual gardener if, after three or four years of following our soil management system, you don't have some of the best soil in the neighborhood.

How Roots Work in the Soil

The connection between your good soil and your flowers is made by the roots of the plant. Roots serve three primary functions for most plants: they anchor the plant; they store food and water; and they serve as an intake and transportation system for water and nutrients from the soil to the rest of the plant.

As a general rule, a plant's root system will penetrate as deeply into the soil as the foliage is high. So a 12-inch-tall zinnia will have roots that go down about 12 inches. This rule does not apply as reliably to woody plants like azaleas, however.

The looser the garden's soil is, the more readily the root systems can spread, becoming heavy and healthy and improving the plant's drought resistance and overall performance. A plant with an expansive root system has a greater ability to absorb water, oxygen, and nutrients from the soil. You can't see healthy roots, but their vigor is reflected in the prolific blooms in your flower bed.

Soil Compaction

Compacted soil is no friend of the flower gardener, yet many gardeners are unaware of the compaction problems they themselves

are causing. Compaction results from pressure from equipment, frequent foot traffic, or even from the weight of a single footstep. It has the effect of strangling the roots of your plants. In compacted soil, water and oxygen are cut off from roots, hindering their growth. This shortage of water and oxygen also means that organic matter cannot decompose properly. You can add all the organic material you want on top, but it won't bring any benefit to soil that's compacted a foot or so deep. As if that weren't enough, compaction discourages the good work done by earthworms.

We strongly recommend that you limit the areas in your flower garden where you allow yourself (or anyone else!) to walk. Set up stepping stones or establish an unobtrusive path and try very hard to avoid tramping randomly in your garden. It doesn't take much compaction to affect plant growth. Research completed by Al Trouse of the United States Department of Agriculture's National Tillage Machinery Laboratory has demonstrated that normal, everyday compaction can slow plant growth to at least one-tenth of what it should be. This kind of compaction can occur just from walking on the beds.

When Charles was visiting a prominent European gardener some years ago, she gave him a private tour of her spectacular formal gardens. At one point he stepped very lightly off the path to get a better look at one of the flowers. Nothing was said, but his hostess quietly pulled a small fork from her back pocket and loosened the spot where he had stepped. That's when his consciousness was raised about compaction in the flower garden.

The time when compaction is most likely to occur, especially in clay soils, is when the ground is wet. This presents problems in the spring when we are all anxious to get out there and start working in the garden. If you develop soil that drains quickly and is thus less prone to compaction, you should be able to start your spring gardening early without endangering the soil's condition.

WHEN IS THE SOIL READY TO WORK?

It's the first nice weekend in spring and you're ready to go out into the garden, but you're not sure whether the garden is ready for you. How can you tell whether the soil is dry enough to work? Here's an age-old guide that can help you decide. Take a handful of soil and squeeze it into a ball. When you open your hand, soil that crumbles apart is ready. Soil that holds together in a ball is still too wet. Practice a little more patience.

The best way to prevent a compaction problem in the first place is to minimize the amount of walking you do in the beds. Later in the chapter, under Double-Digging, we'll show you how to overcome soil compaction that already exists in your garden.

Worms Are Great for the Soil

Flower gardeners often ignore earthworms. Yet earthworms can be significant partners in managing the soil of your 60-Minute Flower Garden. Earthworms produce their weight in castings every day, and worm castings are an absolutely wonderful fertilizer, with nutrients available in a form all plants can use. In a 200-square-foot garden, with a density of only five worms per

Stepping Stones in the Garden: *Strategically placed stepping stones allow you to work in your garden without compacting the soil. Stones that are partially buried and surrounded by foliage remain unobtrusive and don't detract from the look of the garden.*

cubic foot (considered a low population), your earthworms will give you over 35 pounds (about ⅓ pound per worm) of top-grade fertilizer during each gardening year. They not only produce this valuable fertilizer, they also spread it evenly throughout the top 12 inches of soil, and in many cases they will go much deeper, sometimes as far down as 6 feet.

A well-managed soil rich in humus can easily support 25 worms per cubic foot, which, in a 200-square-foot garden, means at least 175 pounds of fertilizer! This fertilizer contains the key plant nutrients nitrogen, phosphorus, and potassium, plus many of the essential micronutrients flowers need to grow and remain healthy. Dead earthworms are also very rich in nitrogen.

Worms make other very significant contributions to your flower garden soil. They have small glands that secrete calcium carbonate, a compound that helps to moderate soil pH. Earthworms can help change acid or alkaline soils toward a neutral pH over time. Worms aerate the soil and improve the moisture penetration in the soil. Remember, roots need oxygen and water to take up their nutrients, and the earthworm makes a major contribution to that process. Finally, by their tunneling, earthworms create access to deeper soil levels for countless smaller creatures, such as predatory mites, springtails, and flatworms, that contribute to the health of the soil.

Believe it or not, the favorite food of the earthworm is dried leaves. Now isn't that convenient, since we recommend chopped leaves as the primary mulching material in our system of soil care? The worms drag dried leaves, tip first, into their burrows and then break them down into plant fertilizer. So your leaf mulch has the added advantage of improving conditions in the earthworm's habitat.

The primary reason we recommend not using dry or granular chemical fertilizers in your flower garden is that they repel earthworms. As these fertilizers become soluble and leach down into the soil, they force the earthworms to seek refuge someplace else. Why put 10 or 20 pounds of dry, granular or powdered, commercial chemical fertilizer into your garden and repel a source of over 100 pounds of superior fertilizer? For us it is a simple economic issue. Supplemental liquid organic fertilizer applied as a foliar spray will not have this negative effect on earthworms. (See Chapter 7 for more on fertilizing the flower garden.)

INTRODUCING WORMS INTO THE FLOWER GARDEN

You may already have a number of earthworms in your garden, but it never hurts to have some more. You can buy earthworms from growers, who advertise in most gardening magazines. Be very sure you get worms that will survive in the garden. Many growers sell worms for composting that will not live in normal garden soil because they need the heat of a compost pile to survive. The most common earthworm, *Lumbricus terrestris*, the ubiquitous night crawler, is a reliable choice for any garden.

When you get your worms, put them in the garden in holes 6 inches wide and 4 to 6 inches deep that are spaced a foot apart. Add some chopped leaves along with the worms and cover them with loose soil. Your worm population will explode over the next few years and your flower garden will thrive.

Soil Temperature

You may not be aware of the role soil temperature plays in the performance of your flower garden. Temperature is important because the microlife of the soil, which is responsible for generating food for plants, doesn't really become active until the soil reaches about 40° to 45°F. For example, the bacteria needed to make nitrogen available to plant roots in a form they can use do not become active until the soil temperature is about 40°F, and they don't reach the height of their activity until the soil temperature climbs to 80°F. Extremely high soil temperatures (above 85°F) will slow down plants' growth mechanisms. Our system of soil care allows you to help the soil reach and maintain its optimum levels throughout the growing season.

Your gardening season doesn't really start with the last spring frost and end with the first fall frost. It starts when the soil temperature reaches 45°F and ends when the soil temperature drops down again to 45°F. There is little correlation between air temperature and soil temperature. You can have a balmy spring day in terms of air temperature, but if the soil temperature hasn't reached 45°F, you shouldn't start to plant your seeds or seedlings.

For example, the set-out date for annuals is usually calculated by adding ten days to the date of the last expected spring frost. We suggest that you are better off using a soil thermometer to determine the set-out day for your annuals. A soil temperature of 50°F or more is best. There is little to be gained from setting plants out prematurely, since they will grow slowly until the soil warms to the optimum level. To keep track of soil temperatures, you can buy a standard soil thermometer at your local hardware store or garden center. You can also order one from many mail-order garden catalogs.

Jeff has gone one step beyond the soil thermometer in applying technology to save time in managing his gardens. He uses a device called Computemp, which allows him to position as many as nine remote temperature sensors all over his property. He can check the current temperature in various locations and the high and low for the previous day by using a convenient read-out device located in his kitchen. This device is connected to each of the sensors by a small wire. He keeps track of the temperature in the vegetable garden soil, in the flower garden soil, in the middle of the compost pile, and in his greenhouse by using this handy device. He finds that it takes a lot of the guesswork out of some of the garden management tasks.

Soil Tests

While our soil management system generally eliminates the need to worry about the pH of your soil and the balance of the major soil nutrients, you do need to check your soil in the very beginning to be sure there are no extreme problems that need addressing. If there is an excess of potassium in your soil, for example, you will want to avoid adding manure and potassium-rich powders. You can't know you have an extreme soil problem without a soil test.

While soil test kits for home use are available, we believe that it's much more convenient to have someone else do the testing. You can have a soil test done by the Cooperative Extension Service (CES) in your state. (You'll find the address listed in the phone book under state or local government offices.) Very often you can get one of these CES soil test packets from your local extension agent. The CES soil test costs only a couple of dollars, and you'll get the results in a matter of weeks. The packet will probably consist of a cloth bag attached to a preaddressed envelope containing a questionnaire for you to fill out about your garden. You must take your soil sample properly for it to be of any practical value. Be sure to follow the directions that come with the packet.

The soil test report will tell you whether the levels of nitrogen, phosphorus, and potassium are low, medium, high, or excessive. Flowers do best in soils where the nutrients are in balanced amounts at the medium to high levels. The test will also give the soil's pH and will often indicate the levels of critical minerals like calcium and magnesium.

Soil pH

A whole lot of fuss is made about pH in many gardening articles and books, but we feel that most folks don't have much to worry about. The pH scale goes from 0 (super-acid) to 14 (super-alkaline), with 7 being considered neutral. Problems in growing flowers will occur only when pH readings are in the extremes—below 5 or above 8. A moderate pH level provides the best environment for the soil-dwelling microorganisms that release nutrients, especially nitrogen, to the roots of the plants. At extreme pH levels these nutrients can be unavailable to the plants, so for best plant growth you should try to keep the flower garden's pH between 6 and 7, a slightly acidic level. Fortunately, many soils naturally fall within this range.

Many flower gardening books recommend that you have two different soil management strategies—one for your acid-loving plants like rhododendrons and one for the other plants such as peonies that prefer a more neutral pH. Well, there is increasing evidence that you don't need to worry about such things once your garden is planted, assuming you add at least 1 inch of compost to your entire garden every year.

A study was done on a property that had soil with a nearly neutral pH. The gardener had planted some rhododendrons and azaleas many years before without taking any special steps to prepare the soil for these acid-loving plants. For all those years this gardener had put 1 inch of compost around each plant every year (compost is almost always nearly neutral in pH). When a researcher went around this gardener's property and took soil samples, he found that the soil around the rhododendrons and azaleas was *acidic* and the rest of the property was still *neutral*. Scientists haven't figured out how, but the plants had managed to create their own acidic environment.

We do agree that when you first plant an acid-loving plant in soil that is neutral, you are wise to add some acidic peat moss to the transplant hole so the plant gets off to a good start. But after that we believe that for the kinds of common plants we are discussing in this book, you can ignore pH issues in your soil management program for the 60-Minute Flower Garden.

Nitrogen, Potassium, Phosphorus

The key nutrients described in the soil test report are nitrogen, phosphorus, and potassium (abbreviated as N, P, and K on fertilizer bags and always listed in the same order; for example, 5-10-5 means 5 percent nitrogen, 10 percent phosphorus, and 5 percent potassium). In some places you'll see potassium called potash and phosphorus called phosphate. Calcium and sometimes magnesium also are mentioned in soil test results. Let's see how our soil management plan addresses plants' needs for these critical nutrients.

In a natural gardening system (one where no chemicals are used), the availability of nitrogen and phosphorus depends on the level of activity of soil microorganisms that make these nutrients available in a form plants can use. To a lesser extent, potassium also depends on these same biological processes that are at work in a healthy soil.

Although nitrogen isn't as critical in the flower garden as it is in the vegetable garden, you still need to provide some for a balanced diet for your plants. Compost, which we'll discuss in more detail later in the chapter, is an excellent source of nitrogen.

The soil's need for phosphorus and potassium can be met by adding some rock powders to your garden every two or three years. Rock powders provide important nutrients very slowly over time, but there is what you might call a lag time between the initial application and the point when the nutrients become available for uptake by the plants. For example, if you put rock phosphate in fairly high amounts on your garden this fall, the plant's roots won't be getting phosphorus until next summer. However, once the nutrient becomes available, the garden will be getting a steady supply of phosphorus from this one application for over two years!

Rock phosphate is sold in many garden centers and is an excellent source of phosphorus. If a soil test reveals a deficiency and you want to correct the problem as quickly as possible, consider adding some rock phosphate to the batches of compost you make. Rock phosphate needs acid to break it down. A garden with the recommended soil pH of 6 to 7 breaks down the rock phosphate rather slowly. Since a compost pile is generally acidic in the beginning stages of its decomposition, it will release more phosphorus sooner. By putting this compost on your garden, you're delivering phosphorus in a form that's ready to be used. If you continue with this enriched-compost treatment for a year or two, the deficiency should be corrected.

A good source of potassium is granite dust or greensand, both available from many garden centers. Again, if your soil test reflects a need for additional potassium, you might add one of these powders to your compost pile for a year or two to speed up the availability of this nutrient in your soil.

Because these rock powders (rock phosphate, greensand, and granite dust) break

down so slowly in the soil, there is little danger of putting too much into your garden. At the same time, you don't need to waste money by using more than you need. A good rule of thumb for these rock powders is to apply about 10 pounds of each kind to 100 square feet of your garden every two to three years. If you have a 200-square-foot garden, a 20-pound bag of rock phosphate and a 20-pound bag of greensand will take care of your phosphorus and potassium needs for two years. Again, the fall is a good time to spread these long-term amendments. This gives them some time to begin breaking down for the next year's garden full of flowers.

Digging the Soil

Preparing your flower garden's soil properly in the beginning is a terribly important step. As you might expect, proper preparation almost always means more work than a haphazard approach. But it really does pay off in lower maintenance later on and in better flowers. There are several ways you can consider preparing the soil once you get out into your new garden site and start mucking about. You can double-dig your garden, which is the best way, or you can rotary-till your site, which is not quite so thorough but does the job.

No matter which method you use, we believe it is essential that when you dig your flower garden you simultaneously add a healthy quantity of organic material to the soil. If you're starting out with very heavy clay soil that has never been used for gardening, you will have to add considerable amounts of organic matter to make that soil as loose and friable as you can. The same rule applies to gardens in very sandy soil that doesn't hold moisture well.

In these situations where the soil is in poor condition in the beginning, you'll need to apply at least 2 to 4 inches of compost, manure, chopped leaves, peat moss, and/or any other organic material that will provide the necessary humus. Double-digging helps to mix in the organic material faster. In the case of both heavy clay and heavy sand, once you've made this initial application of organic materials to correct the situation, the annual soil management program we suggest will be sufficient to keep the soil from reverting to its original undesirable condition.

Double-Digging

Let us describe double-digging for those gardeners who have never done it, since it is the best technique for getting a flower bed in shape. Double-digging is important when establishing a bed for the first time, and it is especially important if you have a hard-pan (compacted) layer to break up below the topsoil.

There is no getting around the fact that double-digging is hard work. But if you are willing to spend 2 to 4 hours double-digging your 200-square-foot garden, the plants' outstanding growth and flowering will reflect the value of the effort.

Double-digging simply means lifting a shovelful of topsoil out of the garden so that you can take a spading fork and loosen, without removing, the second layer of soil below the topsoil. Stick your spading fork down as deeply as you can into this lower layer and then twist and wiggle the fork to loosen up the clumps. As you loosen the subsoil layer you can add some organic matter such as compost or chopped leaves. You'll also work in organic materials as you refill the trenches with the reserved topsoil.

This technique allows you to move systematically down the bed, making consecutive trenches by first loosening the subsoil, then adding organic matter, and finally refilling the trenches with topsoil and more

organic material. Double-digging your beds will raise them about 3 to 4 inches because this technique thoroughly loosens and aerates the soil and allows for the addition of 2 to 4 inches of new organic materials. You can leave the sides of these raised beds in their natural state or you can support them with decorative stones or railroad ties, which help control erosion.

Rotary-Tilling

If hardpan isn't a problem in your garden or if you have a bad back and cannot find someone to double-dig your new flower garden, we would then recommend preparing your garden with a rotary cultivator. You should try to till as deeply as you possibly can, and if you use this method of soil preparation it is even more essential that you add at least 4 inches of organic material to your soil as you till it.

General Guidelines for Digging

No matter whether you use the double-digging method or the rotary-tilling method to prepare the soil, you'll get the best results if you do this job in the fall and then cover the new flower bed with 5 or 6 inches of chopped leaves and let it sit for the winter.

If you're digging a flower bed close to one or more large trees, you'll have to cope with their root systems. You can safely remove any small roots you come across as you dig; clearing those out will reduce the competition, at least for a while, between your flowers and those greedy trees. Very large roots should not be cut or removed, as you might seriously damage the tree's ability to transport food and water. A large root isn't a terrible threat to your flower garden because it is simply a conduit for nutrients picked up by the far-reaching smaller roots. The small roots that you do remove represent only a small portion of the total, so the tree's health isn't really threatened.

Digging among shrubs is okay as long as you remain outside each shrub's dripline (the circular area defined by the spread of the branches). If you already have some perennials in the garden site, avoid digging much closer than 12 inches around them. If the perennial is particularly small, you might be able to dig to within 6 inches of the plant, or until you start seeing roots.

Remember, design your garden space so that you do not walk over any more of the growing area than absolutely necessary. We use stepping stones strategically placed throughout the bed so that we avoid compacting our soil but are still able to maneuver to take care of our routine gardening tasks.

Compost

We have referred to using compost in many sections of this book, so it is time to take a close look at this marvelous stuff and see why it is so important to the 60-Minute Flower Garden. Properly made compost looks just like the dark, almost black, soft, crumbly material you find in the forest just under the top layer of leaves on the forest floor. It looks and feels much like a potting soil mix you might buy from your local gardening store, and it has little odor other than a pleasant woodsy smell. Compost is the by-product of the decomposition of organic materials such as leaves, tree bark, weeds, and grass clippings.

A layer of compost performs several very important functions in our 60-Minute Flower Garden. Researchers at the Connecticut Agricultural Experiment Station have demonstrated that 1 inch of compost on your garden will boost the "yields" of your flowering plants, measured by size and number of blossoms, by a significant percentage.

Compost is a tremendously valuable natural fertilizer. It's an excellent source of nitrogen and provides some potassium and the trace minerals needed by your flower garden. Compost is generally low in phosphorus, so that is why we apply the rock powders to our garden or add them to our compost pile. Compost itself is not a direct fertilizer for the plants. It is food for the billions of microorganisms in the soil that transform the compost into the soluble compounds that can then be absorbed by the roots of the plants.

Compost's most important role is to provide nitrogen to the plants throughout the growing season. You can think of compost as having a half-life of fertility. About half of the nutrients that are present are released for plant use during the first year. Half of the remaining nutrients are released the second year, and so on after that. Most flowers require about ½ pound of nitrogen per 100 square feet. Since we have two and sometimes three successions of flowers in the 60-Minute Flower Garden, we want to have at least 1 pound of nitrogen available per 100 square feet, or 2 pounds for our 200-square-foot model garden. Our yearly addition of compost will provide this nitrogen.

Compost has enormous water storage capabilities. On the surface of a flower bed, a layer of compost will help soak up water rather than let it puddle and run off, washing away nutrients and eroding the soil. As the humus content of your garden's soil increases, its ability to store water and withstand the problems of drought increases immensely. During a long, hot summer, your flowers will come through the season in better shape than those in a neighbor's garden where compost is never used. Boosting your soil's humus content from 2 to 5 percent can quadruple its water-holding capacity. Compost acts as a marvelous soil conditioner, soaking up and holding water in sandy soil and opening up spaces in heavy clay soils through which water can move more easily.

Another interesting attribute of compost is that some of the fatty acids it contains are toxic to certain fungal and bacterial diseases. Research by the Ohio Agricultural Research and Development Center has shown that compost, especially compost made the passive way (see the following section), suppresses harmful root-invading fungi that can cause such diseases as root rot and damping-off. We suspect that research will show us even more, in the years to come, about the disease-prevention benefits of compost.

Foolproof Compost-Making

Compost is produced by billions of microorganisms breaking down raw organic material into humus. These microorganisms require a certain sort of environment in which to multiply and to continue the breakdown process. If you create that environment, you get beautiful compost. If you don't create and maintain that environment, you don't get compost. Now that's pretty simple. Fortunately, the environment you need for making this compost is not all that precise, and you have a great deal of leeway in how you go about building the pile. Essentially, a good compost pile needs four elements: carbon-containing materials, nitrogen-containing materials, oxygen, and moisture.

The 60-Minute Flower Garden needs a layer of organic material every year, and compost is the cheapest source of that material. If you plan to use a lot of compost, you'll probably need to use what is called the active method, rather than the passive method, for making your compost. The passive method is simple—you collect a pile of organic material and let it sit for a few years. You do get compost this way, but it takes a long time and you need to give up space for the pile.

The active method requires that you turn the pile or mix it up a few times during the year so that the breakdown process works faster. You can do this and still easily stay within your 60-minute-a-week time frame.

The compost pile for the 60-Minute Flower Garden gets its carbon and nitrogen from materials normally thrown away without a thought in the suburbs and cities. The oxygen comes from turning the pile a few times, and the water comes from the rain absorbed by the leaves and other dried materials. You'll spend a few hours each year making enough compost for a 200-square-foot garden, but the price is right—it's free!

Great compost can be made from straw, leaves, grass clippings, garden waste, and kitchen scraps. That is all you need. Be especially careful never to use any meat products, bones, or grease in your compost pile, because they will attract rodents and can cause the compost pile to smell bad. A compost pile should *never* smell bad. If it does, you probably have put too much nitrogen material or green stuff in it. A compost pile needs to have much more carbon material (usually dry) than nitrogen material (usually fresh and/or green). Many gardening books recommend a carbon-to-nitrogen ratio of about 30 to 1. Jeff's experience indicates that you can cut that ratio way down to even 10 to 1 if you turn the pile frequently. If the pile smells bad, add more carbon material. If the pile is not heating up, add more nitrogen material. Some experimentation on your part will indicate that there is not much precision in the ratio. (For a list of common carbon and nitrogen composting materials, see the chart on the next page.)

Figuring How Much Compost You'll Need

Earlier we said that compost is a great source of nitrogen for the flowers in your garden. There's no way you can be sure of the nitrogen content of your finished com-

COMPOSTING MATERIALS

CARBON MATERIALS	NITROGEN MATERIALS
Aged sawdust	Fresh grass clippings
Dry leaves	Kitchen scraps
Seaweed	Manure
Straw	Weeds and garden waste

post because of the variety of materials that can be used. For example, compost made from hay is higher in nitrogen than compost made from straw. Leaves have about half the nitrogen that manure has. Among manures, aged chicken manure has about twice as much nitrogen as cow manure. Playing a numbers game and trying to figure out what percentage of nitrogen your compost contains is a waste of time. Our approach is that a 1-inch layer of compost (no matter what it's made from) spread over the garden each spring should provide all the nitrogen needed for good plant growth. If you have plenty of compost, spread a 2-inch layer. With compost, unlike synthetic chemical fertilizers, you never have to worry about overdoing the nitrogen application.

Assuming you'll be putting 1 inch of compost on your garden, you'll need about 120 gallons of compost for each 200 square feet. This adds up to about 17 cubic feet of compost, which is the amount present in a 2-foot by 4-foot by 2-foot pile of finished compost. To end up with a finished pile of those dimensions, you need to start with a pile that's about 4 feet high and 3 to 4 feet across. This is the size pile we have in mind when we discuss compost-making.

A Seasonal System

The composting system we suggest for the 60-Minute Flower Garden is fairly simple. In the fall, you should collect enough leaves to give you a 6- to 12-inch layer of winter mulch over your entire flower bed. Chop these leaves with a shredder or a lawn mower so they don't mat down over the winter. A 12-inch layer of chopped leaves will settle down to a blanket of leaves that is about 4 inches thick by spring. Those chopped leaves are your primary carbon material for a year's supply of compost for the flower garden. By virtue of sitting out in the open all winter, they absorb just the right amount of water for making perfect compost, so there will be no need to add any more water to the pile.

In the spring, remove this winter mulch of chopped leaves from your garden bed and use it to build a compost pile. There are a number of storage devices that will work well for this relatively small-scale composting operation. Check general gardening books and gardening magazines; they very often feature inexpensive, ingenious, and functional compost enclosures. The best size for an efficient compost pile is about 4 feet across and 4 feet high. The pile can be round or square. We don't bother with adding any sticks for aeration, since we turn our pile about every 4 to 6 weeks.

As you collect grass clippings throughout the spring and summer, add them to your pile of leaves. About once a month you should turn your compost pile. Use a spading fork or a shovel to move the pile so that what was on the top is now on the bottom and what was on the outside of the pile is on the inside. During this turning you mix up the grass clippings and leaves, which causes the pile to heat up and begin to rapidly decompose. (This heat produced by an active compost pile kills off weed seeds and some disease

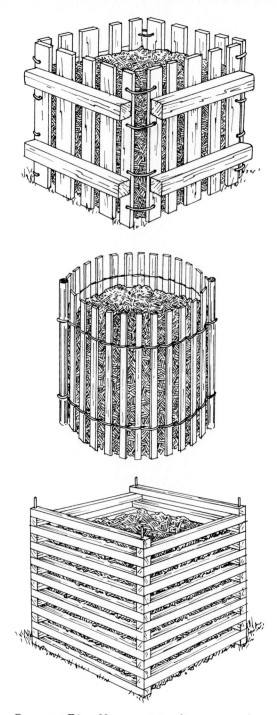

Compost Bins: *Here are just three examples of the kinds of bins you can build to hold your compost. These bins are inexpensive and easy to put together, and they keep your pile neatly contained and out of view.*

organisms.) Remember, the pile should not smell. If it does, it is probably because you have too much grass concentrated in one place and you need to mix that grass with some leaves.

Once you've built the compost pile, you should cover it to keep the rain from soaking it and cooling it down. You can use a piece of plastic held down by a couple of bricks. Jeff and Liz use an old shower curtain liner that has seen better days. You can tell if the pile is working well by sticking your fist about 12 inches into it. If the material feels warm, the pile is decomposing nicely. Jeff keeps track of his compost pile with a soil thermometer so that when the temperature sinks below 100°F he knows it's time to turn it again. You don't need to be this precise unless you are interested in getting finished compost as fast as possible.

Substitutes for Homemade Compost

If you choose not to make compost, you have several options for providing the inch of humus to the flower garden each year. Some communities have their own large-scale composting systems to process various solid waste products that were formerly placed in expensive landfills. This compost is often made available to the general public for free or for a very reasonable fee. Some communities also compost leaves, and the resulting material, called leaf mold, is a great form of humus to add to your flower garden.

A good substitute for compost, at least on the small scale of the 60-Minute Flower Garden, is a mixture of peat humus and processed cow manure, both available at most garden centers. A large bale of peat humus mixed with one or two 50-pound bags of processed cow manure will give you the layer of humus your garden needs each year. Be aware that peat moss is different from peat humus. Peat moss is more acidic than peat humus and is not as desirable as a compost substitute. The pH of peat moss is around 3.2 to 4.5, while peat humus is anywhere between 4.0 and 7.5. Lime should always be added if either form of peat is used as a compost substitute (5 to 10 pounds of lime per bale of peat).

For some folks in certain areas of the country, there is another excellent source of humus available — composted mushroom soil. Mushrooms are grown in composted straw and manure. After the crop is finished, the material is no longer any good for raising mushrooms. This "spent" mushroom soil is an excellent soil conditioner and is usually sold by the mushroom farmers at a very reasonable price. It is best to let fresh mushroom soil age for at least six weeks before adding it to the garden.

Using Compost in the Flower Garden

There are two ways you'll use compost in the flower garden. First, you will place a 1-inch layer across your entire garden at least once a year, ideally in the spring. This means that you will have to hold the compost you make during the growing season over the winter until the next spring. Remember not to leave finished compost exposed to the weather without a covering of some sort; much of its nitrogen value will be leached away by the rain before you get to use it. If you do lay an inch of compost over your garden in the fall, some of its benefits will be lost over the winter. The best strategy is to make your compost during the growing season, when there is plenty of green, nitrogen-rich material available to mix with last year's leaves, and then store it covered until the next spring.

Note that we did not say, "dig this material into the soil." You just lay it on top. If you have a desperate need to at least rake it in a little bit, go ahead if it makes you feel better. You don't really have to spend the energy or the time. The worms and other soil-dwelling organisms will take care of moving your compost down into the ground.

The second way you'll use compost is in the transplanting process. You should always add compost to every hole you prepare for a transplant. Over the years, this addition of compost in your transplant holes will collectively represent a significant supplement of humus to the top 12-inch layer of your garden soil. It also gives your transplants a much better start in life.

Mulch for Flowers

Mulch is a layer of material, usually organic, that covers all the bare soil in the garden. You place this mulch right over the layer of compost we suggested in the previous section. If the idea of mulching a flower garden is new to you, read on, and what we have to say should convince you that mulch belongs on your flower garden (and any other garden sites on your property, for that matter).

A layer of mulch over the surface of a garden greatly reduces the rate of evaporation from the soil. Mulch can reduce moisture loss in a garden by as much as 50 percent, depending on the thickness of the mulch and the material that is used. Mulch may make the difference between your plants making it through a drought in the middle of August or burning up.

If mulch is thick enough, it will prevent most weeds from growing. Those few that do get through are easily pulled, since the soil, if it has been managed according to our system, never gets hard and compacted. A good mulch virtually eliminates the onerous task of weeding the garden.

Research in the past decade has made it clear that mulch has significant impact on soil temperature, and soil temperature is often more important to a plant's growth than air temperature. Organic mulches such as hay or straw will cool the soil by 8 to 12 degrees Fahrenheit, and chopped leaves will cool things down as much as 18 degrees. As we discussed earlier in this chapter, plants don't grow very well when the soil temperature exceeds 85°F. So your ability to keep the soil cool in the middle of the summer will contribute to a healthy family of plants in your flower garden.

Rain beating down on bare garden soil can have some negative effects on your garden. Bare soil tends to become compacted over time, from the pounding of the rain and the drying out of the soil particles in the blazing sun. Mulch protects the surface of the soil from the impact of rain and reduces the compacting process. And by now you should realize that less compaction means healthier roots and a more active population of beneficial microorganisms.

In fact, a mulch will encourage microorganisms to work nearer the surface of the soil, since the soil stays moist and friable. Furthermore, the mulch itself is slowly decomposing, delivering an ongoing nutrient supplement to your garden. Some people worry about the fact that the decomposing mulch is known to tie up nitrogen in the top few inches of the soil. Well, it really isn't an issue unless you're using a sawdust mulch, which we discuss in the next section. The nitrogen lost to the decomposition of the mulch is an insignificant part of the total nitrogen supply available for your plants' roots in a soil supplemented annually with an inch of compost.

Finally, a winter mulch over your entire flower bed helps to stabilize the temperature of the soil, avoiding the rapid fluctuations that can occur in soil that isn't protected. This layer of mulch will not keep the soil from ultimately freezing, but it will protect it from the extreme temperature shifts that occur throughout the winter. This will help keep the populations of beneficial soil mi-

croorganisms stable and flourishing. Winter mulch also reduces freeze damage to roots, prevents further soil compaction, and reduces damage from soil heaving.

You may have heard that slugs enjoy the dark, cool, moist environment under mulch. If you have problems with slugs, that shouldn't deter you from using mulch, because the benefits far outweigh that one liability. We will talk in more detail about controlling slugs in Chapter 8. Here we'll mention one way to control this pest by timing your mulch application. It turns out that slugs are most active and hungry when the air temperature is between 60° and 70°F, and their activity is minimal above 80°F, during the heat of the summer. Consequently, if you live in heavy slug country, you might apply your mulch a little later in the season and take it back off in the early fall to minimize serious slug damage.

Kinds of Mulch

A good mulch for a flower garden will be easy to work with, allow air to pass through, be relatively windproof, hold some moisture, and be attractive. We think chopped leaves are the ideal mulch for the 60-Minute Flower Garden. They're free, generally available in most areas, and form a pleasing backdrop to all the colors and plants in the flower garden.

Use only chopped leaves on a flower garden, since whole leaves get matted and reduce the even flow of water into the soil. Because we recommend that you use leaves gathered in the fall as the winter mulch and then compost those leaves in the spring, you will avoid any potentially serious allelopathic (inhibiting) effects on the plants in your garden. Any chopped leaves you use in the summer will have been collected during the previous fall, so they will have aged enough to eliminate any negative chemical effects on your flower garden.

Peat is another popular organic mulch. However, it does tend to dry out and is hard to rewet. A serious drought can cause it to form a crust that repels water instead of absorbing it. Also, peat is not free. We'd use a leafy mulch instead of peat anytime.

Aged sawdust, grass clippings, pine needles, and shredded bark are also mulches you can consider for the flower beds. Make sure sawdust has aged in a pile exposed to the elements for at least a year before using it. If it hasn't had a chance to age, it will compete for nitrogen—which you would rather have available for your flowers—from the top few inches of soil. Add grass clippings in a thin layer, no more than an inch at a time. Too thick a layer of fresh clippings will decompose and become putrid rather than dry and become an effective mulch. Pine needles are an attractive mulch, but they do tend to make your soil more acid over time. They might not be the best choice in an area with soil that is already somewhat acidic. Shredded bark or wood chips must be laid on pretty thickly to be efficient in weed control and sometimes have negative allelopathic effects on certain plants. We recommend bark mulches only for trees and shrubs that you have tucked in among the flowers in your garden design. If there's no other mulching material available, you can try bark or wood chips around your larger perennials such as peonies and daylilies.

The 60-Minute Flower Garden Soil Management System

The annual approach to soil management that we have outlined in this chapter is extremely easy, takes little time, and goes a long way toward ensuring that you will have beautiful, healthy flowers for many, many years. To summarize, our system involves four basic steps each year, assuming you follow our advice and properly prepare the garden's soil in the first place.

Apply fall/winter mulch and rock powders. The cycle really begins in the fall when the leaves are falling and waiting to be collected and chopped. You need to collect enough leaves to cover the area of your 60-Minute Flower Garden two times with 6 to 12 inches of chopped leaves—now in the fall and again next summer. You'll lay out your winter mulch sometime after the first frost has killed off your herbaceous plants and the garden is ready to be bedded down for the winter. Every other year or so, you will also spread 10 to 20 pounds of rock powders to supplement the soil's supplies of phosphorus and potassium.

Some books recommend that you wait until the ground freezes before you lay the winter mulch, but we feel this is not necessary. The only caution is that in some cases an early mulch may attract rodents that like to feed in the winter on the roots of certain perennials like astilbes and on bulbs like crocuses. (See Chapter 8 to learn how to deal with rodents in your flower beds.)

Apply spring compost. When spring comes, you'll take up the winter mulch that is covering the area of the garden that includes bulbs and early perennials and where you'll be planting early annuals. This allows the soil to warm up faster than if it were left covered with the mulch. These leaves can now be stored in your compost bin in preparation for making your annual supply of compost. Remember, you should have saved some additional chopped leaves somewhere over the winter to serve later in the season as your summer mulch. Leave the mulch under the shrubs and any trees all year long.

This is the same time of year when you apply 1 inch of finished compost over the entire area of the garden. Where you have left the mulch under the shrubs, just put the compost on top. It will disappear before the season is over. As we will discuss in the next chapter, early spring is also the time for laying out your drip irrigation lines.

Make next year's compost. During the spring and early summer months, when grass clippings are most available, you can be making your compost supply for next year.

Apply summer mulch. Sometime in May or early June, soil temperatures are going to be approaching 70°F. That's the time to reapply your chopped leaf mulch to cool the soil into the summer, keep down the weeds, and retain the moisture in the soil. In the fall, you will supplement this summer mulch with some more chopped leaves, and the cycle starts all over again.

Chapter 7

Watering and Feeding the Flower Garden

Watering and feeding the 60-Minute Flower Garden couldn't be simpler. Three times a week you turn on a drip irrigation system, with its automatic shutoff timer, to give your plants a slow, steady, satisfying drink. Once a year you spread a 1-inch layer of compost over the garden to provide it with a nice, balanced diet. Now that's pretty easy! Assuming you follow the other steps in our system, including preparing the soil properly, encouraging earthworms, and using mulch, what we just described is the minimum effort it takes to keep a lovely and healthy flower garden watered and fed.

Obviously, some people would like to go a bit further than just the minimum to make sure that their flowers are particularly healthy and attractive. Therefore, in this chapter we cover all aspects of watering and feeding a flower garden, giving our own biased recommendations as we go. Our approach revolves around using a drip irrigation system and supplementing compost treatments with liquid fertilizer applied as a foliar spray.

Most gardeners in this country tend to underwater their flowers. This occurs for many reasons. A common one is that during July and August, when gardens usually need the most watering, gardeners often find other demands on their time, such as vacations. When flowers don't receive steady watering, they go through a dry/wet/dry cycle that has the net effect of stopping growth, starting growth, and stopping growth, over and over again. This stop/start routine seriously reduces a flower garden's performance. Of course, it's just as easy to overwater the garden. If you give your garden too much water, the soil becomes saturated, reducing the space for that critical element, oxygen. Again, plant growth suffers.

A plant reacts very simply to too little or too much water — it stops growing. When it stops growing, you are losing "production," both in the size of blossoms and in the number of blossoms. The problem is that when a plant starts to wilt from lack of water it has already stopped growing for as much as a day or more. Therefore, the task at hand is to anticipate a plant's water needs *before* its growth slows down, much less stops. The secret to successful watering is *consistency*—trying to keep the water supply as uniform as possible.

Water stress can cause a number of serious problems in the flower garden. Drought-weakened plants are more vulnerable to diseases such as powdery mildew and various blights, and they become prone to pest damage, especially from spider mites.

Using a Rain Gauge

The goal is to give your garden enough additional water to maintain the proper amount of moisture—not too much and not too little—after subtracting how much rain has recently fallen. If you get an inch of rain, you should be able to wait a day or two before worrying about watering your garden. Keeping track of rainfall helps you avoid overwatering your garden. The best way to do that is to mount a rain gauge someplace in or around your garden. Jeff has his fairly close to his back door so he can see it from inside his kitchen. He can check it while it is still raining and, because it is so close to the door, he generally keeps better track of what is happening than if it were located 50 feet out in the backyard. Charles has his rain gauge farther away from the house because there are too many trees near the house to get an accurate reading.

The only thing you must avoid with rain gauges is allowing water in them to freeze. In early spring and late fall, keep a watch for possible overnight freezes after a rain. Most gauges are easily cracked by ice. If you don't have a rain gauge, any straight-sided container will work. Just measure the depth of the water from the bottom.

Rain Gauge: This is the gauge Charles uses to keep track of how much rain has fallen on his garden. When it looks like the plants won't get the 1 inch of water they need each week from rainfall, he knows it's time to check the soil to see if it's time to water.

We keep rough track of our rainfall on a weekly basis and look for ½ to 1 inch a week. If after a few days we have not gotten that much, we know we should be thinking about watering. Neither Jeff nor Charles keeps precise records on paper. Just keeping rough track in your head is enough to make good use of this handy measuring device. Your local newspaper may give you some help by providing information on weekly rainfall. Remember, however, that those figures could differ somewhat from those for your particular garden spot.

60-Minute Garden Watering Guidelines

The soil fills with water from the top down, and it also loses water from the top down. This water is lost in two ways: by evaporation directly from the soil surface and by transpiration by the leaves of the plants that first took the water from the soil. With its chopped-leaf mulch, the 60-Minute Flower Garden has little or no evaporation. Thus, your need for watering is already reduced, compared with the more traditional, unmulched flower gardens that your neighbors have. The objective of your watering efforts is to replace the moisture that is lost through transpiration. The amount of water lost by plants in this way varies with weather conditions, so you'll have little control over it. Transpiration increases with a rise in temperature and with an increase in wind velocity.

The rule of thumb generally accepted by master gardeners like Charles is to see that the garden receives 1 inch of water a week from the rain and/or from watering systems. In arid areas, 2 inches a week is the target. However, this is probably too much water for the 60-Minute Flower Garden. Since our garden loses little or no water from evaporation, the weekly need will be something less than 1 inch, probably between ½ and ¾ inch, depending on the season. A garden located under a tree will probably need more, due to the thirsty tree roots. An inch of water puts ½ gallon of water on each square foot of your garden. Likewise, ½ inch will then put ¼ gallon, or 1 quart, of water on each square foot. In a 200-square-foot

garden, that means you need about 50 to 75 gallons of water a week, less any rain that falls.

Now let's translate those amounts into how often and for how long you'll have to water. To deliver 50 to 75 gallons (less the rainfall), you'll need to water two or three times a week for about 20 minutes on a 200-square-foot garden. (It's better to spread your watering over the week rather than give the plants a single dousing; that makes it easier to maintain a consistent level of moisture without any drastic fluctuations.) Don't follow this rule blindly throughout the entire season, however. In the summer months, during very hot periods with little rain and any kind of breeze, you can go up to a half hour or more two or three times a week. August is the time for maximum growth in the garden, so it is not the time to overlook the water needs of your plants. Feel under the mulch to double-check. It should always feel moist. If it's dry, you've been neglecting your watering duties.

For master gardeners who know which plants need extra water at certain times in their life cycles, this approach to watering can serve as the base. Individual water supplements to certain groups of plants can easily be done by hand in a relatively short period of time. For most of us backyard gardeners, if we get our basic watering program going, our gardens are going to look better than they ever have in the past.

The key to our watering program for the 60-Minute Flower Garden is a drip irrigation system. We believe the drip system offers the best watering method for people who want to have an attractive flower garden but are also pressed for time. When you install a drip system in your flower beds, you virtually eliminate the time it takes to water your garden. Before we launch into our description of what we consider an ideal watering system, let's quickly review the more traditional methods for watering a garden and make some observations about their strengths and weaknesses.

Conventional Watering Methods

Most people water their flower gardens from above, using an oscillating sprinkler or a hand-held hose or watering can of some sort. There are several disadvantages to watering from above. In the first place, it takes a considerable amount of time. Also, when you water this way, you lose about 30 percent of the water to evaporation and runoff. That means that you must add at least 30 percent to the water amount guidelines described in the preceding section. You inevitably use additional water to moisten the mulch each time (water has to penetrate the mulch before it can reach the soil). Using this method to water your plants is very time-consuming and wasteful of a commodity that is becoming more precious with each passing year.

Even if time is of no concern, you should still worry about this watering method because it encourages disease among your flowers. Since the leaves of the plants get wet, certain fungi and other disease spores are encouraged to multiply. Yes, we know that when it rains the leaves get wet. However, if you can avoid wetting the leaves every time you water, you will definitely reduce the danger of certain diseases like mildew.

Watering a 200-square-foot garden with a watering can is an onerous task. In this case you would need to fill a 5-gallon can 10 to 15 times to cover the whole garden. Both Jeff and Charles use a watering can for spot watering, for providing water to transplant holes, and for applying some liquid fertilizers to certain plants. However, neither of us has time to consider using this device as our primary watering method.

Each of these watering techniques will get the job done, but if you are short on time

and if you are conscious of saving water, the drip irrigation system is something you should seriously consider. We recognize, however, that not everyone may be able to use such a system. For gardeners who use conventional methods, here are some commonsense watering principles. First, always water deeply so that the soil is moistened at least 12 inches down (dig to check this). Apply about an inch of water a week. If possible, water in the morning, so foliage has a chance to dry (this minimizes disease problems). And last, avoid watering at midday, because too much water will be lost to evaporation.

Drip Irrigation in the Flower Garden

Drip irrigation is not a new idea. German farmers developed a kind of drip system over 100 years ago. They laid pipe for water underground in their fields in such a way that the joints did not quite connect. This allowed water to seep into the earth down to the roots of their crops. Forty years ago, Symka Blass, an Israeli engineer, developed the idea of using special valves, or emitters, in a hose to release water one drop at a time. Since then drip irrigation has become a more and more popular watering method in commercial agriculture, since it saves enormous amounts of water and in the long run is cheaper than traditional watering systems.

Benefits for Flowers and Gardeners

Drip irrigation systems offer a number of important benefits to backyard flower gardeners and to the flowers that are growing in their gardens. To start, a drip system uses much less water than the traditional sprinkler system. You can assume that you will save at least 30 percent, and in some cases 50 percent, of the water you would use with other methods of watering, such as sprinklers. Water in a drip system has no chance to evaporate or run off because it is completely absorbed by the soil and never touches the leaves of the plants.

The timesaving benefit should appeal to lots of gardeners. You can water your garden with a drip system in 10 seconds, the time it takes to turn it on. The best drip systems operate with a mechanical timer device that allows you to set the timer to a specified watering period, after which the timer automatically shuts the water off.

Another big plus is that your flowers will look better. Research has demonstrated that drip irrigation systems, especially those used in conjunction with mulch, increase the productivity of a garden. In a flower garden this means that plants blossom earlier, show increased growth, and have larger

blossoms. The plants will also be healthier. Because water never touches the leaves, many moisture-related diseases are avoided with a drip system. Problems such as rust, mildew, and blossom damage are all reduced in gardens using drip irrigation. And don't worry that a drip system will mar the good looks of your flower garden. All drip systems can be covered by mulch and most can even be buried.

An advantage just recently being appreciated is the cooling effect a drip system has on the soil. A properly managed drip irrigation system can be used to help keep down soil temperatures in the heat of the summer. Your garden will look better because plants grow more efficiently in cooler soil.

Finally, a drip irrigation system reduces the problem of soil compaction in the beds. When the soil is saturated with large amounts of water at once, its structure is weakened

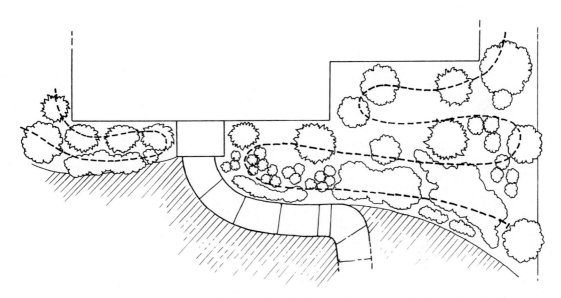

Drip Irrigation in the Flower Garden: *The dotted lines show how the hose for the drip system is laid out among all the plants in these two flower beds. The system works best when the loops of the hose are set no more than 2 feet apart. The hose can be covered with mulch so it is discreetly hidden from sight.*

somewhat and compaction occurs as a natural result. Drip irrigation avoids this problem because the water is introduced into the soil so slowly that the structure of the soil is not affected.

A top-quality drip irrigation system will cost you about $.25 to $.40 a square foot, or $50 to $80 for a 200-square-foot garden. You can expect a system to last for decades and take very little maintenance. It is easy to expand as you develop more garden areas.

Four Types of Drip Irrigation Systems

The first task in developing a drip irrigation system is to select the type of system best suited for your flower garden. As you might expect, when you ask two gardeners, you get two different opinions. Jeff favors the emitter system and Charles thinks the soaker hoses are best. So that you can make the best choice for *your* garden, let's review all the options.

A major problem inhibiting flower gardeners from installing drip systems is the technical fog found in most catalogs and articles about drip irrigation. Most drip irrigation supply companies direct their efforts toward large commercial applications and consequently must offer a broad range of types of equipment and must get into fairly sophisticated technical calculations in designing those large systems. The home flower garden system, on the other hand, is pretty simple and easy to understand if we sweep away some of that technical terminology and advanced mathematical calculations.

There are four types of drip systems available to the flower gardener. They include the drip soaker lines, the porous soaker lines, the spaghetti-type lines, and the emitter system.

Drip Soakers

The drip soaker system comes in two models. One is simply a plastic or rubber hose with lots of holes punched in it that allow the water to drip out along the hose's entire length. You simply lay the hose along the bed and turn on the water just a little bit so that it doesn't squirt out of the holes but rather drips slowly into the ground.

These hoses are found in most garden supply stores. They are used mostly for watering shrubs and hedges. Drip soakers have a number of disadvantages for flower gardens. Their most serious problem is that you can't control how much water is released into all parts of the garden. If you have more than one length of hose in a system, regulating pressure along the length of the hose is difficult. Pressure is controlled by how much you turn the valve at the faucet. You will have more water coming out close to the faucet and much less water coming out at the far end of the system. These drip soaker hoses are difficult to put down in a bed without having kinks develop at the bending points. We wouldn't recommend these simple drip soaker hoses for the 60-Minute Flower Garden.

The other model of drip soaker hose, usually made of PVC tubing with a twin-wall design, is definitely an option to consider in the flower garden. This is essentially a tube within a tube. Water from the feeder line enters via the inside tube and moves through the length of that inner tube. When pressure is equalized, water moves into the outer tube through holes spaced every 5 feet in the inner tube. The outer tube has perforations every 12 inches, through which water seeps into the soil. This system is relatively inexpensive and is almost maintenance free. We recommend this system for your 60-Minute Flower Garden.

Porous Drip Soaker System

The canvas soaker hose, which simply sweats water along its entire length, was the earliest version of the porous soaker hose.

It is difficult to control how much water is being released. This hose also has the added disadvantage of needing to be dried out after every use to reduce deterioration. You can see how this soaker hose is pretty impractical for regular use in your garden.

Technology has given us two other porous soakers. Du Pont has developed one made of white plastic tubing that feels something like paper. It is very light and it sweats water along its whole length. There are several companies marketing this product, and it works very well for some watering applications. The disadvantage is that it is very vulnerable to ultraviolet rays from the sun and therefore should be used under a mulch. Even with that precaution, this tubing won't last more than two or three seasons before it breaks down with lots of leaks.

Another porous soaker hose recently developed offers a much more practical option for flower gardeners. Made from recycled automobile tires, this durable hose has millions of little air spaces or holes that allow it to sweat along its entire length. One version of this porous soaker hose, sold under the name Hydropore, waters plants within 1 foot on either side. Perhaps this type of hose's biggest attraction, besides its durability, is its simplicity of operation. All you do is snake it out around your flower bed, attach it to a regular hose with a mechanical timer at the faucet, and turn on the timer.

"Spaghetti" Drip System

This system gets its name from the spaghetti-like hoses that attach to a main feeder line and drip water into the soil. "Spaghetti" drip systems were designed primarily for commercial greenhouse and nursery operations using thousands of pots to grow small plants. These "spaghetti" lines can be led to each potted plant, which makes watering a large number of pots at the same time very easy. In the flower garden, "spaghetti" lines can get clogged and are also vulnerable to rodent damage. They aren't very practical for the flower garden when compared with the porous hose or standard emitter system.

Emitter Drip System

This system is simply a series of narrow hoses laid throughout the garden. Each hose has embedded in it a number of evenly spaced nozzles, or emitters, that release water into the soil one drop at a time. These emitters come in several designs, making the system very flexible for almost all watering applications from a 20-acre orchard to our 200-square-foot 60-Minute Flower Garden. The emitter system allows the gardener to have more precise control of the water distribution throughout the garden, because he can choose the type of emitter and determine the spacing between the emitters. This is a very reliable system, but it is definitely more complicated to install than the porous hose or the twin-wall hose. The emitters are also susceptible to clogging, so you must be sure to use the filter that comes with the kit to keep clogging to a minimum.

Designing Your Drip Irrigation System

Before you install a drip irrigation system in your garden, you need to decide whether to start off with a kit with all the basic parts included or whether to buy all the parts of your drip system and fabricate it yourself. The kits will cover a specified number of square feet, anywhere from 100 to 400. Sometimes they don't include what we consider important parts, such as pressure regulators, backflow valves, and filters. On the other hand, they give you the basics you need to try out drip irrigation in at least a part of your garden.

Components of a System

It isn't very difficult to design a drip system for your flower garden. To decipher the jargon of the drip irrigation companies all you need to do is figure out what you need for your system. There are four basic components: the head (where you connect your system to a water source); the main supply line or lines (they carry water to the garden from the faucet); the laterals or feeder lines (they carry the water to the plants); and, if needed, the emitters that are embedded in the feeder lines. Once you understand the function of these four components, you are ready to read and understand the catalogs and brochures of most of the drip irrigation companies.

Another feature you should consider, and which we feel is invaluable, is a timing device. There are three kinds of timing devices that will work on either an emitter system or a porous hose system. The simplest and least expensive is a mechanical timer connected to a valve that you hook up to the head of the system. Whenever you want to water, you turn the timer to the desired length of time (usually up to an hour) and walk away. There are other timers that are battery operated; these allow you to schedule your watering over a period of time, such as over a week. A timer like this will turn the system on and off automatically without your having to be there—perfect for when you are on vacation. The most sophisticated device has the capability to measure the moisture content of the soil; when that level drops below what is an appropriate amount, the system turns itself on. The monitor then turns the system off when the desired moisture level is reached.

We use the simple mechanical timer in our gardens and it works very well. We believe some kind of timer is valuable because it allows you to forget about keeping track of how long you wanted to water and when you wanted to turn off the system. It does that chore for you, saving you time and bother. Most gardeners tend to not water their gardens enough. Anything you can do to make watering less of a chore will improve the chances of getting to that task often enough to keep your garden thriving.

Matching the System to Your Garden

A drip irrigation system is not necessarily suited for every 60-Minute Flower Garden we described in Chapter 3. Laying out and using a drip system in a Woodland Garden would be impractical. But that doesn't pose a problem, since this garden contains plants that generally have low watering requirements. It doesn't need the more intensive watering treatment of a drip system to do well. The Decorative Home Garden, the Herbaceous Flower Border, and the Bank Garden will all thrive with a drip system.

When designing a drip irrigation system, it is very important to work with a reasonably accurate drawing of your garden layout. Check Chapter 2 for our discussion about preparing a sketch of your flower garden. This drawing will help you determine how much hose or tubing you need, and if you use emitters, how far apart you should place them on the tubing. Most of the companies that sell drip irrigation equipment will help you with this planning. Usually, if you send them a scale drawing of your garden, they will send you a layout of the drip system and a complete parts list for your review.

Installing the Drip System in the Garden

The best time to install a drip system in the 60-Minute Flower Garden is when you first build the garden. If you're past that point, a system can be easily installed in an existing garden. Normally, you would install your drip lines on top of the beds and then cover them with your mulch. Some of the porous and twin-wall systems can be buried just below the surface of the soil and left there.

If you're installing a system with flexible PVC tubing, it is much easier to work with the tubing when it is warm. Let it sit out in the sun for a few hours or dip the ends in boiling water just before trying to attach pieces together.

You can set up a drip system for a 200-square-foot garden in a few hours. Remember not to tighten plastic fittings with a wrench, or you will strip the threads. Where you have plastic screw fittings, a piece of Teflon tape wrapped around the male fitting helps to keep leaks down with just hand tightening. You can buy emitter systems with the emitters already installed, or you can install them yourself.

Using the Drip Irrigation System

No matter whether you use a porous hose, a twin-wall system, or an emitter system, running it for roughly 1 hour should meet your 60-Minute Flower Garden's weekly water requirements. The output rates of each system will vary somewhat, but 1 hour is a good general guideline for those of us who don't want to get too scientifically precise.

Now, watering the garden only once a week is not necessarily a good idea. Maintaining a consistent moisture level is more important than quantity. You don't want the plants to go through a dry/wet/dry cycle over and over again. So if there's a dry spell with no rain, you could spread the watering over three times a week with a 20-minute session each time. That would ensure that the garden receives sufficient water and maintains a more consistent level of moisture. Some people water their gardens daily, and that means a 10-minute watering session with the drip system. Jeff prefers to water two or three times a week, keeping track of how much rain he gets. If he gets ½ inch of rain, he'll wait two days and start his 20-minute watering cycle again.

Feeding the 60-Minute Flower Garden

In Chapter 6 you were introduced to our general approach to soil management for the 60-Minute Flower Garden. The major nutrient source for flowering plant growth is put into the beds in the spring in the form of compost. The slow breakdown of that material, along with biennial applications of rock powders, provides virtually all of the nutrients the flowers need to be healthy and prolific, assuming you have a strong earthworm population in the garden.

Consequently, any feeding done during the growing season provides a supplement to that primary nutrient resource. In-season feeding isn't necessary for normal, healthy plant growth, but it will definitely make a difference if you apply it properly and at the right times. These supplemental feedings are much like the vitamin supplements we humans take to get extra nutrients in times of stress or to make up for deficiencies in our diets. The vitamin is not replacing a good diet, it is simply a supplement to it. Supplemental plant feedings, in either dry or liquid form, act the same way. These feedings take very little extra time (especially when you use our methods), can be accomplished within the 60-minute-a-week time frame, and will often make the difference between a very nice flower garden and a spectacular one.

Using Dry Fertilizers

We have already made our case in Chapter 6 for why we don't use dry, synthetic chemical fertilizers on our flower garden. While they do provide plants with the key NPK nutrients, they also repel the earthworm population, which is capable of producing enormous amounts of valuable fertilizer. At the same time, some gardeners may prefer to add what are called organic fertilizers, such as bloodmeal or cottonseed meal for nitrogen, phosphate rock powder for phosphorus, and wood ashes for potassium. Although these amendments are excellent slow-release fertilizers for the flower garden, we recommend that you consider using liquid fertilizers for your supplements. We feel you will get better results for your efforts.

Using Liquid Fertilizers

Plants take up nutrients 20 to 30 times faster when they are offered in liquid form than when they are offered in powdered form. This is true whether the liquid is applied to the roots or whether it is sprayed on the plant foliage. There are many fertilizers sold in garden centers that can be mixed with water and applied in liquid form. Our favorite is fish emulsion, because it has a much broader spectrum of micronutrients than other fertilizers we are familiar with. You can also use homemade manure or compost tea, which is a good source of nitrogen and costs nothing to make. Brew a batch of manure or compost tea by filling a burlap sack with one or both materials and letting it soak in a 50-gallon drum of water for a week or so. The resulting brownish water, or tea, contains nutrients easily taken up by your plants.

Feeding through the Soil

Most people, when they think of feeding plants, think about applying the fertilizer to the soil, where the roots will take it up. One way of delivering liquid fertilizers to plant roots is through an emitter-type drip irrigation system. That way the plants get a dose of nutrients along with the water that's being carried by the drip system. This may sound quick and easy, but from experience we really would recommend that instead you use the foliar method we describe in the next section. Feeding through a drip system can lead to clogged emitters, and the procedure for introducing the liquid fertilizer into the system can be messy and time-consuming.

Foliar Feeding

There has been in recent years an increasing interest in foliar feeding of flowers, especially on a commercial scale. This involves applying diluted liquid fertilizer directly onto the leaves of plants, using a device that can produce a mistlike spray. As we mentioned earlier, plants take up the nutrients very quickly when they're applied this way. The plants show rapid and significant gains very soon after a spraying. Young leaves are more able to absorb nutrients than the mature leaves on a plant.

We think foliar feeding is superior to feeding through the soil because there is absolutely no waste of fertilizer. While liquid fertilizer applied to the soil is more efficient in terms of waste than dry fertililzer, there is still a portion of that fertilizer that is leached down through the soil and is not picked up by the plants. With a foliar spray, all the fertilizer gets to the plant.

Foliar feeding does require purchasing a piece of spray equipment. Sprayers suitable for home-scale growers are available in many garden supply centers and catalogs. Once you have your sprayer, the preparation of the liquid mix and the actual spraying of the 60-Minute Flower Garden will take no more than 15 minutes every month or so. This is a modest time investment for the dramatic improvement a foliar spraying program will make in the health and quality of your flower garden.

How Much to Feed?

There are no clear rules for determining the best frequency for foliar feeding. Some gardeners give their plants a shot of liquid fertilizer every time they water. We supplement our basic soil maintenance program with foliar sprays about once every two weeks. If you spray only once every month, you will still make a noticeable difference in your garden's appearance.

Feeding through a foliar system is most effective if you apply the nutrients in the early part of the day. This gives the plants the whole day to absorb what they need. You should avoid spraying at midday when the sunlight is most intense and in the evening when damp plants encourage fungal growth and other disease problems.

Enhancing the 60-Minute Flower Garden

For most of us, our flower gardens are a long way from the sea. But horticultural research is showing that we should bring a part of the sea to our gardens—in the form of seaweed—to enhance the beauty and health of the flowers.

For over 2,000 years, gardeners and farmers around the world who live near the seacoast have been using seaweed to improve their soils and their crops. They recognized that plants grow better in soil fortified with composted seaweed and with a seaweed mulch. No one really understood why seaweed was so good for the garden, but it was obvious that it was. Over the past 20 years, researchers have begun to discover what this wonderful relationship between seaweed and plants is all about.

What they've found is that seaweed is more than a fertilizer (although it does have some plant food value). Its special characteristic is that it acts as a catalyst, or enhancer of growth, by giving the plant the ability to very effectively absorb nutrients from the soil. Various liquefied seaweed or kelp emulsions have been used as foliar sprays on plants and have caused very signficant increases in plant growth and performance. Similarly, liquid seaweed emulsions added directly to the soil have increased its microbial activity, accelerating the process of freeing nutrients for plants.

What does this mean for your flower garden? Research indicates that just two or three applications of very dilute liquid seaweed emulsion, applied as a foliar spray, will improve plant growth, increase the plants' capacity to withstand drought, and reduce incidence of disease. The plants' enhanced performance should show up in your garden as more and brighter blooms, lusher foliage, and overall vigor and health.

Chapter 8

Managing Pests in the Flower Garden

There is nothing in a gardener's life that is more discouraging and frustrating than to come out one morning to find the annuals you transplanted last evening seriously damaged by insects or rabbits or some other dastardly pest that has invaded the sanctity of the flower bed. At first you're likely to feel helpless, but that feeling will soon be followed by anger and a deep desire to wipe that pest from the face of the earth, or at least from your garden. Insects, weeds, diseases, and four-legged pests can be problems in any flower garden, even to the point of discouraging you from having a garden at all. Fortunately, as long as you know how to handle them, pest problems don't have to turn into a catastrophe. We 60-Minute Flower Gardeners view pests from the perspective of prevention, balance, and control of problems. We aren't driven by the need to completely eradicate the problems.

To understand this approach to garden pests, think of the way many of us are viewing our personal health. We're discovering that it makes more sense and is more cost-effective to spend some money to keep well (by exercising and by eating properly) than

to wait to get sick and then spend money to treat the illness. Likewise, in the 60-Minute Flower Garden it is cheaper and more effective to *prevent* weed, insect, disease, and other pest problems than it is to wait to take action until disaster has struck. However, the first challenge for the gardener is to get rid of the notion that there should be *no* pest damage whatsoever in the garden. A few holes in an odd leaf or two won't hurt a thing. You need to learn to tolerate those minor problems but be ready to take action so that they don't turn into major ones — where there are no leaves left because of insect attack or disease, for example.

We suggest you consider using what we call Backyard Pest Management techniques in your 60-Minute Flower Garden. We have coined this term from the pest-control approach called Integrated Pest Management (IPM), which is used in commercial agriculture and by some home gardeners. We have adapted many of the IPM practices to be more appropriate for the scale of pest management in backyard gardens, which is why we call our approach BPM, for Backyard Pest Management. BPM in the home

150

garden is concerned with *controlling* pests rather than eradicating or exterminating them—a very different approach from the traditional one.

BPM relies on various biological, physical, and natural chemical methods to control pest problems in the garden. As you use this approach, no matter what type of pest you're dealing with, you follow the same sequence: identify your particular pest problem; monitor the problem; and use control measures that will deal specifically with the problem in your garden.

Using Backyard Pest Management in the Flower Garden

The general BPM system for the 60-Minute Flower Garden revolves around eight basic steps. They are listed in order of priority from the best prevention activities to modest control measures to the steps of last resort to save the plant. The philosophy is that it is better to prevent pest damage than to have to fight it after the pests have arrived. The last two steps are taken only when the other steps have failed. Our experience has shown that after a few years of following this approach, the final steps of using sprays and botanical poisons will seldom be necessary. As you read through the chapter you'll see that different combinations of these eight basic steps are employed to deal with insects, weeds, diseases, or animal pests.

Don't be alarmed by the length of this list. It isn't as complicated as it may sound. After a few seasons you should become comfortable and skillful in using all these steps effectively. Many beginning gardeners start with step nine, which isn't even on our list. This drastic step is to use chemical herbicides, insecticides, or fungicides designed

Eight Steps in BPM

1. Maintain garden hygiene.
2. Build soil health.
3. Identify the pest and learn its habits.
4. Use pest- and disease-resistant varieties.
5. Use biological controls.
6. Use physical controls.
7. Use natural sprays.
8. Use botanical poisons.

to wipe out *all* of the weeds, bugs, or diseases within striking distance. In our opinion, steps one through eight yield far better results in the long run, but they do take several years to begin to have their full impact. Fortunately, these steps take less time every year as the overall influence of BPM is felt in the garden's ecosystem. The rest of this chapter will present our BPM approach to each of the four types of pests in the flower garden—weeds, insects, diseases, and animals.

Dealing with Insects

While insects rank as the American gardener's number one problem (according to a National Gardening Association survey), they are not nearly the concern for the flower gardener that they are for the vegetable gardener. After all, the vegetable gardener wants to be able to bring something appetizing and edible into the kitchen. Flower gardeners don't have that same requirement, but you can't ignore the insect pests in your garden entirely or you will definitely find damage to the blossoms and the plants that will diminish the garden's beauty.

A healthy flower garden has both good bugs and bad bugs living in balance as part of your yard's ecosystem. The bad guys are kept in control by the predators, or good bugs. Traditional attitudes about insects maintain that any insect pest in the garden is one insect too many. This approach calls for eradicating the entire population of insect pests rather than simply controlling them. By indiscriminately wiping out the pests, the predators are also diminished because their food supply is gone. The garden is made defenseless by these attacks and by the gardener's lack of understanding of how nature works. What we want to show you is that, for example, you need to have some aphids in the garden at all times or the lady-bugs (the predators) will have nothing to eat. Your task is to keep the aphid population down to a level that causes only a minimal, acceptable amount of damage to your flowers while maintaining a healthy balance of pests and predators in your garden's eco-system. We have found the following BPM steps to be very effective in keeping our insect problems at a low level.

Practice Good Garden Hygiene

Good garden hygiene means simply keeping the garden in a condition that minimizes the opportunities for insects to breed and multiply. Don't allow any piles of rotting weeds or flower refuse to lie around the garden. Neither should you let stagnant water or piles of rotting wood or objects that can harbor insects sit around the garden.

Maintain Good Soil Health

Good, healthy soil produces healthy plants, and healthy plants are able to withstand insect attack. Insect pests tend to bother plants that are weakened for some reason, such as poor soil conditions, unbalanced nutrients, lack of water, or disease problems. Healthy soil will support an active population of beneficial microorganisms in

the top 6 inches. This population includes all kinds of predators that will attack insect pest larvae. Every predator you can maintain saves you time in pest control later.

Identify the Bad Bugs

Some beginning gardeners are overwhelmed by the prospect of controlling insect activity in the garden. They know there are hundreds of thousands of different insects, so how can they possibly deal with them all? That's really the wrong impression of the situation. Few flower gardens will have many more than five insect pests that cause what could become serious damage. Of those, only two or three are particularly serious threats to the plants in a healthy garden.

When you realize that the numbers of insect pests are not so overwhelming, you can begin to imagine learning enough about those few bad bugs to begin gaining control of the situation. Books on insect pests list hundreds of different beetles, bugs, and caterpillars that can potentially raise havoc with your flowers. The fact of the matter is that most of those insects don't even live in your area. Your first task is to identify the pests that reside in your own backyard.

If you're an experienced gardener, you probably already know the three to five insect pests that occasionally attack your little garden kingdom. If you're a beginner and can't figure out why your hosta is laced with holes, you won't find a solution to the problem until you identify the source—the insect pest making the holes. We suggest three basic steps to insect identification, with an optional fourth.

Learn how to spot the critters. Jeff couldn't figure out how Charles was able to spot the smaller insect pests such as aphids and mites so much more easily than he was. Then Jeff realized that while he must wear glasses to read, he didn't wear his glasses outside in the garden and consequently couldn't see those small creatures even if they were right under his nose. He now wears his glasses when he is checking the garden for insect pests. Jeff also learned that the time of day is critical. Some insects are nocturnal and feed at night. To catch them you must check damaged plants after dark with a flashlight. Observation skills come from experience. All you have to do to practice is be in your garden.

Insect Pests Common to Flower Gardens*

Aphid
Cutworm (on annuals)
Inchworm
Japanese beetle
Leaf hopper
Leaf miner
Looper
Mealybug (in warmer climates)
Scale
Spider mite
Tent caterpillar
Thrip
Whitefly

*Although many gardeners consider slugs to be insects, we don't classify them that way; they're discussed later under Dealing with Other Assorted Pests.

Insect Pests: Sooner or later, most flower gardeners encounter these troublesome pests. Good garden hygiene, knowledge of the insect and its habits, a good garden ecosystem with natural predators, and other natural control measures can keep your flowers looking good.

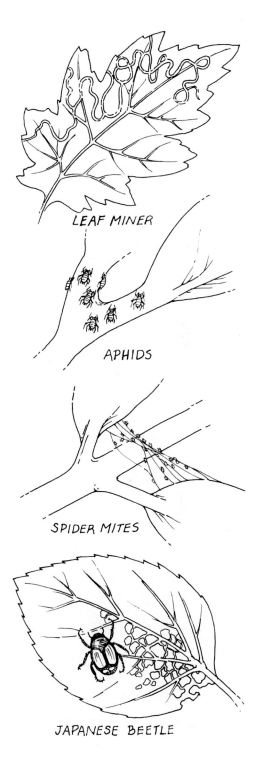

LEAF MINER

APHIDS

SPIDER MITES

JAPANESE BEETLE

Buy a good insect guide. Find one with lots of color photographs of insect pests (see the Recommended Reading list later in the book for some good titles).

Talk to friends or neighbors who have flower gardens. They may have had the same problem and figured out a solution years ago. If all else fails, call your local extension agent, who can often identify the insect just from your description over the phone. If that doesn't work, the agent may come to see your garden or ask you to bring a specimen to the office. Either way, the agent will know which bug is ventilating your hosta.

Use insect-monitoring traps. While plain old observation skills are a good way to spot the emergence of a particular insect pest, monitoring traps are starting to come on the market that will make this task easy and save some time as well. If you know you have a particular insect, it is possible to buy a trap that will catch it when it first emerges, giving you an important clue that the pest is about to attack the garden. Traps for Japanese beetles, aphids, and whiteflies are available commercially. (Later, under Use Physical Controls, we will give you some pointers on how you can make your own whitefly and aphid traps.)

Use Biological Controls

Biological insect controls include a whole range of natural resources that are available to most gardeners. These include insect-fighting viruses and bacteria, predatory or beneficial insects, birds, and even toads. The principle behind biological control is simple. The more of these beneficial predators you have in your garden, the fewer insect pests will be found. At the same time, it is critical that you have at least *some* insect pests so the predators have something to eat, otherwise they will go away. All of these helpers work day and night, saving

you the time and bother of having to deal with insect pests yourself—a real advantage for the 60-Minute Flower Gardener.

Enlist the aid of helpful microbes. Just like humans, insect pests are vulnerable to many diseases, and these are often caused by soil-dwelling microorganisms. Many insect pest larvae never see the light of day because they are done in by these disease-causing organisms before they can emerge. By maintaining healthy, well-balanced soil you can ensure that there are plenty of these beneficial microbes present.

It's also possible to introduce some microbes into your garden to attack particular pest problems. One of these is *Bacillus thuringiensis*, known as BT. It is available under the trade names Biotrol, Dipel, and Thuricide. BT is a type of naturally occurring bacteria that cause disease in certain caterpillars, including the cutworm, tent caterpillar, looper, and inchworm. When you dust BT onto infested plants, the caterpillars eat it and it enters their stomachs, where it penetrates the lining. BT then multiplies in the bloodstream. The caterpillars stop feeding, become paralyzed, gradually weaken and grow sick, and finally die. BT is harmless to humans, other warm-blooded animals, and benefical insects.

Bacillus popilliae, commonly called the milky spore disease, is another helpful microbe. It is very effective against bad infestations of Japanese beetles while being harmless to everything else.

Call on beneficial insects. Virtually every one of the insect pests in your garden has more than a few insect predators just waiting to consume it. The prowess of the ladybug and the praying mantis in devouring untold numbers of other insects is generally well known to gardeners. Ladybugs are particularly good at fighting aphids, and praying mantises will eat anything, even the beneficial insects. These two garden heavyweights have plenty of company. Lacewings, dozens of varieties of parasitic wasps, and even predatory mites also control their share of harmful insects.

As helpful as they are, we don't particularly recommend purchasing beneficial predatory insects for dealing with pest problems outdoors in the flower garden (they do, however, have some value in a greenhouse environment). The biggest problem is keeping these hired helpers in your own yard and preventing their migration all over the neighborhood and into the next town. If you wish to try this technique, you should read about the procedures very carefully, and even then you have no guarantee of keeping your predators in your yard.

Instead of importing predators, we prefer to invite those already in the area to visit and stay in our garden. To do this, we create an environment in our yard that is varied and healthy, with a steady source of food—that is, insect pests. Jeff doesn't have hordes of ladybugs, but even a few can help with insect control. Charles spots a number of praying mantises among his flowers every year, and occasionally finds an egg case. We both know we have lots of spiders, and we assume we have other insect predators that we never even see. We are fairly confident that we have a good population of predators, since we don't have any serious populations of insect pests.

Invite toads and birds into the garden. Toads eat more than 100 insects a *day* and in just one growing season can knock off more than 10,000 insects, free of charge! Toads relish all sorts of insects, including some of the ones that most commonly plague flower gardens, like cutworms, caterpillars, and beetles. They are also one of the few creatures that will feast on slugs. With a food preference list like that, every flower garden should have a whole toad family. While toads are not found in all parts of the country, in those sections where they do reside the gardener can encourage them to stay with a few simple features. Build a little toad house from a clay pot half buried on its side. Make a shallow "pond" from a sunken pie plate or dish that you keep filled with water.

Songbirds are incredibly efficient insect controllers. A house wren can eliminate 800 to 1,000 insects in a day during the 12 weeks it is feeding its young. An oriole was seen eating more than 100 caterpillars in less than an hour! The more birds you have that consider your garden as their territory, the fewer insect pests you'll find throughout the growing season and the less time you'll need to spend worrying about bugs. Songbirds and toads are excellent partners, since the birds work when the toads are asleep and vice versa, giving you 24-hour coverage.

Many of us feed birds in the winter because we don't want them to go hungry; however, few gardeners have ever considered actually *managing* their property's bird population in order to control insect pests in their garden. The way you build your bird population is to increase their food supply, give them access to water, and provide them with shelter in the form of shrubs and birdhouses. In the Recommended Reading list we have included some excellent references that will help you attract more songbirds to your flower garden.

Use Physical Controls

There are all kinds of physical controls that have been developed over the years to keep down the population of insect pests in the flower garden. The two we recommend here are ones we have found to be particularly effective.

Handpick bugs. If your BPM program is working well, you will still have some insect pests among your prize flowers, but they should be few in number. Very often, what is left over after the birds, toads, and beneficial insects have done their job can be picked off your plants by hand. Caterpillars and Japanese beetles are examples of pests that can be handpicked, since they are fairly easy to spot and don't move too fast.

The time to handpick insect pests is early in their season before they can do much damage. Knowing their emergence times is a great help in preparing for particular culprits.

Trap insect pests. You can use traps for two purposes. As we described earlier, you can trap to signal the arrival of an insect in your garden. Then you can use other methods to control it. Or you can try to trap the insect in sufficient numbers so that the trapping is in fact controlling the insect population. Jeff and Charles both use commercial Japanese beetle traps to control the beetle population. If you use a trap like this, be very careful about where you locate it. Research has shown that some beetles are attracted to the trap but miss the bag and fall to the ground, stunned. You don't want your bag to be any closer than 50 feet from a flower garden, especially one that contains plants like roses that are vulnerable to Japanese beetle attack.

Whiteflies can be a real problem in the flower garden. As we mentioned earlier, there are ready-made traps you can buy. You might find it just as easy to make your own. One trap, used effectively by greenhouse owners, is a ball or board painted bright yellow, about the same shade as the high-visibility yellow used on school buses. The whitefly just loves that color and will be attracted to the yellow surface. The trap is created by coating the ball or board with a sticky substance such as mineral oil, motor oil, or a commercial product like Tanglefoot. Every few days, wipe off the layer of whiteflies

stuck fast to the board and recoat your trap. This trap is most effective early in the season when the whiteflies are just starting to increase their ranks. To catch the most whiteflies, hang your yellow traps as close to the target plant as you can. These traps will also snare flying aphids.

Apply Natural Sprays

For the most part, you will need these tools only when everything else fails (although there is one sort of spray you can use as a preventive measure). After a few years of BPM, you will seldom have to resort to sprays to control insects. However, when the problem gets serious enough, don't hesitate to bring natural sprays and even botanical poisons into the fray.

Natural sprays, in contrast to what are called chemical sprays or pesticides, include such deterrents as dormant oil sprays, soapy water, and seaweed emulsion.

Spray as a preventive technique. Most owners of fruit trees are familiar with using dormant oil sprays in the very early spring. These petroleum-based oil sprays create a film over the entire tree and suffocate many pests by blocking their pores. These sprays, when applied properly, don't harm the trees, beneficial insects, or people. While traditionally viewed as a tool only for the fruit grower, dormant oil spray can now be considered a useful tool in the flower garden as well.

Recent developments in oil sprays now mean that they can be used year-round to fight scale, mites, mealybugs, whiteflies, aphids, leaf rollers, and treehoppers on woody ornamentals such as rhododendrons and azaleas. The older dormant oil sprays were much heavier or more viscous and could not be used on leaves without harming them. The newer type, "superior horticultural spray oil," is lighter and less viscous and evaporates much more quickly from leaves and stems. Be sure to use these oil sprays as directed and don't try to invent your own formula with motor oil.

Take advantage of soap sprays. Certain soaps have fatty acids in them that kill insects by disrupting their metabolism. These commercial insecticidal soaps, such as Safer's Insecticidal Soap, should not be confused with the soaps we use in the bathroom and laundry. Insecticidal soaps are applied as a foliar spray and act only on direct contact with the insect. Commercial insecticidal soap sprays are effective against spider mites, aphids, mealybugs, whiteflies, soft scale, earwigs, and grasshoppers. At the same time, these sprays do not harm honeybees, ladybugs, parasitic wasps, birds, or humans.

Use seaweed emulsion for extra protection. Recent studies indicate the value of using seaweed emulsion to control nematodes, the microscopic worms that attack the root systems of many plants in the flower garden. It was found that flushing nematode-infested soil with a solution of 1 tablespoon of liquid seaweed in 2 gallons of water significantly reduced nematode damage. This treatment doesn't actually kill the worms but rather gives the plants the ability to resist the effects of the nematodes.

Use Botanical Poisons as a Last Resort

Botanical poisons should be your very last resort in the battle of the bugs. While they are considered natural insecticides and for the most part are derived from plant materials, they still kill, often without discriminating between harmful pests and beneficial insects. They're generally harmless to humans and animals a few days after their application; however, they can be hazardous to people if they are not handled properly and according to directions on their packages. Two widely available botanical poisons are pyrethrum and rotenone.

Dealing with Weeds

The same survey that tells us insects are problem number one shows that weed control is the second most serious concern for gardeners, especially in the flower garden. Liz defines weeds as those plants that, when damaged, don't die. It often seems as though when we accidentally mishandle a cherished annual or perennial it will die, but the injured weed continues to appear indomitable.

Weeds offer flower gardeners a number of problems. In the first place, they are generally unattractive and spoil the appearance of the flower garden. Weeds definitely compete with flowers for nutrients and water, especially if they're allowed to mature. Dead weeds with hollow stems left to winter-over can become rooming houses for aphids and other harmful insect pests. Weeds can also be host to certain plant diseases. Groundsel, for example, is a host to various wilts, mildews, and rusts that can strike down your flowers.

Annual versus Perennial Weeds

Before we get to our BPM system for weed control, we want to make a major distinction between annual and perennial weeds. Both types can be pests in the flower garden, but they offer very different kinds of problems. Most weeds that you see in a garden are annuals. While they seem to survive all rudeness during the growing season, they do eventually die at the end of the season. However, if you allow them to, they spread thousands of seeds to guarantee their presence the next year. Annual weeds are highly prolific and produce enormous numbers of seeds per plant. For example, a single chickweed will produce 15,000 seeds, shepherd's purse will put out 40,000 seeds per plant, and good old lamb's-quarters is right up there with 70,000 seeds. As you might guess, the key to controlling annual weeds is to control their *seeds.*

It is the perennial weeds that can be the most serious problem in a flower garden, and they need very direct attention. Perennial weeds often have amazing root systems that make them extremely difficult to eliminate. Leafy spurge, for example, has roots that grow 4 to 8 feet deep, while Canada thistle's roots may penetrate to depths of 20 feet! It's no wonder that these root systems are very difficult to pull up cleanly. To control perennial weeds you must control their roots. In most cases, if you leave just a little bit of the root in the ground, the weed will return. If you happen to rotary-till a perennial weed root into many small pieces, you are propagating that villain and creating a much more serious weed problem for yourself. Many of the perennial weeds will grow right up through a heavy mulch. Perennial weeds must be dealt a serious blow right in the beginning when you are building your flower garden.

Build a Weedless Garden

It makes little sense to create a flower garden in the middle of a perennial weed bed without first eliminating those troublesome pests. If you don't, you will be fighting an uphill weed-control battle for years. If you're building your 60-Minute Flower Garden where there was formerly grass sod or where there were shrubs, it's unlikely that you'll face a serious perennial weed problem. You can proceed with soil preparation as we described in Chapter 6. If, on the other hand, your new garden site is infested with a heavy growth of perennial weeds that may have been there for a few years, you're facing a more involved situation.

The best way to deal with a serious perennial weed infestation is to cover the garden site and leave it fallow for a whole year. Blanket the area with a layer of overlapped newspapers and top that with several inches of bark or sawdust mulch. This lengthy procedure will eliminate virtually all of your toughest perennial weeds.

However, most of us are not willing to wait that long, so we recommend that you try to dig as many of the perennial weeds as you can from the site. Use a hefty trowel or even a shovel to dig down as far as possible. Remember, you need to get as much of the root system out of the soil as you can to really eliminate these persistent plants. Then, during that first year after you've planted the garden, you need to be very diligent

Weeding Tool: *A narrow, pointed tool like the one shown here is your best defense against ongoing battles with perennial weeds. Use the tool to dig as much of the root system out of the soil as possible.*

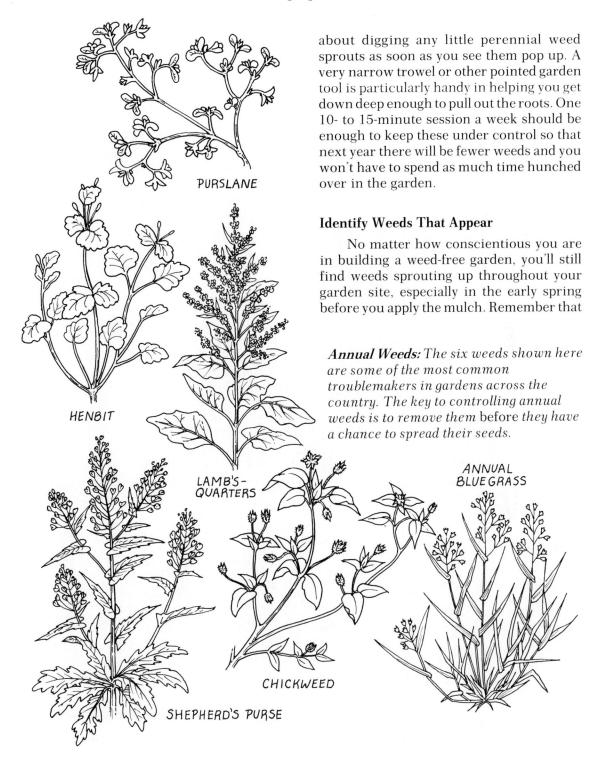

PURSLANE

HENBIT

LAMB'S-QUARTERS

SHEPHERD'S PURSE

CHICKWEED

ANNUAL BLUEGRASS

about digging any little perennial weed sprouts as soon as you see them pop up. A very narrow trowel or other pointed garden tool is particularly handy in helping you get down deep enough to pull out the roots. One 10- to 15-minute session a week should be enough to keep these under control so that next year there will be fewer weeds and you won't have to spend as much time hunched over in the garden.

Identify Weeds That Appear

No matter how conscientious you are in building a weed-free garden, you'll still find weeds sprouting up throughout your garden site, especially in the early spring before you apply the mulch. Remember that

Annual Weeds: *The six weeds shown here are some of the most common troublemakers in gardens across the country. The key to controlling annual weeds is to remove them* before *they have a chance to spread their seeds.*

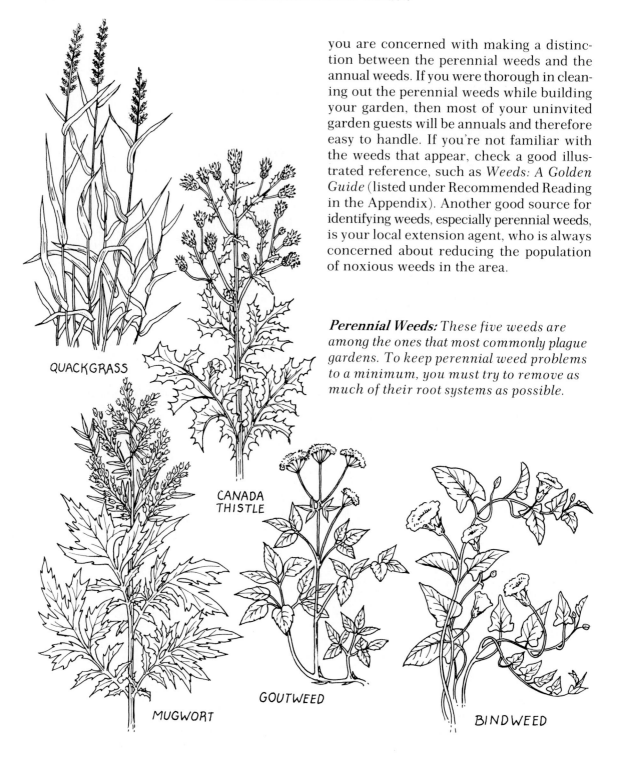

QUACKGRASS

CANADA
THISTLE

MUGWORT

GOUTWEED

BINDWEED

you are concerned with making a distinction between the perennial weeds and the annual weeds. If you were thorough in cleaning out the perennial weeds while building your garden, then most of your uninvited garden guests will be annuals and therefore easy to handle. If you're not familiar with the weeds that appear, check a good illustrated reference, such as *Weeds: A Golden Guide* (listed under Recommended Reading in the Appendix). Another good source for identifying weeds, especially perennial weeds, is your local extension agent, who is always concerned about reducing the population of noxious weeds in the area.

Perennial Weeds: These five weeds are among the ones that most commonly plague gardens. To keep perennial weed problems to a minimum, you must try to remove as much of their root systems as possible.

Use Physical Controls

There are two basic physical controls that can decrease the weed population in your 60-Minute Flower Garden. One is to break the reproductive cycle of the weeds already in your garden, and the other is to try to avoid introducing new ones. This applies to both annual and perennial weeds.

An effective way to break the reproductive cycle of weeds is to pull those that do appear as soon as possible so no seeds are produced and spread through the garden. The general rule of thumb for both annual and perennial weeds is to get them out of the garden within the first three weeks of their growth. Jeff and Charles have found that if you pull a few weeds each time you are in the garden, even if just for 3 or 4 minutes, the weed pulling never becomes an odious chore. Try very hard to pull up the roots, rather than just breaking off the stem (remember the tools recommended earlier).

In general, if you are able to keep all the weeds that do appear pulled from your garden, you will have only about half as many weeds the next year and half again the third year, until you reach the point where weeds are a very minor issue in your flower garden (somewhere between five and seven years down the road). About half the weed seeds in the soil die each year without germinating. If you are preventing new weed seeds, or at least minimizing new arrivals, then your seed population is shrinking by half every year until it becomes inconsequential.

If you use mulch, and you should, in the manner we suggested in Chapter 6, you won't have many annual weeds appearing, especially later in the season. Mulch keeps light from reaching the weed seeds, thus preventing their germination. By using mulch, instead of waiting five to seven years for weeds to phase themselves out of your garden it should take only two or three years. We have found that a 2- to 4-inch layer of mulch will deter most annual weeds. However, you need to be careful that you are not reintroducing weed seeds into your flower garden with seed-filled compost and mulch. Chopped leaves will have no weed seeds, and compost prepared by the active method should have only a few.

Dealing with Diseases

First the bad news: There are thousands of diseases that can attack the plants in your garden. Fungi, bacteria, viruses, and nematodes are all possible sources of infection. Environmental stress, air pollution, pesticide toxicity, and nutritional imbalances can also cause diseases. In other words, worrying about diseases could become a very complicated, full-time job! Understanding all these potential disease problems would require a lot more knowledge than any of us are willing to take the time to learn.

Now here's the good news: *All* of these potential diseases are unlikely to strike your flower garden. From year to year you may have to deal with only a handful of disease-related problems. Flower gardeners have much less to worry about in terms of ailing plants than vegetable gardeners do.

It is beyond the scope of our book to be able to help you identify disease symptoms in your garden. What we can do is tell you how to take preventive measures in the hope that symptoms will never appear. However, if your plants are showing signs that they're not well, call your local extension agent for a reliable diagnosis and suggestions for a cure. You can also consult one of the books we list under Recommended Reading.

We can recommend three major steps for preventing diseases in your 60-Minute Flower Garden—maintain good garden hygiene, build healthy soil, and use disease-resistant varieties of plants. This is the simplest approach and is generally very effective.

Maintain Garden Hygiene

By far the most effective disease-prevention measure in the garden is plain old hygiene. Keeping the garden free of rotting weeds or wilted flower plants goes a long way toward preventing the spread of disease. Plants that have begun to rot or show signs of disease should be disposed of in the trash! Even though the heat of the compost pile can kill many disease organisms, don't take the chance of inadvertently infecting your garden with a batch of not-quite-clean compost.

If your zinnias have been blossoming and are now looking shabby with mildew, simply pull them out and put them in the trash. Fill the spot with some other annuals or put some mulch in place. By no means should you leave the diseased plants sitting there to get worse. The next year you may want to find a substitute for zinnias in that spot or choose a mildew-resistant variety such as 'Old Mexico.' And of course, cleaning up the garden at the end of the season is essential to minimizing disease problems the following year.

Garden hygiene is also served by making sure there is sufficient air movement throughout the garden site. Leave at least a foot of space between your garden and any solid wall or structure. Don't pack your plants so close together that there is little or no air circulation. When air can't move easily through the plants, disease spores can multiply rapidly.

The method of watering you use can contribute greatly to your garden's level of health. As we discussed in Chapter 7, using a drip irrigation system to water your flower garden will greatly reduce the incidence of disease. Many disease spores need moist conditions to grow, which is exactly what watering from above with a sprinkler system can help create.

Build Healthy Soil

We don't want to belabor the point, but healthy soil leads to healthy plants that are better able to withstand any diseases. Chapter 6 tells you everything you need to know about establishing and maintaining good garden soil.

Use Disease-Resistant Varieties

Some gardeners sidestep diseases by trying to plant only those varieties of flowers that are disease resistant. We agree with that approach. Every year there are more of these resistant varieties appearing on the market. Someday it may be possible to fill a garden with nothing but disease-resistant varieties. In the meantime, when you have a choice between varieties of a particular flower, we'd recommend that you favor the one with the most disease resistance. You can learn about a particular variety's disease resistance from the catalog description or from your local nursery.

Dealing with Other Assorted Pests

Now that you've learned how to deal with such pests as insects, weeds, and diseases, you're left with the category of "everything else." Pests in this category can range from the slimy and somewhat repulsive slug to the excited but innocent three-year-old child who charges through your flowers in pursuit of a butterfly. This section is a rather broad look at assorted animal pests, since they vary so much from garden to garden. We still suggest you use our BPM philosophy to deal with these "other" pests: first try to prevent them and use poisons or other lethal methods only as a last resort. Of course, we don't expect you to poison the three-year-old child, but the parents might be educated about controlling children near a flower garden.

Rather than give you any detailed BPM strategies for animal pests in general, we will cover a few of the more common and frustrating pests as best we can. Controlling animal pests in the garden is an area that is still a challenge. There are few guaranteed solutions. Charles is at war with the squirrels in his neighborhood that are decimating his bulbs. With all of his training and experience, he has yet to find a solution to that problem.

Slugs

In many parts of the country, slugs can pose a serious problem to flower gardens. Unfortunately, there are few sure-fire solutions. In this section we'll give you the best ideas we know for keeping these creatures at bay.

Allies you can enlist in your battle include the slug's natural enemies: skunks, centipedes, ground beetles, firefly larvae, and most especially, toads and garter snakes. You can even help your plants develop a natural defense against slug attack. Research shows that very healthy plants with a high nitrogen content produce an enzyme that slugs don't like to eat. So if you use a foliar spray of fish emulsion or seaweed emulsion every few weeks during slug season, you can reduce slug damage levels considerably.

In areas where slugs are rampant, you can at least include some plants in your garden that don't interest them. For example, slugs will usually not bother with azaleas, daffodils, fuchsias, freesias, holly bushes, hibiscus, rhododendrons, and most poppies.

Trapping remains the most popular way to keep slug numbers down. By now most gardeners have heard about the beer-and-pie-plate trap. A shallow dish or pie plate is set flush into the soil with a cup or so of beer in it. The slugs are attracted to the yeast in the beer and drown. The weakness of this tactic is that you must refill the plate after a rain, and even without rain it loses its value after a few days. Other traps may prove more effective. Slugs work at night, so they seek cool shade during the day. You can trap them under boards, overturned grapefruit rinds, or almost anything else that gives them protection. They're easier to dispose of when they're gathered together in one place.

While traps can be helpful in reducing the slug population, your goal should be to set up some kind of barrier to eliminate the problem entirely. Slugs avoid areas that are dusty and scratchy. Some people have found that they can protect their plants with a sprinkling of sand, lime, wood ashes, or cinders. You can either form a ring of these materials around the base of the plant or dust the leaves with them. The most effective dusting material by far is diatomaceous earth, which is made from the remains of ancient algae. This dusty powder consists of tiny, razor-sharp particles that cause many tiny abrasions in the slug's body, resulting in death by dehydration. Diatomaceous earth remains effective after a rain and is not harmful to anything else in your garden. Sprinkle a band of diatomaceous earth around the slug-infested target area, and you should have no more troubles. We also suggest simultaneously using trapping methods so you can reduce your slug population while you are repelling them.

Gardener Neva Beach, who lives in Mendocino, California, developed an effective slug fence for her vegetable garden using ¼-inch hardware cloth. This fence should work just as well for flowers. She cuts the hardware cloth into strips 8 inches wide, making sure to cut down the middle of the squares to leave sharp points on the edges of the strips. Then she mounts these strips on the outside face of her boxed beds so that the sharp points along the edge stick up about 1 inch above the edge of the bed. Slugs can't easily crawl up the mesh, and if they do manage to get to the top, they can't crawl over the tiny wire spikes.

To adapt this technique for the flower garden, simply surround those plants threatened by slugs with little fences made of hardware cloth. Instead of attaching them to a wooden bed, sink the fences into the soil.

Moles and Gophers

Moles are really helpful creatures that inadvertently interfere with the way we like to maintain our yards. Moles eat all kinds of grubs and worms that can be harmful to our gardens. However, they dig endless tunnels through our lawns and gardens to find those grubs. The tunnels are the problem, not the mole. Nevertheless, moles can be a serious nuisance and need to be dealt with. By dumping certain materials into a mole's hole, you can often get him to move to another neighborhood. Many gardeners have had success with filling mole holes with used cat litter to repel the little diggers. However, if such methods are not successful, you may have to resort to more drastic measures.

An intriguing scheme to control moles comes from the Dawes Arboretum in Cincinnati, Ohio. It appears that moles are fatally attracted to the flavor of Wrigley's Juicy Fruit gum. Making sure that no human odor is on the freshly unwrapped gum (work with your hands in plastic bags), roll up five or ten sticks of gum and place them inside an active tunnel at 4- to 6-inch intervals. Moles eat some of it and die, because their digestive tracts cannot handle this common sub-

stance. This approach to ridding your garden of moles should take only a few days to be effective.

Some gardeners report that putting castor beans in gopher holes has been successful in killing that particular pest.

You can also use a gasoline-driven lawn mower to fumigate gopher or mole tunnels if your yard has been invaded. You will need a piece of flexible metal exhaust material, around 10 feet long. Find a way to attach one end of the flexible tube to fit snugly over the mower's exhaust pipe. Put a few drops of oil on the inside of the flexible tube at the lawn mower end to produce a little bit of smoke. This will go into the mole or gopher tunnel and come up at escape holes. Cover those holes with soil. The fumigation process is simple. Move the soil away from the entrance of the mole or gopher hole so you can place the end of the tube down into the hole. Then take some soil and pile it around the tube to make it as airtight as possible at the entrance. Turn on the lawn mower and let it run for 10 to 15 minutes. The carbon monoxide exhaust will kill the gophers or moles quickly and painlessly in their tunnels.

Rabbits

Jeff believes that one of the best ways to deal with rabbits is to own a cat. In a study done in Sweden, domesticated house cats were found to be just as effective as feral, or wild, cats in controlling wild rabbits, field mice, and voles. Although they were fed in the house, they preferred natural prey when it was available. Jeff and Liz have two cats, and Jeff is convinced that the male cat has left its markings around the edge of the property to stake its territory, which has served to repel the rabbits. Jeff's next door neighbor is plagued by rabbits, while Jeff and Liz have never had one incident of rabbit damage and have seen a rabbit in their yard only once.

Some Final Words

We've covered a lot of territory in this chapter, but if you think about the total BPM process, it isn't very time-consuming to manage, especially after the first year when you've had a chance to identify the few serious pests you'll have to cope with.

During those few minutes you spend each day or so watering, feeding, and tending the garden, put your observation skills to good use. They can become your best weapon against the flower garden's pests. Once you see an increase in aphid activity or some signs of plant disease or an impending weed invasion, you'll know how to respond quickly to avoid any serious problems. As long as you keep your eyes open and visit your garden often, you should be able to nip any problems in the bud, before they have a chance to become serious. Learning about how all the various creatures, good and bad, fit into the amazingly complex ecosystem of your flower bed can be one of the more enjoyable and satisfying parts of your gardening experience.

Chapter 9
Putting It All Together

Flower gardening can be a lifelong hobby filled with years of new experiences, delightful discoveries, and insights that can help you maintain a beautiful and healthy flower garden. You'll never really stop learning about gardening. As a starting point for your wonderful adventures in the garden, there are a number of basic techniques for planting, propagating, and maintaining a 60-Minute Flower Garden that will stand you in good stead. Flower gardening only becomes complicated when you decide to specialize in a certain kind of garden and/or try to raise flowers that are not easy to grow. The 60-Minute Flower Garden avoids these pitfalls. You can have a thriving, beautiful garden with just the basic points we outline in this chapter. As the years go by, you'll continue to refine your techniques and become a more sophisticated flower gardener.

To help you fit all the pieces together, in this chapter we feature a master plan for seasonal activities that you can use as a model for your own garden schedule. And because we believe that flower gardening shouldn't be all work and no play, we give you some ideas on how to have fun and enjoy the flowers you've grown.

Planting and Managing the 60-Minute Flower Garden

No matter which type of 60-Minute Flower Garden you select from the basic models we presented in Chapter 5, most of the gardening tricks and tips are the same. The differences in techniques come with the different types of plants rather than with the different types of gardens. Shrubs are treated differently than bulbs, for example, and annuals need special treatment that perennials don't.

Because we have given you garden design techniques to produce a low-maintenance garden, your 60-Minute Flower Garden management tasks are relatively modest. The next four sections will offer you tips and tricks for planting and managing perennials, annuals, bulbs, and shrubs.

Planting and Managing Perennials

Perennials make few demands on the flower gardener. About all you do is plant them and then periodically divide them to restore the plants' vigor. There's no yearly

166

replanting, which is why they're so popular in a low-maintenance garden.

Bare-Root Planting

Perennials often arrive from mail-order nurseries with their bare roots wrapped in wood shavings in a plastic bag. Open the box immediately. If there are any leaves on the plants, stand them up in the box to keep the air circulating around them. Keep the roots covered and moist so they don't dry out. If you receive a small box of dormant hardy perennials, you can hold those over in a refrigerator. In any case, you should make an effort to get these plants in the garden as soon as possible.

To plant bare-rooted perennials, dig a hole large enough to spread the roots comfortably without crowding them. Build a mound of soil in the bottom that comes almost up to the top of the hole. As you set the plant in place, spread the roots over this mound. You must position the plant so that the place where the roots come together (the crown) is just below the soilline. When leaves begin to emerge they will be right there, ready to push above the soil. Fill the hole with soil that has been enhanced with some kind of organic material and water thoroughly.

Planting Rhizomes

Some perennials, such as bearded iris, bergenia, and Solomon's seal, grow from rhizomes, or horizontal underground stems. Plant rhizomes so that they are just below the soil surface but are completely covered with soil. Bearded irises need slightly different treatment; plant them so that about one-third to one-half of the rhizome lies partially exposed above the surface of the soil. Spread the roots, which will help to anchor the rhizome. Water well and keep moist until the plant is well established.

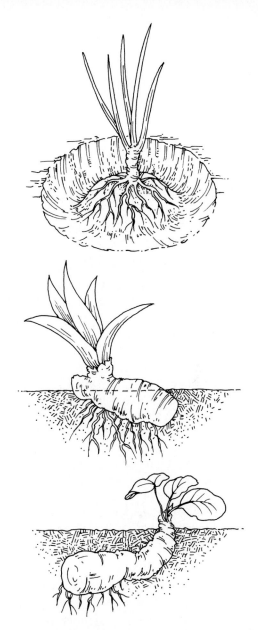

Perennial Planting: *At top is a bare-rooted perennial with its roots spread comfortably over a mound of soil. It is positioned so that its crown will be just below the soilline when the hole is filled. In the center is a bearded iris rhizome planted so that roughly one-third is exposed above the soil. Other rhizomes, such as the bergenia shown at bottom, need to be planted right below the soil surface and completely covered.*

Container Plants

Many young perennial plants are purchased from garden centers in containers. To give these a home in the garden, gently remove each plant from its container and pull or loosen the outer roots before setting it in the ground. Your planting hole should be much larger than the diameter of the container. Cover the roots with soil, press down snugly, and water generously.

Transplanting Established Perennials

The primary question about transplanting a perennial is, When do you do it? The best time is in the early spring. However, if you do things right, you can transplant successfully in the early fall. The plant must have a good root system to begin with, and you must carefully dig it up with a heavy ball of soil around the roots. A bare-rooted perennial has less chance of survival if it is transplanted in the fall. Even if you mulch it thoroughly, it will be in danger of being killed by frost heaving during the winter.

No matter when you're transplanting, be sure to plant the perennial at the same depth it was in its previous location. Water the plant thoroughly and protect it with mulch.

Propagating Perennials

Most perennials are propagated, or re-produced, by division. (Perennials can also be started from seed, which is discussed later under Homegrown Seedlings.) Division means taking a full-grown plant that has mushroomed in size and breaking it up into smaller pieces. You divide your perennials for two reasons. First, it's an easy way to get free plants to expand your garden or to fill in spaces in the existing site. Second, most perennials will stay healthier if they are divided periodically to give them new vigor. When they get too old and crowded,

their centers begin to die out. When you divide them you use only the vigorous outside parts of the clump and throw away the old center section.

Different perennials prefer different schedules for division. Asters and phlox need dividing every three to five years. Astilbes, daylilies, Autumn Joy sedum, and irises are divided every five to seven years. And some plants, like peonies and gas plants, need dividing rarely, if ever.

Getting the timing right. Gardeners usually divide perennials in the spring to avoid

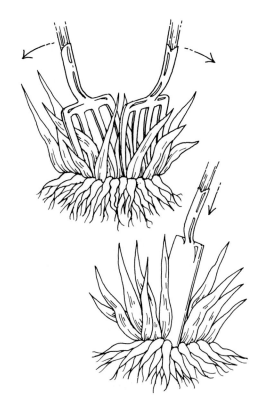

Dividing Perennials: *You have two options when the time comes to split clumps of perennials. You can pry them apart with two spading forks set back to back, as shown at top, or you can slice them apart with a spade.*

the frost-heaving risk that threatens fall-planted divisions. Fall transplants will not have time to develop sufficient root systems to anchor them in soil that's often subjected to the pressures of frost heaving. There are a few cases where you can make an exception to the spring-division rule. Early-blooming perennials like shasta daisies and clustered bellflowers can be divided after they bloom or in early September. Irises do best when divided between July and September. However, late-blooming perennials such as asters and Japanese anemones don't recover if they're divided in the fall, so they absolutely must be attended to in the spring.

Perennials can take fairly rough treatment in the division process. You can pry the crowns apart by using two spading forks back to back, or you can split the clump with a spade. Just place the spade at the spot where you wish to divide and then push it through the clump of roots with your foot. A few perennials, such as bearded irises, are easy to pull apart with your hands, but most need a tool like a fork or a spade.

Remember that many ground covers, which are perennials, can be divided with great success. For example, a 3-square-foot patch of mature pachysandra can be broken up to cover an area of about 9 square feet with no trouble at all. Plant each set of leaves separately and space them 4 to 6 inches apart. Coil the long white rhizomes and cover them with soil. Be sure to apply a good mulch, which is a must for healthy pachysandra. Remove all weeds from the site before planting the pachysandra, and keep up the weeding while the plants are merging.

Planting and Managing Annuals

Annuals are going to go into the garden in one of three forms: as bulbs, as seedlings, or as seeds.

Planting Annual Bulbs

What we conveniently refer to as annual bulbs come in the form of rhizomes (cannas), corms (gladiolus), and tubers (dahlias). Unlike hardy bulbs that can stay in the garden all year long, annual bulbs must be removed from the flower bed each fall and stored inside over the winter. You can plant annual bulbs with a trowel or a special bulb planter, making sure you sink them to the proper depth and space them correctly. (See The Best Plants for the 60-Minute Flower Garden in the Appendix for these planting guidelines.)

Don't forget to remove annual bulbs from the soil around the time of the first frost and store them in a cool place. Gladiolus prefer a cool, dry storage area like an unheated attic and do just fine in a plain old paper bag. Dahlias and cannas like to be stored nestled in dry peat moss or chopped leaves in a box placed in a cool, dry place.

When you harvest your annual bulbs you'll find that many have multiplied during the growing season. Leave their clumps intact over the winter and break them up when you replant in the spring. When you divide your dahlias, be especially careful to include with each tuber a piece of the central base of stem, because that is where the buds are located. If you simply break off the tuber without that little piece of central stem, the tuber will never grow. Separate dahlia tubers with a sharp knife or pruner to make sure you get that essential piece of stem.

Planting Seedlings

Transplanting annuals from the local nursery or from your own seed-starting efforts is very easy. (Look at the section Home-grown Seedlings later in this chapter for tips on how to get from seed to seedling stage.) You don't have to worry about spreading the roots as much as you do with perennial transplants. In most cases, annual transplants are young seedlings in small containers, so they can be removed from the containers and popped right into the prepared soil. Be sure to plant them close enough to create a grouping of color but far enough apart so that they won't overcrowd each other as they mature.

Direct-Seeding Annuals

Some people like to direct-seed their favorite annuals rather than raise seedlings in their house or buy them from the local garden center. There is nothing wrong with this approach except that it will delay the floral display somewhat. A plant started from seed right in the garden will take longer to bloom than one that was introduced as a seedling.

Charles learned a trick from English gardeners for determining spacing when direct-seeding flowers. This trick reduces the time it takes to thin the bed later. Follow the instructions on the flower seed packet for outdoor planting times and prepare the area in which you want a particular variety of annual. On the seed packet, find the recommended spacing between mature plants. Use that distance as your space between rows. Within the row, set the seeds somewhat closer to provide extras to replace the ones that inevitably fail to grow. When the seedlings come up, you'll have a bed of annuals that are almost correctly spaced. All you need to do then is a bit of thinning to get your final layout. You can either thin the seedlings to be directly across from each other in rows or stagger the rows for a less rigid look. For this approach to be successful, you must use varieties than can be sown directly in the garden, such as nasturtiums, spider flowers, and zinnias.

Propagating Annuals

Most annuals are so easy to find in the local garden center that you may not find it worth the energy to try to propagate them yourself. However, you may reconsider when you realize that a few common annuals are unbelievably easy to propagate by rooting cuttings. Coleus, impatiens, begonias, and geraniums will produce roots when you stick a 3- to 5-inch-long cutting in a glass of water and set it in a well-lit window. As soon as some roots are showing, plant these cuttings in pots or directly into the garden, where they should be kept shaded for the first three or four days.

Another way to root annuals avoids the possibility of having the stems rot before the roots develop. This calls for setting your cuttings in some kind of soilless rooting medium such as vermiculite. Thoroughly moisten the vermiculite and dip the end of each cutting in a commercial root stimulator or rooting hormone before sticking it down into the medium. Keep the vermiculite moist but not wet. Roots should appear in about two to three weeks.

Charles uses a very simple device for rooting cuttings this way. To create a mini-greenhouse, he cuts the top off a gallon plastic jug and fills it one-third to one-half full with rooting medium. Then, after setting the cuttings into the medium, he covers the large opening with clear plastic wrap, leaving the hole in the handle open for air circulation. A thin line of rubber cement around the top edge of this device will hold the plastic wrap in place. Be sure to let the cement dry before applying the plastic so that any fumes will have a chance to escape. Charles sets the jug in a window with bright light but no direct sun. He checks it weekly and waters as needed with a mist sprayer to keep the medium moist but not soggy.

His minigreenhouse doesn't take up too much space and can handle 8 to 12 cuttings at a time.

Managing Biennials

Biennials fall between annuals and perennials in terms of their life span. They are hardy and live for just two years, flowering in the second year before they die. If they live a third year, the flowers will be small and disappointing. The best biennials provide plenty of seed that will automatically come up in your flower garden, giving you another generation of plants. Learn to recognize these young biennial seedlings, because they are your future flowers.

Charles manages biennials like foxgloves and sweet Williams in his garden on the following schedule. Flowers appear in early summer and then make lots of seeds. He allows some seed to fall to the ground and then pulls out all the old plants. Soon the young seedlings appear in the garden. When they're large enough to handle, he transplants these into their permanent positions between perennials. He weeds out the extras so they won't crowd other flowers in the garden. With good care, by the end of the summer these seedlings will grow into large, healthy plants. The following year, these plants will give another gorgeous display of flowers in early summer and the cycle is repeated all over again.

Because biennials are short-lived, they are useful as temporary fillers in the flower garden. When you assess your beds in the fall or spring, consider filling in some of the empty spaces with biennial seedlings that have popped up in your garden. With care, they transplant easily in these seasons. With little effort, these free plants will reward you with a rich display of color.

Planting and Managing Hardy Bulbs

You can have beautiful bulbs year after year if you remember to follow just five well-timed steps: plant the bulbs properly; cut off all blossoms after they fade; allow the leaves and stems to remain as long as they are green; add a mulch only after the fall freeze arrives to avoid rodent damage; and feed the bulbs in *both* the fall and early spring.

Planting Specifics

Planting depth is fairly important for hardy bulbs such as tulips, daffodils, and hyacinths. As a general rule, bulbs are planted at a depth equal to about three times the bulb's height. Measure the planting depth from the bottom of the hole, not from the top of the bulb. Some experts have found that planting tulips 9 inches deep, rather than 6 inches, increases their life span significantly. Crocuses and other early-flowering bulbs should be planted 4 inches deep and 3 inches apart. Most daffodils, tulips, and larger bulbs go 5 to 9 inches deep with the same distance between plants.

Fall is the time when you should be busy planting hardy bulbs. Daffodils and narcissus need to be planted in early fall because they need time to develop a good root system before it gets cold. Most other bulbs can be planted in midfall and some, such as tulips, can be planted in late fall up until the ground freezes. Fall-blooming bulbs (colchicum and autumn crocus, for example) should be planted in late August if possible, or as soon as you can get them in the fall. If you forget to plant your bulbs until late fall, it's better to plant them anyway than to save them until spring. They are likely to dry out and die if you try to hold them over.

Dividing Bulbs

As long as your bulbs continue to flower satisfactorily, you shouldn't worry about splitting them up. However, if you wish to spread the wealth or if your bulbs are not flowering as well as they used to (meaning fewer and smaller flowers), you can dig them up and divide them.

It is best to divide and transplant hardy bulbs just as the leaves turn yellow in May or June or so. You can replant them right away, or you can store them and replant them in the fall. Before storing, wash the bulbs in water and then dry them thoroughly by spreading them out in full shade for a week. Then put them in something that breathes, like paper bags or nylon stockings (no plastic bags). To store, keep them at about 65° to 70°F in a dry place.

Now that we've given you the general rule, we'll tell you about the exception. Some hardy bulbs, such as daffodils, snowdrops, and winter aconite, can be divided and transplanted right after blossoming while they still have green foliage. This is an advantage because you can do it while you're thinking about it, rather than having to remember to do it later. In fact, for some bulbs, this summer transplanting actually works better.

Feeding Bulbs

There is a belief that you don't have to feed bulbs because they supposedly contain all the nutrients they need for good growth. Research has proven this to be false. Bulbs need to be fed both in the fall (every fall, not just when they are planted) and in the spring when they produce their foliage and blossoms.

Another piece of conventional wisdom that has been proven faulty by research is that adding bone meal to the bulb's planting hole gives it important nutrients. Bone meal isn't what it used to be some 25 years ago.

Today, companies processing bone meal steam the bones to extract gelatin and other nitrogen-rich by-products. Experiments have shown that the remaining phosphorus in today's diminished bone meal is much less beneficial to bulbs than the phosphorus in bone meal made more than 25 years ago.

When you plant a bulb, replace the recommended handful of bone meal with a small handful of rock phosphate, which releases phosphorus very slowly into the soil. Then in the fall and again in the spring you can give your bulbs a side-dressing of any organic fertilizer combination having an NPK ratio of roughly 10-10-5. A mixture of bloodmeal, rock phosphate, and greensand will do the trick. Daffodils like a bigger share of potassium, so some extra greensand or wood ashes will keep them happy.

Good Grooming

Remove the flower heads from most hardy bulb plants promptly when their blooming is completed. That will prevent the formation of seeds, which can take stored food away from the bulbs and reduce flowering for the next spring. (For more on this technique, see Dead-Heading Flowers later in the chapter.)

On the other hand, never cut off bulb foliage or flower stems while they are still green and actively growing. Removing the leaves too early stops bulb growth and may keep the plant from flowering next season. Allow the foliage and stem to remain until they naturally begin to yellow and die. At that time it's safe to clip them off.

When the leaves have begun to turn yellow in June, you're free to plant annuals right on top of the bulbs, without harming them at all. In fact, this should be part of your plan so that the garden continues to have an eye-catching array of colors.

Planting and Managing Shrubs

Most of the shrubs that are best suited for a 60-Minute Flower Garden will be smaller plants that are relatively easy to handle, even for the beginning gardener. There are only a few guidelines you need to follow to plant a shrub successfully. First, you should always plant it at the same depth it was previously growing, never deeper. The hole you dig for the shrub must be two to three times the size of the root ball. That gives you plenty of room to enrich the soil with compost or some other organic material. It is better to have the hole too big than too small. If you have already prepared the bed for your garden as we recommended in Chapter 6, no extra work is necessary to get the soil in shape.

Bare-Root Planting

Shrubs often come from a mail-order nursery in a bare-rooted condition. The shrub's roots will be packed in damp organic material of some kind and wrapped in a plastic bag. Before you plant any shrub with bare roots you should prune back the top by one-third to one-half to compensate for the loss of parts of the root system. You can cut off whole branches and/or prune back portions of each branch to accomplish this. After pruning, soak the shrub for at least 24 hours in water fortified with a root stimulator compound (readily available at any garden center).

When you plant your bare-rooted shrub, spread the roots out in the big hole over a mound of soil that is high enough to bring the stem to surface level. Fill the hole with soil that contains at least 25 percent organic material such as compost, peat humus, or leaf mold. Work the soil in between the roots and firm it as you go. After the hole is filled, tamp the soil down firmly to get rid of the air pockets and then water heavily. Any newly transplanted shrub should be kept moist throughout the entire first season in its new location.

Container or Balled-and-Burlapped Shrubs

The temptation with a shrub like an azalea that comes in a container or a burlap-covered ball is to remove the outer covering, dig a hole, and plunk the shrub into the hole as is. Avoid the temptation! Many containerized shrubs will be potbound as a result of having their roots compressed in a tight ball. Often many of the roots are wrapped around the circumference of the root ball. It is terribly important to spread out those roots before you plant the shrub, otherwise they won't grow properly. Then you can place the shrub in the hole in the same manner described for the bare-rooted shrub.

Some nurseries still recommend that a shrub with a burlap wrapping (called B and B, for balled and burlapped) can be planted as is. The conventional wisdom is that the burlap rots and the roots spread out naturally. Research has shown that such is not the case. You must assist the shrub and spread the roots away from the plant, especially those that are wrapped around the circumference of the root ball.

Charles sets the burlap-covered root ball into the prepared hole and then cuts away all but the very bottom piece of burlap. He spreads the roots and fills the hole, leaving the one piece of burlap on the bottom. He uses this approach to minimize the loss of whatever soil is still inside the root ball.

Transplanting Shrubs

As we mentioned in Chapter 2, small shrubs are easy to move from site to site in your garden room. Early fall is the best time for moving most shrubs, giving them an opportunity to generate some more roots and get settled before winter sets in. Follow the same planting techniques outlined for the burlap-covered shrubs from a nursery. Adding compost and using lots of water are keys to success.

Pruning Shrubs

Shrubs, like perennial flowers, are wonderfully low-care plants. Pruning is about the only maintenance activity you'll spend time on during the season. The first rule in pruning shrubs is: *Never* use hedge clippers. These will give your shrub a tight, overly manicured, unnatural appearance. Instead, use a hand pruning tool that allows you to discriminate between branches, leaving the healthy ones and removing the weak and dead ones.

Another rule to remember is that you prune spring- and summer-flowering shrubs at different times. With spring-flowering shrubs like azaleas, spireas, and forsythias, prune right after they bloom in late spring. If you prune these shrubs too late in the summer, you'll cut off next year's flower buds and defeat the whole reason for having them in your garden. This pruning does not have to be an annual ritual; you prune spring shrubs only if they've gotten too large or if there is dead wood to be cleaned out.

On the other hand, summmer-flowering shrubs like buddleias and shrubby cinquefoil should be pruned hard every year. Pruning hard means you cut them back to at least half their height in the early spring, which helps to maintain their size and keep them neat. This approach to pruning removes dead wood and twigs, encourages stronger

Dos and Don'ts of Shrub Pruning: *On the left you see the results of years of overzealous pruning. The forsythia has taken on a round, overmanicured, dense shape. The forsythia on the right, which was pruned more judiciously, has a more natural and pleasing shape that will enhance the looks of a flower garden.*

growth, and promotes abundant flowering each year.

Homegrown Seedlings

We recommend that if you are a beginning flower gardener you don't get involved with starting your own seedlings at the same time you are trying to design your very first garden. We do believe, however, that after a few years of buying all your plants and seeing the limited choice you have at your local nursery, you may feel some incentive to grow some of your own plants. Annuals are most commonly raised by gardeners, but perennials can be started from seed as well. What you need then is a technique for growing flower seedlings that isn't complicated, doesn't take much time, and produces healthy young plants as you need them throughout the entire growing season. Summarized here is the seedling system Jeff has been using with good results in his 60-Minute Flower Garden.

Jeff starts his seeds in soil blocks. He's a fan of these blocks because they are so handy to work with. They make transplanting very easy for the gardener, and they lessen the stress of transplanting for the seedling (transplant shock can set back growth for two to three weeks). In addition, they take little time each week to manage.

Soil blocks are widely available in garden centers and through garden catalogs. They're usually made of peat and are wrapped in some kind of netting. You can also make your own blocks with a special press and raw materials like peat moss, soil, sharp sand, and water. Once you invest in the press you can make unlimited numbers of soil blocks at a very low cost. (The Resources Guide lists companies that sell these presses.)

If you're just beginning to raise your own seedlings, we recommend that you ex-

periment with the commercial soil blocks for a year. Then you can decide whether you want to start producing your own blocks with a press.

Jeff uses fluorescent lights all year long to start seedlings. They give enough light to produce healthy, strong young plants with very little trouble. For most gardeners, we recommend setting up just one fixture with two 48-inch fluorescent tubes. Regular fluorescent bulbs will do—there's no need to invest in the special "grow light" bulbs. Because you may want batches of seedlings during spring and early summer, you might want to establish some kind of permanent installation that allows you to raise and lower the lights easily.

The basement is where Jeff locates his seedling nursery, for several reasons. The temperature stays between 60° and 70°F year-round, which is ideal for seedlings. There's water available and he has ample space. Folks without basements might want to build a seedling bench that's attractive enough to share space in the family room or other living quarters. The light fixture must be adjustable so that you can move it up and down to maintain the proper distance between the plants and the light.

Make sure the lights are on for 14 to 16 hours a day, every day. Anything less and the seedlings are not going to grow strong and healthy. When seedlings are just little sprouts, the lights should be no more than 3 inches away. As the plants get their first true leaves, you can move the lights up to about 4 inches. Jeff sets the lights at 6 inches when the seedlings are a few inches tall so that he can disperse light evenly to all his plants, even those on the edge of the shelf. He uses an automatic timer to turn his lights on and off. A timer costs about $10 and it eliminates one more thing you have to remember to do, which of course saves you time.

Before he sets out any seedlings, Jeff always makes sure to harden them off, or get them used to conditions outside in the garden. Starting a week before he wants to plant them, he begins leaving the seedlings outside in an area protected from strong sun and strong winds. When the time comes to transplant, he sets the seedling, cube and all, into the prepared hole in the garden.

Planting and Managing a Meadow Garden

We didn't include a discussion of the Meadow Garden in the Gallery of Flower Garden Designs in Chapter 5 because we felt it didn't quite fit. We didn't create a detailed plan for this garden as we did for the others because the Meadow Garden's loose, relatively unconstructed form really isn't appropriate for a detailed drawing. And providing a list of suggested plants is almost impossible, since the region you live in will really determine which plants are best for your Meadow Garden.

But this garden does merit a special set of directions for basic soil preparation, planting, and maintenance since it is so unique and different from the rest of the gardens we discuss in the book. That's why we've provided this special section in this chapter.

The most important requirement in building a Meadow Garden is to try to eliminate as many perennial weeds and weed seeds as possible before planting the site. If they aren't eliminated, they can quickly multiply and spoil the general appearance of the garden (see Dealing with Weeds in Chapter 8). Preparing the soil for the Meadow Garden isn't as intensive as the process we described for other flower gardens in Chapter 6. The types of flowers and grasses used in a Meadow Garden are tough, often native,

annual and perennial plants that don't require the high-quality, rich soils needed by cultivated flower garden plants.

Assuming you have purged the garden site of perennial weeds, we suggest you rotary-till it twice. The first time you will till as deeply as you can without turning up any subsoil. Then you should wait at least two weeks to give the annual weeds a chance to sprout and show their heads. By tilling the site the second time at a very shallow setting (about 1 to 2 inches deep), you will kill most of the annual weeds and only a few will come back later. If you want to give the weeds another shot, wait two or three weeks before you plant the flower seeds and rake the site thoroughly just before you plant. This will take care of a good share of the second generation of annual weeds. Your Meadow Garden flowers and plants will eventually choke out most of the annual weeds that do manage to come back.

Most gardeners will use a commercially packaged mixture of wildflower seeds to start their Meadow Gardens. A few years later they may wish to add specific flowers that they have come to admire. It is critical that you select a wildflower seed mix that is appropriate to your region. Most reliable wildflower seed companies offer a number of mixes specially designed for particular regions of the country, such as the Northeast and the Midwest. Most mixes come with planting instructions. The main trick is to spread the seeds evenly throughout the site. Some gardeners mix their seeds with damp sand or sawdust and spread that mixture. After you have planted your seeds, water the site just as you would a newly seeded lawn. It shouldn't be allowed to dry out.

Remember that most of the color in a Meadow Garden in the first year will come from the annuals in your mix. In the following years more of the display will come from perennials as they become established. The annuals will reseed themselves naturally, so you don't have to plant any seeds after the first year. During your Meadow Garden's first fall, you may wish to add some hardy bulbs such as daffodils, crocuses, and snow-drops to give some early spring interest to the display.

A Meadow Garden is a very low-main-tenance garden, but that doesn't mean it's a no-work garden. One thing you won't have to do is fertilize; this garden will actually do better if you skip the fertilizer. You may need to do a little hand weeding period-ically to pick out some annual weeds, but that isn't a very demanding job. The pri-mary maintenance task for the Meadow Gar-den is its annual mowing. It should be mowed down to 2 to 4 inches sometime in the late fall or early winter, but definitely before anything begins to grow in the spring. This annual mowing is required to keep woody plants from taking over the meadow and dominating the flowers. If the residue of the mowing is particularly heavy, you should remove it so that it doesn't mat down and prevent some of the more tender wildflow-ers from poking through in the spring. Be-sides, these Meadow Garden clippings make terrific compost.

Improving Your Garden's Display

Carefully designing your garden and get-ting the flowers in the ground properly are the important first steps in making sure your flower bed will be an attractive one. But these aren't the only steps. Flower gar-deners have developed a number of tricks to make sure their flowers look especially attrac-tive and showy throughout the whole sea-son. Staking and dead-heading are two common techniques used to enhance the appearance of the flower garden.

Staking Flowers

Some flowers, like queen-of-the-prairie and goat's-beard, can stand tall without assis-tance. However, most flowers that are taller than 24 inches can be knocked over by the weight of their blossoms or by heavy rains or winds. These are the ones that look more attractive if they're supported or staked in some fashion.

You can rig your own staking system with bamboo sticks and string, or you can purchase ready-made staking devices that are sold in some garden centers and through catalogs.

Most garden centers sell packs of dark green bamboo sticks, ranging from 24 to 48 inches long, that serve well as stakes for tall flowers. Never use unsightly white string or cloth to tie up your plants. Green twine or paper-coated wire is best for tying plants to stakes. Tie them lightly so you don't dam-age the stems.

There are two approaches to staking flow-ers—individual stakes for single-stemmed plants like delphiniums or group staking for multistemmed plants like zinnias and bee balm. The best technique for single plants is to wrap the string around the stake once, then circle it lightly around the plant before coming back to the stake to tie the knot. Tie the plant to the stake about two-thirds to three-quarters of the way up the stem.

When you need to stake a clump of flowers, don't simply run some string around the outside of the clump; that won't look natural and will detract from your garden's appearance. Charles has developed a special staking technique that he has used success-fully for years. Place a number of bamboo stakes about 8 inches apart around the out-side edge of the straggling clump of plants. Using a ball of green twine that fits comfort-ably in your hand, tie the end to a stake and

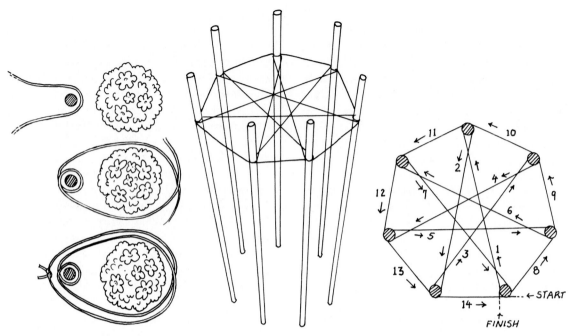

Staking Methods: *At left is an overhead view of how to stake a single-stemmed flower.*
Wrap the string around the stake, then circle it around the plant before coming back to
the stake to tie the knot. In the center and at right is the staking technique to use
for a clump of flowers. Surround the clump with at least four stakes set 8 inches apart.
With twine, weave from opposite stake to opposite stake through the mass of stems
until you've connected all the stakes in what looks like a star pattern (use the numbers
and arrows in the illustration as your guide).

pass it through the middle of the clump, then wrap it around the opposite stake a couple of times before passing it through the plants to another stake on the opposite side. Do this until all the stakes are connected. The final step is to loosely circle the clump and connect the stakes along the perimeter. This creates a matrix of string that will support a clump of flowers in a very natural fashion from the middle as well as from the sides. The leaves should hide the stakes and twine. Charles recommends that you set up this support system right before the plants start to flop over (probably as the flower buds show color), or just before bad weather, which can knock over the plants, is expected.

Dead-Heading Flowers

Blossoms that are past their prime and drying up will have a subtle but negative effect on the general appearance of the garden. If you go to all the trouble of designing and building a flower garden, you'll want it to look as nice as possible at all times. Dead-heading is a relatively minor task, but it has a major impact on the appearance of your 60-Minute Flower Garden.

Dead-heading is the process of removing faded blossoms from your bulbs, perennials, and annuals. You do this mainly to keep your garden looking neat, but there's another important reason—it gives you more flowers in the garden. Many plants are stimulated to blossom longer and more profusely when their old flowers are removed. On perennials, this technique works with varying degrees of success, depending on the type of plant. For example, the balloon flower will produce many more buds with dead-heading, while an astilbe will flower only once no matter whether you dead-head or not.

Since annuals flower over a longer season, they tend to respond better to dead-heading than perennials do. Zinnias are an example of an annual that will really respond to dead-heading. Petunias, pansies, and impatiens produce so many blossoms that dead-heading really isn't needed to spur the plants on even more, but the appearance of the flower bed will still be improved if you remove the old blossoms.

Remember also to dead-head the larger hardy bulbs, which will help them get stronger for next year. With the smaller bulbs such as crocus, Siberian squill, and snowdrop, there's no need to clip the old flowers, and it's too much trouble anyway.

The Year in the Flower Garden

Once you have designed and built your 60-Minute Flower Garden, you can look forward to spending about an hour a week maintaining it in a healthy and beautifully showy condition throughout most of the year. The secret to keeping within the 60-minute time frame is to spread your flower gardening tasks fairly evenly over the whole year, rather than doing nothing for four weeks and then having to spend four or five hours in one hot day to catch up.

The tasks involved in managing an existing flower garden are fairly predictable and occur each year at about the same time. You can plan a very rational maintenance schedule for the whole year that won't vary much from year to year.

On the next page is an outline of the tasks required to maintain an existing 60-Minute Flower Garden that you can use to develop your own schedule. We've broken the year down into five seasons. Under each season we've grouped the tasks into the general categories of planting, propagation, and culture and maintenance. Some of these tasks, of course, will vary by season, depending on where in the United States you live. But taken as a general guide, this yearly schedule should help you get a feel for the relative workloads in each season.

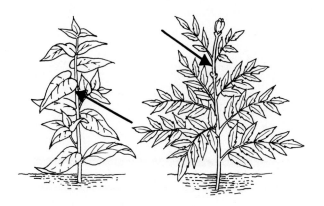

Pruning Young Flowers: *The arrows show where to pinch back growth on a young zinnia (left) and marigold (right) to encourage more branches to form. Sacrificing a few early blossoms for a bushy plant shape pays off in the end, since more branches can ultimately give you more flowers throughout the season.*

Early Spring Season

Planting

- Plant early frost-tolerant annuals.

Propagation

- Divide and transplant snowdrops and daffodils immediately after they finish flowering.
- Plant new bare-rooted perennials.
- Divide and replant established perennials.

Culture and Maintenance

- As soon as first spring bulbs (such as snowdrops, snow crocuses, and winter aconite) show their color, remove the winter mulch from the bed; leave the mulch around shrubs and tender perennials.
- Loosen soil and add a 1-inch layer of compost.
- Install drip irrigation system if it was removed last fall.
- Dead-head tulips and daffodils after blossoming.
- Correct garden design problems and planting arrangements by moving clumps of perennials, biennials, or small shrubs to a better spot.

Midspring to Late Spring Season

Planting

- In late spring plant summer annuals.
- Plant annual bulbs when soil is warm (about 55°F).

Culture and Maintenance

- In midspring add mulch for weed control.
- In late spring begin looking for insect pests.
- Begin foliar feeding.

Summer Season

Planting

- Plant fall-flowering bulbs.
- Plant late crop of annuals for late summer to fall bloom.
- Transplant biennial seedlings to their permanent positions.

Culture and Maintenance

- Stake plants before they have a chance to fall over.
- Watch watering needs carefully.
- Dead-head and do minor weeding.
- After some seed has fallen, pull out biennials that have finished flowering.

Fall Season

Planting

- Sink containers of fall chrysanthemums in the garden for temporary color.
- Plant daffodils in September/October.
- Plant new perennial additions to the garden from very late summer to early fall.
- Plant tulips and crocuses in midfall to late fall.

Propagation

- Divide and replant early-blooming perennials.

Culture and Maintenance

- Spread rock powders every two years.
- Remove all weeds that have sneaked into the garden.
- Clean out the perennial bed; cut back plant stems to 3 or 4 inches and remove the old foliage from the bed entirely.
- Correct garden design problems and planting arrangements by moving clumps of perennials, biennials, or small shrubs to a better spot.
- Apply winter mulch after the ground freezes.
- Dig and store annual bulbs.

Winter Season

Culture and Maintenance

- Watch for rodents that may have moved in under the winter mulch.
- Watch for frost heaving and replant if necessary.
- Clean up and shape your trees and shrubs by removing dead or unwanted branches.

Keeping Track of the 60-Minute Flower Garden

From our experience, it seems that vegetable gardeners are a bit more obsessed about keeping records of their gardening activities than flower gardeners. But as a flower gardener you do have reason to keep track of what's going on, if only to be able to remember the names of the perennials and shrubs that you've placed with such loving care in your 60-Minute Flower Garden. Jeff has real problems remembering all the different varieties of the many plants that make up his flower garden, so he and Liz depend on unobtrusive labels stuck in the ground to keep things straight. Charles, with his vast gardens, has both permanent labels on his plants and over 2,000 3-by-5 cards on file to keep track of the enormous number of trees, shrubs, flowers, and other plants he has on his property. Few people are going to need that kind of detail or have that kind of dedication.

One way to keep a record is to use the back of your garden plan for notes to yourself when you decide you'd like to move the hosta next fall or maybe add some dusty miller next spring. A spiral notebook can become a garden diary. Or you might use a calendar with good-sized spaces for each weekday; save the annotated calendar from each year and you'll have a convenient library of seasonal notes to refer to.

Labels in the garden can be as much of a problem as a help. If they are too obvious, they can become unsightly and draw your eye away from the plants. If they are too small, they can't be read without getting down on your hands and knees. Also, they can take a beating from the elements. If they aren't weatherproof, the rain can wash off the writing or the sun can bleach them and cause the names to fade away.

Liz and Jeff have had good luck with labels made of heavy-duty aluminum foil

Plant Label: *This type of all-weather, all-season metal label is a good choice for the flower garden. Because you can insert it directly into the soil, it is a good marker to use on perennials, which die back in the fall.*

with small wires for attaching the label to the plant. You use a dull pencil to make an impression in the foil which is then impervious to the weather and fairly easy to read without having to bend over too far. If you use these labels, you can't tie them to a perennial since it dies back in the winter. Take a coat hanger and fashion a little mast that can be stuck in the ground right in the middle of the clump of perennials. Then tie the label to the mast. (Look in the Resources Guide for several sources of these and other plant labels.)

Computers in the Garden

For people like Charles with very large and complex flower gardens, the home computer offers excellent relief from the laborious 3-by-5 card file for keeping track of many varieties and plants. There are simple data management programs available for any of the home computers on the market that can be used for keeping garden records and for keeping track of the gardening schedule.

Jeff uses his computer to keep a file of new varieties of flowers and vegetables that he reads about throughout the year in his gardening magazines. When the flood of seed catalogs comes in December and January, he already has a good idea about any new plants he might like to try.

Within the next few years there will be programs for home computers that will allow the flower gardener to map out his garden on the computer screen in the appropriate colors. He'll also be able to move things around to see how the garden might look in different seasons. The program will automatically translate a map of the garden into a three-dimensional view from the front of the garden. Computer graphics in full color will make it easier to visualize all the various possibilities for the flower garden.

Bringing the Beauty of the Garden Inside

You can transport the beauty of your flower garden into your home if you know a few tricks about keeping cut flowers looking fresh or about drying flowers for year-round display.

There's nothing more refreshing and pleasant than to walk into a home that has freshly cut flowers tastefully arranged in an attractive container. Flowers add an extra dimension of beauty to any room. People without gardens have to pay dearly for the luxury of having cut flowers, but with a 60-Minute Flower Garden you can have freshly cut flowers anytime you want—they're yours for the taking. While some flowers will last longer than others, virtually any flower in your garden can be cut for display inside your home. Go back to page 67 for our list of some of the most popular garden flowers for cutting.

Keeping Cut Flowers in Good Shape

You can affect how long your cut flowers will last by the way you cut them in the garden. Always use a very sharp knife, scissors, or pruning tool to cut the stems on an angle. The very best time to cut flowers is early in the day before the dew has dried. The other option, for those of you who leave for work early in the morning, is to cut your flowers in the evening. In either case, Charles recommends carrying a bucket of fresh water out to the garden so you can immediately plunge the stems into water.

You should always cut off all the leaves on the part of the stem that is going to be underwater in the vase. Those leaves will rot and foul the water, which will shorten the life of your flowers. In almost all cases, cut flowers will last significantly longer if you add some commercial floral preservative to your water right at the beginning. There are a number of different brands of preservatives, and you'll find at least one in almost any flower shop or garden center.

Another trick to add to the longevity of your bouquet is to replace the water in the container with fresh water and more preservative every day and to mist the bouquet each morning. Keep your arrangement out of direct sun, away from heat sources, and out of drafts. If you have a suitable place, set your bouquet in a cool spot at night while everyone is asleep. This will help keep the flowers looking fresher longer. Few people have a root cellar as Jeff and Liz do, but a low arrangement can certainly spend the night in the refrigerator. Even a basement will be cool enough to make some difference in the staying power of your cut flowers.

Drying Flowers

Drying fresh flowers for long-lasting bouquets is relatively easy to learn, but it takes years of practice to get good at it. We strongly recommend that you buy a book and/or take a class on the subject to really learn all the techniques you need to dry flowers successfully. Here we'll simply provide some very basic pointers that can help you get started.

Most of the flowers in your 60-Minute Flower Garden can be dried, but some are easier than others. We gave you a list of these on page 67. You should harvest flowers for drying just before their peak, when the colors are the brightest and the flowers are firm. For the best results, cut the flowers on a dry day after the dew has burned off.

You don't need much fancy equipment to dry flowers. Many people get excellent results by simply hanging bunches of flowers to dry in the attic. Other people swear by using some kind of drying agent such as silica gel. You bury your flowers in a box filled with silica gel crystals and let them absorb the flowers' moisture. It takes some practice to learn how to adjust the drying periods for large or small blossoms, tight buds or open blooms, and leaves and stems, but this is a hobby where practicing is great fun.

The general principle in drying flowers is that the quicker you dry the flower, the better will be its final color. Air drying takes weeks and sometimes months, silica gel by itself can do the job in less than a week, and a microwave oven takes only a few minutes. Yes, you can dry flowers in a microwave. Before you try this on your own, though, you must do some reading on the special techniques that are needed or talk to someone who's done it.

Drying the flowers is just half the fun. Once they're dry, you have the delightful opportunity to make attractive dried flower arrangements. As you can see, your adventure in starting a 60-Minute Flower Garden can lead to all kinds of new experiences and new hobbies. Since you'll be spending only an hour a week in the garden, that leaves you plenty of time to have fun doing other things!

Grand Finale

By now we hope you've been sufficiently inspired to go out and create a 60-Minute Flower Garden in your own yard. We've tried throughout the book to give you the tools and information you need to design and build an easy-care flower garden that is beautiful and satisfying virtually all year long.

At a time in our world's history when tension and stress seem to be the norm rather than the exception, we can't think of a better way to find some relief than by spending an hour or so a week mucking about in your own little piece of the earth that exists for no other reason than to be beautiful. Some of the unenlightened among us might feel that a flower garden has no practical value whatsoever. You can't eat it, you can't ride in it, and you can't wear it. However, that same bit of ground can offer all of us and our neighbors rich feelings of joy and peace in a way that few other things in our world can. Peace!

The Best Plants for the 60-Minute Flower Garden

There are literally thousands of varieties of plants readily available from local nurseries or from any of hundreds of reliable flower gardening catalogs. You may be wondering how you can choose among them to find the best plants for your garden. To help make your plant selection process an easy one, Charles has developed this chart, which lists 173 plants that satisfy the following criteria: They're readily available throughout most of the country; they'll grow in most areas of the country; and they're relatively easy to grow.

Charles's list is in no way complete. If all the plants that meet the stated requirements were included in this chart, we'd be back up to 1,000 plants. The 173 plants in Charles's list, in addition to meeting the criteria, represent enough variety to allow you to design any one of the 60-Minute Flower Gardens we discuss in the book, without overwhelming you with too many options in each category. This list is offered as a sound beginning. If your favorite variety is missing or if your neighbor offers you an unlisted perennial that he says grows extremely well, then by all means include those in your plan. Our chart is simply a good place to start.

To make sure you know how to take full advantage of all this chart has to offer, we're going to give you some pointers on how to use it. To start, the plants are listed in alphabetical order by their common name. The botanical name is given second. If you know only the botanical name of a plant you're interested in, go to the Plant Name Index on page 257. There you'll be able to scan down the column of botanical names until you come to the one you're interested in. Look across to the neighboring column for the common name. Then you're ready to look for that plant's entry in the chart.

If you are a beginning gardener, you might find the following color-coding procedure helpful in identifying the plants you want to consider for your 60-Minute Flower Garden. You'll need a set of highlighting pens, which can be purchased in most stationery or art supply stores. A set often includes six colors. The ink in these pens doesn't cover up the print on a page; it simply leaves a transparent color to highlight a word or passage.

Step one: Identify the plants that will grow in your geographic area. To do this you must first determine your hardiness zone from the Hardiness Zone Map on page 250. Then take a highlighter pen (orange, for example) and highlight the "Zones" sections on the chart that include your zone number.

Step two: Select the appropriate light conditions. Using the box on page 16 that gives the definitions of four light conditions in the garden (full sun, partial sun, partial shade, and full shade), determine the light conditions that prevail in the garden site you're planning. Now check the plants that you've highlighted for appropriate hardiness zone to find those that fit your light requirements; with a different color pen, highlight the "Light Requirements" for each of these.

These two very simple steps give you all the plants included in our chart that you can possibly consider in planning your garden. As we have mentioned before, these are not the only plants that are available to you, but they can be considered reliable options.

Step three: For this step you need three different colors of highlighting pens — perhaps a pink, a yellow, and a blue. You want to sort through the group of suitable plants by size, keeping in mind that the same type of plant can come in many sizes, depending on the particular varieties. Go through the entries for plants that you have already indicated in the chart and highlight the "Size" section with pink whenever you find a plant that is taller than 36 inches. Go through

again and mark the mid-sized plants with yellow; these are from 15 to 36 inches tall. Finally, go through and mark with your blue highlighter all those plants that are less than 15 inches tall.

You have now narrowed down the total list of plants in the chart and have set up quick indicators about their size. It should be fairly easy for you to find the tall perennials for the background of your new flower garden or the low-growing annuals to fill in the foreground. You can now go back to Chapter 5 and, following the guidelines we present there, begin to select your plants.

Before you get started, here are explanations of some of the terms used throughout the chart.

Hardiness: The terms *very hardy* and *hardy* for perennials are tied to their cold-hardiness, not to their ease of growth. For annuals the terms *hardy, half-hardy,* and *tender* are used. These are explained fully on page 56.

Light requirements: See the box mentioned above for a discussion of the four basic light conditions used here. They are listed in order, with the preferred condition given first. The term *deciduous shade* means shade created by trees that lose their leaves in winter, thereby allowing sun to reach early spring flowers.

Growing requirements: *Adaptable* means the plant is able to tolerate most average soil conditions. *Dry soil* indicates that a plant cannot tolerate soaking wet soil for very long and can withstand some drought; for best growth, however, this plant still needs periodic watering.

Propagation: Planting depth for bulbs means the depth from the *bottom* of the hole.

Size	Appearance	Bloom Period	Light Requirements	Growing Requirements
AGERATUM (FLOSSFLOWER)		*Ageratum houstonianum*		
15 in. tall; 15-in. spread.	Blue, purple, or white flowers; oval, bright green foliage.	June-Oct. Faintly scented.	Full sun; partial sun; partial shade.	Rich, moist soil.
AGERATUM, HARDY		*Eupatorium coelestinum*		
24 in. tall; 24-in. spread.	Light blue flowers; green foliage.	Aug.-Sept.	Full sun; partial sun; partial shade.	Very adaptable.
AJUGA	*Ajuga reptans*			
6 in. tall; 8-in. spread.	Blue or white flowers; green, bronze, or variegated foliage.	May-June.	Partial shade to full shade.	Well-drained soil or plants will die out.

Look for: 'Alba'—white flowers; 'Burgundy Glow'—variegated with white, bronze, and green; *A. pyramidalis*—nonspreading.

Size	Appearance	Bloom Period	Light Requirements	Growing Requirements
ALYSSUM, SWEET		*Lobularia maritima*		
4-8 in. tall; 6-in. spread.	White, rose, or purple flowers; green foliage with fine texture.	May-Oct. Faint sweet scent.	Full sun; partial sun; partial shade.	Poor, light, well-drained soil.
AMARYLLIS, HARDY (RESURRECTION LILY)			*Lycoris squamigera*	
24 in. tall; 8-in. spread.	Pink flowers on tall stems; straplike green foliage.	Aug.	Full sun to partial sun; deciduous shade.	Deep, rich soil; plant 6 in. deep.
AMSONIA	*Amsonia tabernaemontana*			
24 in. tall; 18-in. spread.	Light blue flowers; narrow green leaves.	May-June.	Full sun to partial shade.	Very adaptable.

Propagation	Garden Types	Uses	Notes
Tender Annual	**Zones —**		
Sow seed indoors in March, germinates in 5 days; also by cuttings.	Sunny or shady garden; Bank Garden.	Middle or foreground of bed; edging; good fresh-cut flower.	Avoid hot, dry sites; remove old flowers to prolong bloom.
Hardy Perennial	**Zones 5-8**		
By division, cuttings, or seed.	Sunny or shady garden.	Middle of bed; good fresh-cut flower.	Light blue flowers in early fall are good companions for chrysanthemums. Watch out for very invasive rhizomes. Pinch midsummer for compact growth.
Very Hardy Perennial	**Zones 2-8**		
By division or seed.	Shady garden; Woodland Garden.	Ground cover; foreground of bed; edging.	Invasive ground cover but easily pulled to keep under control. Self-seeds freely.
Hardy Annual	**Zones —**		
Sow seed indoors in March, or sow outdoors when soil can be worked in spring.	Sunny or partly shady garden; Bank Garden.	Foreground of bed; edging.	Cut back, feed, and water to rejuvenate and renew bloom. Start early indoors for use with spring bulbs.
Hardy Bulb	**Zones 5-10**		
By division.	Sunny or shady garden with deciduous shade; Woodland Garden.	Middle or foreground of bed; good fresh-cut flower.	Leaves grow in spring and die down in June; flower stalk appears without leaves in Aug. Best grown among a low ground cover.
Very Hardy Perennial	**Zones 3-8**		
By division or seed.	Sunny garden.	Middle of bed.	A native plant with yellow fall color.

Size	Appearance	Bloom Period	Light Requirements	Growing Requirements

ANEMONE, GREEK (GREEK WINDFLOWER)   *Anemone blanda*

| 4 in. tall; 3-in. spread. | Blue, white, or pink flowers; finely cut green foliage. | March–April. | Full sun to partial sun; deciduous shade. | Well-drained, limey soil, kept dry in summer. |

ANEMONE, JAPANESE   *Anemone hybrida*

| 60 in. tall; 24-in. spread. | Pink, rose, or white flowers with golden stamens; flowers taller than green foliage; coarse leaves. | Sept.–Oct. | Full sun; partial sun; partial shade. | Rich, well-drained, moist soil. |

Look for: 'Honorine Jobert' (also called 'Alba')—white single flowers; 'September Charm'—pink single flowers; 'Margarette'—double rosy pink flowers; 'Prince Henry' —double rose-red flowers.

ANEMONE, POPPY-FLOWERED   *Anemone coronaria*

| 12-18 in. tall; 8-in. spread. | Blue, red, pink, or white flowers; deeply cut green foliage. | April–May. | Full sun to partial sun. | Rich, well-drained soil containing lime with neutral to alkaline pH; prefers dry soil in summer. |

Look for: Commonly offered hybrids 'de Caen' and 'St. Brigid.'

ASTER, CHINA   *Callistephus chinensis*

| 36 in. tall; 12-in. spread. | Blue, purple, pink, or white flowers; green foliage with moderately coarse texture. | June–July. | Full sun to partial sun. | Rich soil. |

ASTILBE   *Astilbe arendsii*

| 24-48 in. tall; 24-36-in. spread. | Pink, white, or red flowers; green foliage with ferny texture. | June–July. | Partial sun to partial shade. | Rich, moist soil. |

Propagation	Garden Types	Uses	Notes
Hardy Bulb	**Zones 6-10**		
By division or seed; plant 4 in. deep.	Sunny or shady garden; Woodland Garden, Bank Garden.	Foreground of bed.	Flowers must have the sun shining on them to open. Soak corms in water overnight before planting to improve results.
Hardy Perennial	**Zones 5-8**		
By division or root cuttings.	Sunny or shady garden; Woodland Garden.	Background or middle of bed; good fresh-cut flower.	Provide winter mulch in North.
Moderately Hardy Bulb	**Zones 8-10**		
By division; plant 3 in. deep.	Sunny garden; Bank Garden.	Foreground of bed; good fresh-cut flower.	Large-flowered but unfortunately not hardy in the North. Flame anemone (*A. flugens*) is scarlet and is the hardiest (to Zone 5).
Half-Hardy Annual	**Zones —**		
Sow seed outdoors after danger of frost; prefers not to be transplanted.	Sunny garden.	Middle of bed; good for cutting fresh or drying.	Plant a succession for continuous supply of cut flowers into late summer since China asters don't rebloom after cutting.
Very Hardy Perennial	**Zones 4-8**		
By division.	Shady garden; Woodland Garden.	Middle or foreground of bed; ground cover; good for cutting fresh or drying.	Will grow in full sun only with constant moisture. Many hybrids available with varying heights, colors, and bloom times.

Size	Appearance	Bloom Period	Light Requirements	Growing Requirements

BABY'S BREATH   *Gypsophila paniculata*

Size	Appearance	Bloom Period	Light Requirements	Growing Requirements
36 in. tall; 24-in. spread.	Masses of tiny white or pink flowers; gray-green, narrow leaves with fine texture.	June–Aug.	Full sun to partial sun.	Light, well-drained soil with lime; prefers neutral to alkaline pH.

Look for: 'Bristol Fairy'—outstanding white double flowers; can spread 4 ft. Also double pink varieties available.

BACHELOR'S BUTTONS (CORNFLOWER)   *Centaurea cyanus*

Size	Appearance	Bloom Period	Light Requirements	Growing Requirements
24 in. tall; 8-in. spread.	Blue, pink, or white flowers; green foliage with moderately coarse texture.	April–June.	Full sun; partial sun; partial shade.	Poor, dry soil.

BALLOON FLOWER   *Platycodon grandiflorus*

Size	Appearance	Bloom Period	Light Requirements	Growing Requirements
10-24 in. tall; 15-in. spread.	Deep blue, white, or pink flowers; green foliage with moderately coarse texture.	July–Aug.	Full sun to partial sun.	Well-drained soil.

Look for: 'Apoyama'—10 in. tall, deep blue, widely sold; 'Mariesii—15 in., deep blue; 'Shell Pink'—24 in., pale pink.

BALSAM   *Impatiens balsamina*

Size	Appearance	Bloom Period	Light Requirements	Growing Requirements
8-24 in. tall; 10-in. spread.	Pink, salmon, red, or white flowers; green foliage with moderately coarse texture.	May–Oct.	Full sun to partial sun.	Very adaptable; prefers moist soil.

BARRENWORT   *Epimedium rubrum*

Size	Appearance	Bloom Period	Light Requirements	Growing Requirements
12 in. tall; 12-in. spread.	Masses of small red and white flowers; heart-shaped leaves on wiry stems.	April.	Partial shade to full shade.	Average to rich soil; drought tolerant in shade.

Look for: *E. versicolor* 'Sulphureum'—yellow flowers. *E. youngianum* 'Niveum'—white flowers.

Propagation	Garden Types	Uses	Notes
Very Hardy Perennial	**Zones 4-8**		
By division or direct-sown seed; dislikes transplanting.	Sunny garden.	Middle of bed; good for cutting fresh or drying.	Sprawling plant needs staking but can be used to cover bare spots of spring bloomers like poppies and bulbs.
Hardy Annual	**Zones —**		
Direct-sow outdoors fall to early spring; germinates in 5-20 days; mulch lightly for winter; dislikes transplanting.	Sunny or shady garden.	Background or middle of bed; good for cutting fresh or drying.	A cool-season annual that fades with summer heat. For best results sow very early. Good source of early cut flowers.
Very Hardy Perennial	**Zones 3-8**		
By division or seed.	Sunny garden.	Middle of bed; good fresh-cut flower.	Among the best midsummer blue perennials; needs staking. Dig deeply to transplant. Remove seedpods to prolong bloom.
Tender Annual	**Zones —**		
Sow indoors in March, germinates in 4-5 days; sow outdoors in May when soil is thoroughly warm.	Sunny garden.	Middle or foreground of bed; good fresh-cut flower.	Dwarf varieties suited for edging. Prefers full sun, except in areas with hot summers where afternoon shade is beneficial.
Very Hardy Perennial	**Zones 4-7**		
By division.	Shady garden; Woodland Garden, Bank Garden.	Foreground of bed; edging; ground cover; good fresh-cut foliage.	One of the best ground covers for dry shade.

Size	Appearance	Bloom Period	Light Requirements	Growing Requirements

BEE BALM (BERGAMOT)   *Monarda didyma*

Size	Appearance	Bloom Period	Light Requirements	Growing Requirements
36 in. tall; 12-in. spread.	Red, pink, or white flowers; green foliage.	June–July.	Full sun; partial sun; partial shade.	Rich moist soil; good air circulation reduces mildew on leaves.

Look for: 'Adam'—red; 'Cambridge Scarlet'—red; 'Croftway Pink'—clear pink; 'Mahogany'—wine-red; 'Snow White'—pure white.

BEGONIA, BEDDING   *Begonia semperflorens*

Size	Appearance	Bloom Period	Light Requirements	Growing Requirements
12 in. tall; 12-in. spread.	Small pink, red, or white flowers; rounded green or bronze foliage.	Continuous.	Full sun; partial sun; partial shade.	Very adaptable but prefers rich, moist soil.

BEGONIA, TUBEROUS   *Begonia tuberhybrida*

Size	Appearance	Bloom Period	Light Requirements	Growing Requirements
12–18 in. tall; 12-in. spread.	Large flowers of all colors except blue; large green foliage.	May–Oct.	Partial sun; partial shade; full shade.	Rich, moist, well-drained soil.

BELLFLOWER, CLUSTERED   *Campanula glomerata*

Size	Appearance	Bloom Period	Light Requirements	Growing Requirements
12–36 in. tall; 24-in. spread.	Deep blue or white flowers; green foliage.	June–July.	Full sun; partial sun; partial shade.	Well-drained soil, kept on the dry side.

Look for: 'Alba'—white; 'Joan Elliot'—deep violet-blue, 18 in. tall; 'Superba'—violet-blue, 24 in. tall.

BELLFLOWER, PEACH-LEAVED   *Campanula persicifolia*

Size	Appearance	Bloom Period	Light Requirements	Growing Requirements
36 in. tall; 12-in. spread.	Blue or white flowers; green foliage lower than the flowers.	June–July.	Full sun; partial sun; partial shade.	Prefers moist soil.

BERGENIA (MEGASEA)   *Bergenia cordifolia*

Size	Appearance	Bloom Period	Light Requirements	Growing Requirements
12 in. tall; 12-in. spread.	Pink flowers; coarse, round green foliage.	April–May.	Partial shade; partial sun; full sun.	Very adaptable.

Propagation	Garden Types	Uses	Notes
Very Hardy Perennial	**Zones 4-9**		
By division in spring (fall transplanting is risky) or by seed.	Sunny or shady garden.	Background or middle of bed; good fresh-cut flower.	Shallow rhizomes spread rapidly but are easily pulled. Cut out old, unsightly stems when finished blooming.
Tender Annual	**Zones —**		
Sow seed indoors Jan.-Feb. and set out plants when all danger of frost is past; also by cuttings.	Sunny or shady garden; Woodland Garden, Bank Garden.	Foreground of bed; edging.	Very heat resistant. Wide selection of varieties combine all flower colors with green or bronze foliage.
Annual Bulb	**Zones —**		
Start tubers indoors in April or outdoors when soil is warm; also by seed or cuttings.	Shady garden; Woodland Garden.	Middle or foreground of bed; edging.	In hot climates shade from afternoon sun; best to stake brittle stems.
Very Hardy Perennial	**Zones 3-8**		
By division in spring or just after blooming; also by seed.	Sunny garden.	Middle or foreground of bed; good fresh-cut flower.	Rhizomes less invasive in poor soil.
Very Hardy Perennial	**Zones 3-8**		
By division.	Sunny or shady garden; Bank Garden.	Middle or foreground of bed; good fresh-cut flower.	Will flower longer if dead blossoms are removed.
Very Hardy Perennial	**Zones 3-8**		
By division.	Sunny or shady garden; Bank Garden.	Foreground of bed; ground cover; edging.	*B. crassifolia* is very similar. Large leaves provide bold textural contrast.

Size	Appearance	Bloom Period	Light Requirements	Growing Requirements
BLACK-EYED SUSAN (CONEFLOWER) *Rudbeckia fulgida*				
24 in. tall; 18-in. spread.	Bright yellow flowers with dark centers; broad-leaved green foliage.	July–Sept.	Full sun to partial sun.	Well-drained soil.

Look for: 'Goldsturm'—one of the best perennials available today.

Size	Appearance	Bloom Period	Light Requirements	Growing Requirements
BLANKET FLOWER (GAILLARDIA) *Gaillardia grandiflora*				
12–30 in. tall; 12–18-in. spread.	Red and/or yellow flowers; green foliage.	June–Oct.	Full sun.	Poor, sandy, well-drained, dry soil.

Look for: 'Burgundy'—wine-red, 30 in. tall; 'Goblin'—red and yellow, most common variety, 12 in. tall; 'Yellow Queen'—yellow, 30 in. tall.

Size	Appearance	Bloom Period	Light Requirements	Growing Requirements
BLEEDING HEART, COMMON *Dicentra spectabilis*				
30 in. tall; 24-in. spread.	Pink or white flowers; green foliage with fernlike texture.	May–June.	Partial shade; partial sun; full sun.	Rich, moist soil.

Look for: The common variety is pink; 'Alba' and 'Pantaloons' are white.

Size	Appearance	Bloom Period	Light Requirements	Growing Requirements
BLEEDING HEART, FRINGED *Dicentra eximia*				
12 in. tall; 12-in. spread.	Pink or white flowers; fernlike green foliage.	April–Sept.	Partial shade; partial sun; full sun.	Rich, well-drained soil; prefers moist soil but can withstand summer drought.

Look for: 'Luxurient'—actually a hybrid, probably the best and most widely available.

Size	Appearance	Bloom Period	Light Requirements	Growing Requirements
BLOODROOT *Sanguinaria canadensis*				
6 in. tall; 8-in. spread.	White flowers; rounded green foliage.	April–May.	Partial sun; partial shade; full deciduous shade.	Rich soil, prefers acid pH.

Propagation	Garden Types	Uses	Notes
Very Hardy Perennial	**Zones 3-9**		
By division or seed.	Sunny garden.	Middle or foreground of bed; ground cover; good fresh-cut flower.	Broad, ground-hugging foliage forms tight ground cover to choke out weeds; doesn't need staking.
Very Hardy Perennial	**Zones 3-9**		
By division, root cuttings, or seed.	Sunny garden; Bank Garden.	Middle or foreground of bed; good fresh-cut flower.	One of longest-blooming perennials. Sow seed early to grow as annual; must have lots of sun; needs good drainage to overwinter.
Very Hardy Perennial	**Zones 3-7**		
By division or seed.	Sunny or shady garden; Woodland Garden.	Background or middle of bed; good fresh-cut flower.	Dies down in summer, so plant behind later-flowering perennial to cover empty space. Dig deeply to transplant. Often self-seeds.
Very Hardy Perennial	**Zones 3-7**		
By division or seed.	Sunny or shady garden; Woodland Garden, Bank Garden.	Middle or foreground of bed; ground cover; edging; good fresh-cut flower.	Blooms continuously with adequate moisture. Several named varieties, some with grayish leaves.
Very Hardy Perennial	**Zones 3-8**		
By division or seed.	Shady garden; Woodland Garden, Bank Garden.	Foreground of bed.	Prefers a site with deciduous shade for shelter from summer sun; goes dormant in summer. A native plant.

Size	Appearance	Bloom Period	Light Requirements	Growing Requirements
BOLTONIA *Boltonia asteroides*				
48-84 in. tall; 12-24-in. spread.	White flowers; green foliage with moderate texture.	Aug.-Sept.	Full sun to partial sun.	Very adaptable.

Look for: 'Snowbank'—an improved form only 48-60 in. tall that seldom needs staking.

BROWALLIA *Browallia americana*				
12 in. tall; 12-in. spread.	Blue or white flowers; green foliage.	July-Oct.	Partial sun to partial shade.	Average to poor soil.
BUGBANE *Cimicifuga racemosa*				
72 in. tall; 24-in. spread.	White flowers; large, coarse green leaves about half the height of the flowers.	July-Aug.	Partial sun; partial shade; full shade.	Rich, moist soil; prefers acid pH.
BUTTERFLY WEED *Asclepias tuberosa*				
24 in. tall; 12-in. spread.	Orange flowers; narrow green foliage.	July-Aug.	Full sun.	Poor, well-drained soil; drought tolerant.
CALADIUM *Caladium* hybrids				
12 in. tall, 12-in. spread.	Insignificant flowers; large, heart-shaped leaves colored with pink, red, green, and white.		Partial sun; partial shade; full shade.	Rich, moist soil.
CALENDULA (POT MARIGOLD) *Calendula officinalis*				
18-24 in. tall; 12-in. spread.	Yellow or orange flowers; green foliage.	July-Oct.	Full sun; partial sun; partial shade.	Rich, moist soil.

Propagation	Garden Types	Uses	Notes
Very Hardy Perennial	**Zones 3-8**		
By division or seed.	Sunny garden.	Background or middle of bed.	Similar to the Michaelmas daisy.
Half-Hardy Annual	**Zones —**		
Sow seed indoors in March, germinates in 2 weeks; also by cuttings.	Sunny or shady garden; Bank Garden.	Middle or foreground of bed; edging; good fresh-cut flower.	Shade from hot afternoon sun for best blooming.
Very Hardy Perennial	**Zones 3-9**		
By division or seed.	Shady garden; Woodland Garden.	Background or middle of bed; good fresh-cut flower.	A native plant that seldom needs division; avoid hot afternoon sun. Peculiar scent of foliage can be used to ward off bugs.
Very Hardy Perennial	**Zones 3-8**		
By division, transplant only in spring as growth begins; also by seed.	Sunny garden; Bank Garden.	Middle or foreground of bed; good fresh-cut flower.	A brilliantly colored native; sometimes available in yellow and red.
Annual Bulb	**Zones —**		
By division of tubers; start indoors in April in warm place, set out in late May when soil is warm.	Shade garden; Woodland Garden.	Middle or foreground of bed; edging.	Don't set out too early, as cold will set back plants. Store dormant tubers in cool cellar. Remove flowers for better leaf display.
Half-Hardy Annual	**Zones —**		
Sow seed indoors and set out as soon as soil can be worked.	Sunny or shady garden; Bank Garden.	Middle or foreground of bed; good for cutting fresh or drying.	Best in areas with cool summers; makes a good showing well into fall. Cut faded flowers to continue bloom.

Size	Appearance	Bloom Period	Light Requirements	Growing Requirements
CAMASSIA *Camassia leichtlinii*				
24-36 in. tall; 10-in. spread.	Blue, cream, or white flowers; straplike green foliage.	May.	Full sun; partial sun; partial shade.	Rich, moist soil. Noteworthy for its ability to grow in wet, poorly drained, clayey soils.
CANNA *Canna generalis*				
36-60 in. tall; 36-in. spread.	Red, pink, orange, or yellow flowers above large, wide, dark green leaves.	June-Oct.	Full sun.	Rich soil.
CHRYSANTHEMUM *Chrysanthemum morifolium*				
12-36 in. tall; 24-in. spread.	White, yellow, orange, red, or pink flowers; green foliage.	Aug.-Oct.	Full sun.	Rich, well-drained soil.
CLEMATIS, BLUE-TUBE *Clematis heracleifolia*				
36 in. tall; 48-in. spread.	Pale to medium blue flowers; coarse green foliage.	Aug.-Sept.	Full sun; partial sun; partial shade.	Rich, well-drained soil.

Look for: *C. heracleifolia* var. *davidiana* is a noteworthy variety.

Size	Appearance	Bloom Period	Light Requirements	Growing Requirements
COCK'S-COMB, PLUMED *Celosia cristata* var. *plumosa*				
12-36 in. tall; 8-12 in. spread.	Red, yellow, orange, or pink flowers; green foliage.	June-Sept.	Full sun.	Very adaptable to any well-drained soil.
COLCHICUM *Colchicum* spp.				
8 in. tall; 8-in. spread.	Large, pink, crocuslike flowers; coarse green foliage.	Sept.	Full sun to partial sun; deciduous shade.	Well-drained soil; tolerates clay.

Look for: Best species *C. autumnale, C. byzantinum, C. speciosum;* best hybrids 'Lilac Wonder,' 'The Giant,' 'Violet Queen,' and 'Waterlily' (double).

Propagation	Garden Types	Uses	Notes
Very Hardy Bulb	**Zones 3-10**		
By division or seed; plant 6 in. deep.	Sunny or shady garden; Woodland Garden.	Middle of bed; good fresh-cut flower.	Native bulb that blooms after most spring bulbs; plant with daffodils to extend seasonal color.
Annual Bulb	**Zones —**		
By division; plant tuberous rhizomes when soil has warmed in spring.	Sunny garden.	Background or middle of bed.	Roots are dug in fall and stored dormant indoors over winter; divide in spring. Japanese beetles may be a problem.
Very Hardy Perennial	**Zones 4-8**		
By cuttings, division, or seed.	Sunny garden.	Middle of bed; good fresh-cut flower.	Pinch 2 or 3 times before mid-July for bushy, compact growth; best divided each spring. Provide winter mulch in North. Many types and colors available.
Very Hardy Perennial	**Zones 3-9**		
By cuttings, division, or seed.	Sunny or shady garden.	Background or middle of bed; good for cutting fresh or drying.	Not a vine, but an almost woody perennial; long-lasting, sweet-scented flowers.
Half-Hardy Annual	**Zones —**		
Sow seed early indoors or sow outdoors after danger of heavy frost.	Sunny garden.	Background to foreground of bed or edging, depending on variety; good for cutting fresh or drying.	Pest-free and dependable for a long season of color in hot summers.
Very Hardy Bulb	**Zones 4-10**		
By division; plant 6 in. deep.	Sunny or shady garden; Woodland Garden, Bank Garden.	Foreground of bed; good fresh-cut flower.	Leaves appear in spring, die away by summer, and flowers (but no leaves) appear in Sept. Very effective planted among pachysandra.

Size	Appearance	Bloom Period	Light Requirements	Growing Requirements

COLEUS (FLAME NETTLE)   *Coleus hybridus*

Size	Appearance	Bloom Period	Light Requirements	Growing Requirements
24 in. tall; 18-in. spread.	Insignificant blue flowers; leaves variegated with green, red, pink, and yellow.	–	Full sun; partial sun; partial shade.	Rich, moist soil.

COLUMBINE, LONG-SPURRED   *Aquilegia 'McKana Hybrids'*

Size	Appearance	Bloom Period	Light Requirements	Growing Requirements
24-36 in. tall; 18-in. spread.	Red, pink, white, yellow, blue, and purple, often bi-colored flowers; green foliage with fine texture.	May-June.	Partial shade; partial sun; full sun.	Well-drained soil.

CONEFLOWER, PURPLE   *Echinacea purpurea*

Size	Appearance	Bloom Period	Light Requirements	Growing Requirements
36 in. tall; 18-in. spread.	Pink flowers with orange center; green foliage.	July-Sept.	Full sun to partial sun.	Well-drained soil; drought tolerant.

Look for: 'Bright Star' and 'The King'—more brightly colored selections; 'White Lustre'—white flowers.

CORAL BELLS   *Heuchera sanguinea*

Size	Appearance	Bloom Period	Light Requirements	Growing Requirements
12-24 in. tall; 12-in. spread.	Pink, white, or red flowers; low, rounded green foliage.	May-July.	Full sun; partial sun; partial shade.	Rich, moist, well-drained soil.

Look for: 'Chatterbox'—pink, 18 in. tall; 'June Bride'—white, 15 in. tall; 'Pluie De Feu'—red, 24 in. tall.

COREOPSIS (TICKSEED)   *Coreopsis lanceolata*

Size	Appearance	Bloom Period	Light Requirements	Growing Requirements
24 in. tall; 12-in. spread.	Golden yellow flowers; narrow green foliage.	June-Oct.	Full sun.	Well-drained soil; drought tolerant.

Look for: 'Sunray'—award winner with bountiful flowering habit.

COREOPSIS, THREAD-LEAF   *Coreopsis verticillata*

Size	Appearance	Bloom Period	Light Requirements	Growing Requirements
24 in. tall; 18-in. spread.	Yellow flowers; feathery green foliage.	June-Aug.	Full sun to partial sun.	Poor, well-drained soil.

Look for: 'Golden Showers'—golden yellow, tall, common; 'Moonbeam'—the best, pale yellow, 15 in. tall, long flowering.

Propagation	Garden Types	Uses	Notes

Tender Annual   Zones —

Sow seed indoors in March; also by cuttings.	Sunny or shady garden; Woodland Garden, Bank Garden.	Middle or foreground of bed; edging; good fresh-cut foliage.	Pinch for compact plants; remove flowers for better foliage display.

Very Hardy Perennial   Zones 3-8

By seed.	Sunny or shady garden; Woodland Garden, Bank Garden.	Middle or foreground of bed; good for cutting fresh or drying (seedpod).	Replace this short-lived perennial with seedlings. Poor drainage encourages rot. Shorter types available for Bank Garden.

Very Hardy Perennial   Zones 3-9

By division or seed.	Sunny garden.	Background or middle of bed; good for cutting fresh or drying.	Also known as *Rudbeckia purpurea*. On poor, dry soils usually doesn't need staking.

Very Hardy Perennial   Zones 3-8

By division or seed.	Sunny or shady garden; Bank Garden.	Middle or foreground of bed; edging; good fresh-cut flower.	Low foliage and airy flower stems are nice featured toward front of bed.

Very Hardy Perennial   Zones 4-9

By division or seed.	Sunny garden; Bank Garden.	Middle or foreground of bed; good fresh-cut flower.	Long-blooming, short-lived perennial; easily grown from seed and will bloom first year; similar to *C. grandiflora*.

Very Hardy Perennial   Zones 3-9

By division or seed.	Sunny garden.	Middle or foreground of bed; good fresh-cut flower.	Spreading rhizomes troublesome only in moist, sandy soils.

Size	Appearance	Bloom Period	Light Requirements	Growing Requirements

CORNFLOWER, HARDY   *Centaurea montana*

24 in. tall; 24-in. spread.	Blue flowers; green foliage.	May–July.	Full sun to partial sun.	Poor, well-drained soil.

COSMOS   *Cosmos bipinnatus*

72 in. tall; 12-in. spread.	Crimson, pink, or white flowers; feathery green foliage.	June–Oct.	Full sun to partial sun.	Poor, sandy, or ordinary soil, kept on the dry side.

Look for: 'Sensation Mix'—earlier flowering and can be direct-sown outdoors.

COSMOS, KLONDYKE   *Cosmos sulphureus*

30 in. tall; 12-in. spread.	Yellow, orange, or red flowers; fine-textured green foliage.	June–Oct.	Full sun.	Poor, sandy or ordinary soil, kept on the dry side.

Look for: 'Sunny Red'—AAS Award winner, scarlet, long flowering, and tolerant of neglect, 12-14 in. tall; 'Sunny Yellow'—yellow, 12-14 in. tall.

CROCUS, AUTUMN   *Crocus zonatus*

3 in. tall; 3-in. spread.	Lilac flowers; grassy green foliage.	Oct.	Deciduous shade; full sun; partial sun.	Rich soil.

Look for: *C. speciosus*—deep bluish purple and better but less commonly sold.

CROCUS, DUTCH   *Crocus vernus* hybrids

4 in. tall; 4-in. spread.	Purple or white flowers; grassy, fine-textured green foliage.	March–April.	Deciduous shade; full sun; partial sun.	Rich soil.

Look for: Snow crocus (*C. chrysanthus*)—smaller but earlier blooming, Feb.–April, brighter colors of yellow, cream, and blue, smaller flowers.

Propagation	Garden Types	Uses	Notes
Very Hardy Perennial	**Zones 4-8**		
By division or seed.	Sunny garden.	Middle or foreground of bed; good fresh-cut flower.	Cut down as soon as new growth appears at base for substantial second bloom period. Seeds itself freely.
Half-Hardy Annual	**Zones —**		
Sow seed indoors 6 weeks before setting out; sow outdoors after last frost.	Sunny garden.	Background of bed; good fresh-cut flower.	Rich soil encourages excessive height, delays bloom; pinch out terminal bud at 18 in. for bushiness; remove old flowers to prolong bloom.
Half-Hardy Annual	**Zones —**		
Sow seed indoors 6 weeks before setting out; sow outdoors after last frost.	Sunny garden; Bank Garden.	Middle or foreground of bed; good fresh-cut flower.	Require careful transplanting or grow in individual pots. Sow again in late spring for late summer bloom.
Hardy Bulb	**Zones 5-9**		
By division; plant 4 in. deep.	Sunny or shady garden; Woodland Garden, Bank Garden.	Foreground of bed; good fresh-cut flower.	Correct name is now *C. kotschyanus*, although still sold under *C. zonatus*. Plant under low ground cover so that flowers will not be hidden by taller foliage.
Very Hardy Bulb	**Zones 3-9**		
By division or seed; plant 4 in. deep.	Sunny or shady garden; Woodland Garden, Bank Garden.	Foreground of bed; under deciduous shrubs; good fresh-cut flower.	Many hybrids available in varying shades of purple and white, often with stripes. Largest-flowered crocus and latest to bloom.

Size	Appearance	Bloom Period	Light Requirements	Growing Requirements

CROWN IMPERIAL   *Fritillaria imperialis*

Size	Appearance	Bloom Period	Light Requirements	Growing Requirements
30-48 in. tall; 12-in. spread.	Red, orange, or yellow flowers; narrow green foliage.	April.	Full sun; partial sun; partial shade.	Rich, well-drained soil.

DAFFODIL (NARCISSUS)   *Narcissus* hybrids

Size	Appearance	Bloom Period	Light Requirements	Growing Requirements
4-15 in. tall; 4-8-in. spread.	Yellow, orange, and/or white flowers; straplike green foliage.	March-April.	Deciduous shade; partial sun; full sun.	Rich soil.

DAHLIA   *Dahlia* hybrids

Size	Appearance	Bloom Period	Light Requirements	Growing Requirements
24-72 in. tall; 24-in. spread.	Red, orange, yellow, lavender, or white flowers; husky plants with dark green foliage.	June-Oct.	Full sun to partial sun.	Rich, moist soil.

DAHLIA, BEDDING   *Dahlia* hybrids

Size	Appearance	Bloom Period	Light Requirements	Growing Requirements
18 in. tall; 12-in. spread.	Red, yellow, pink, or lavender flowers; green foliage.	June-Oct.	Full sun.	Rich soil.

DAISY, GLORIOSA   *Rudbeckia hirta* hybrids

Size	Appearance	Bloom Period	Light Requirements	Growing Requirements
36 in. tall; 12-in. spread.	Yellow, orange, and rust flowers; green foliage.	June-Sept.	Full sun to partial sun.	Well-drained soil; drought tolerant.

DAISY, MICHAELMAS   *Aster* hybrids

Size	Appearance	Bloom Period	Light Requirements	Growing Requirements
12-60 in. tall; 12-in. spread.	Blue, white, pink, or lavender flowers; green foliage.	Aug.-Sept.	Full sun.	Adaptable to most conditions; good air circulation reduces leaf diseases.

Propagation	Garden Types	Uses	Notes
Hardy Bulb	**Zones 5-10**		
By division; plant 8 in. deep.	Sunny or shady garden; Bank Garden.	Middle of bed; good fresh-cut flower.	Popular, expensive, and not the easiest to grow; it will thrive in just the right spot. Plant has a skunky odor.
Very Hardy Bulb	**Zones 4-10**		
By division; plant 4-8 in. deep.	Sunny or shady garden; Woodland Garden, Bank Garden.	Middle or foreground of bed; good fresh-cut flower.	Hot locations promote end rot during summer; mulch helps to keep soil cool. Among the easiest and showiest of garden bulbs.
Annual Bulb	**Zones —**		
Divide tubers in spring and replant; be sure piece of central stem and bud is attached to each tuber.	Sunny garden.	Background or middle of bed; good fresh-cut flower.	Hybrids available with different flower types, including peony flowered, cactus, and pompon; most need staking.
Half-Hardy Annual	**Zones —**		
Sow seed indoors in March; also by division.	Sunny garden; Bank Garden.	Middle or foreground of bed; edging; good fresh-cut flower.	Roots may be stored for winter, divided, and replanted in spring.
Hardy Annual	**Zones —**		
Sow seed outdoors when soil is warm, or indoors 8-10 weeks before last frost, for earlier bloom.	Sunny garden.	Middle of bed; good fresh-cut flower.	Heat tolerant. Cut dead flowers to prolong bloom. Tall varieties need staking.
Very Hardy Perennial	**Zones 4-9**		
By division.	Sunny garden; Bank Garden.	Background or foreground of bed; edging, depending on variety.	Pinch tall (36-60 in.) varieties twice before mid-July for bushiness. Dwarfs (12-15 in.) self-branching. Most not good for cutting; 'Harrington's Pink' is an exception.

205

Size	Appearance	Bloom Period	Light Requirements	Growing Requirements

DAISY, PAINTED (PYRETHRUM)   *Chrysanthemum coccineum*

Size	Appearance	Bloom Period	Light Requirements	Growing Requirements
24 in. tall; 12-in. spread.	Pink, red, or white flowers; fernlike green foliage.	May–July.	Full sun; partial sun; partial shade.	Well-drained soil.

DAISY, SHASTA   *Chrysanthemum superbum*

Size	Appearance	Bloom Period	Light Requirements	Growing Requirements
24-36 in. tall; 12-in. spread.	White flowers; green foliage.	June–Aug.	Full sun; partial sun; partial shade.	Rich, well-drained soil.

Look for: 'Alaska'—commonly grown seed, variable growth habits, needs staking; 'Starburst'—new hybrid with large flowers on strong, straight stems, unusually uniform from seed.

DAYLILY   *Hemerocallis* hybrids

Size	Appearance	Bloom Period	Light Requirements	Growing Requirements
12-48 in. tall; 24-in. spread.	Red, pink, yellow, orange, and/or purple flowers; low, straplike green foliage.	May–Sept. A few varieties sweetly scented.	Full sun; partial sun; partial shade.	Well-drained soil.

Look for: 'Bertie Ferrif'—20 in. tall, orange; 'Fairy Tale Pink'—24 in. tall; 'Pardon Me'—18 in. tall, red, repeat bloomer; 'Russian Rhapsody'—30 in. tall, lavender; 'Stella de Oro'—18 in. tall, golden yellow, repeat bloomer.

DEAD-NETTLE   *Lamium maculatum*

Size	Appearance	Bloom Period	Light Requirements	Growing Requirements
8 in. tall; 12-in. spread.	Pink or white flowers; variegated silver leaves.	April–Aug.	Partial sun; partial shade; full shade.	Adapts to dry shade conditions in average soil.

Look for: 'Beacon Silver'—silver leaves with green edges, pink flowers; 'White Nancy'—a white-flowered sport of 'Beacon Silver'; 'Herman's Pride'—leaves speckled with silver, yellow flowers.

DELPHINIUM (LARKSPUR)   *Delphinium elatum* **hybrids**

Size	Appearance	Bloom Period	Light Requirements	Growing Requirements
30-72 in. tall; 24-in. spread.	Blue, purple, white, or pink flowers; green foliage.	June–July.	Full sun to partial sun.	Rich, well-drained soil.

Look for: 'Pacific Coast Strains'—elegant, 60-72 in. tall, available in single color strains; 'Connecticut Yankee Strains'—30 in. tall; *D. belladonna*—48 in. tall, continuous bloom.

Propagation	Garden Types	Uses	Notes
Very Hardy Perennial	**Zones 4-9**		
By seed or division.	Sunny or shady garden.	Middle of bed; good fresh-cut flower.	Also called *Pyrethrum coccineum.* Short-lived plant; divide every 2-3 years to prolong life span.
Hardy Perennial	**Zones 5-9**		
By division or seed.	Sunny garden.	Background or middle of bed; good fresh-cut flower.	Divide every 2-3 years or plant will die out. Many varieties available, some with double or frilled flowers, some with shorter growth.
Very Hardy Perennial	**Zones 3-8**		
By division or seed.	Sunny or shady garden.	Middle or foreground of bed; edging; good fresh-cut flower.	Many hybrids available with varying bloom season and color. A few new hybrids are everblooming, but most last about a month.
Very Hardy Perennial	**Zones 4-9**		
By cuttings or division.	Shady garden; Woodland Garden, Bank Garden.	Foreground of bed; ground cover; edging.	Excellent ground cover, not invasive like the common dead-nettle.
Very Hardy Perennial	**Zones 3-7**		
By seed.	Sunny garden.	Background or middle of bed; good for cutting fresh or drying.	Short-lived perennial. In areas with hot summers, grow as annual started indoors in early winter, set out in early spring. Most need staking.

Size	Appearance	Bloom Period	Light Requirements	Growing Requirements
DUSTY MILLER *Senecio cineraria*				
12 in. tall; 12-in. spread.	Insignificant yellow flowers; fernlike silver-gray foliage.	—	Full sun to partial sun.	Well-drained soil; drought tolerant.
EUROPEAN GINGER *Asarum europeum*				
6 in. tall; 12-in. spread.	Insignificant flowers; rounded, kidney-shaped, dark green foliage.	—	Partial shade to full shade.	Rich, moist soil.
FERN Many genera				
12-24 in. tall; 12-24-in. spread.	No flowers; foliage light to dark green, some with silvery markings, usually deciduous.	—	Full shade to partial shade.	Rich soil. Some will take fairly dry conditions when shaded.

Look for: Christmas fern — 24 × 24 in., dark green, evergreen; Japanese painted fern — 12 × 12 in., silvery; lady fern — 24 × 24 in., lacy light green foliage; maidenhair fern — light green.

Size	Appearance	Bloom Period	Light Requirements	Growing Requirements
FOAM FLOWER *Tiarella cordifolia*				
12 in. tall; 8-in. spread.	White flowers; green foliage.	May-June.	Partial shade to full shade.	Rich soil, prefers acid pH; moderately drought tolerant.

Look for: *T. wherryi* — similar but nonspreading.

Size	Appearance	Bloom Period	Light Requirements	Growing Requirements
FORGET-ME-NOT *Myosotis sylvatica*				
9 in. tall; 6-in. spread.	Tiny blue, pink, or white flowers; narrow, emerald green foliage.	April-June.	Full sun; partial sun; partial shade.	Rich, moist, well-drained soil.

Look for: 'Victoria' — most popular blue variety.

Size	Appearance	Bloom Period	Light Requirements	Growing Requirements
FOUR-O'CLOCK *Mirabilis jalapa*				
30 in. tall; 24-in. spread.	Red, yellow, pink, lavender, or white flowers; bright green foliage.	July-Oct. Sweetly scented.	Full sun; partial sun; partial shade.	Very adaptable; drought tolerant.

Propagation	Garden Types	Uses	Notes

Hardy Annual   Zones 7-10

Sow seed indoors in April, germinates in 5-20 days; also by cuttings.	Sunny garden; Bank Garden.	Middle or foreground of bed; edging; foliage good for cutting fresh or drying.	Prized for its silver-gray foliage. Actually a short-lived perennial, hardy south of Zone 7.

Very Hardy Perennial   Zones 4-8

By division.	Shady garden; Woodland Garden, Bank Garden.	Foreground of bed; ground cover; edging.	Evergreen in the South. Spreads by creeping rhizomes. Not the same as edible ginger.

Perennial   Zones 3-8

By division or spores.	Shady border; Woodland Garden; shady Bank Garden.	Back, middle, or foreground of bed; ground cover; edging. Foliage good for cutting fresh.	Adds a delightful textural contrast to other shade plants.

Very Hardy Perennial   Zones 3-8

By division or seed.	Shady garden; Woodland Garden, Bank Garden.	Foreground of bed; ground cover; edging.	Spreads by runners; may be invasive but is easy to pull out.

Hardy Annual/Biennial   Zones —

As annual, sow seed indoors in Feb.; as biennial (in South), sow in July; often seeds itself in the garden.	Sunny or shady garden; Woodland Garden, Bank Garden.	Middle or foreground of bed; edging; good fresh-cut flower.	Popular for clusters of tiny, sky-blue flowers. Early blooming, so often planted among daffodils, tulips, and early perennials.

Half-Hardy Annual   Zones —

Sow seed indoors in late March, germinates in 10 days.	Sunny or shady garden.	Background or middle of bed.	Flowers open around 4 o'clock. Store tuberous roots for the winter like dahlias. Guard against Japanese beetles.

209

Size	Appearance	Bloom Period	Light Requirements	Growing Requirements

FOXGLOVE *Digitalis purpurea*

Size	Appearance	Bloom Period	Light Requirements	Growing Requirements
24-60 in. tall; 18-in. spread.	Purple, lavender, pink, or white flowers; coarse green foliage.	June-July.	Full sun; partial sun; partial shade.	Rich soil; moderately drought tolerant.

Look for: 'Excelsior'—good biennial strain; 'Foxy'—can be grown as an annual.

GAS PLANT *Dictamnus albus*

Size	Appearance	Bloom Period	Light Requirements	Growing Requirements
30 in. tall; 36-in. spread.	Pink or white flowers; moderately coarse green foliage.	June.	Full sun.	Rich, well-drained, moist soil.

GAY-FEATHER *Liatris pycnostachya*

Size	Appearance	Bloom Period	Light Requirements	Growing Requirements
60 in. tall; 12-in. spread.	Purple or white flowers; narrow green foliage.	July-Sept.	Full sun.	Rich, well-drained soil; drought tolerant.

Look for: 'Alba'—white; 'September Glory'—purple; 'White Spire'—white; last two bloom in late Sept.

GAZANIA *Gazania ringens*

Size	Appearance	Bloom Period	Light Requirements	Growing Requirements
8-10 in. tall; 8-in. spread.	Yellow, cream, orange, pink, and bronze flowers; green foliage.	May-Oct.	Full sun.	Sandy, well-drained soil; drought tolerant.

GERANIUM, HARDY *Geranium himalayense*

Size	Appearance	Bloom Period	Light Requirements	Growing Requirements
15 in. tall; 12-in. spread.	Blue flowers; green foliage.	June-July.	Full sun; partial sun; partial shade.	Moist, well-drained soil.

Look for: 'Johnson's Blue'—an excellent hybrid, very similar to *G. himalayense*.

GERANIUM, HARDY *Geranium maculatum*

Size	Appearance	Bloom Period	Light Requirements	Growing Requirements
24 in. tall; 18-in. spread.	Lilac-pink flowers; green foliage.	May.	Partial sun to partial shade.	Rich soil.

Propagation	Garden Types	Uses	Notes

Hardy Biennial/Annual — Zone 4

Propagation	Garden Types	Uses	Notes
Sow seed indoors 8-10 weeks before last frost.	Sunny or shady garden; Woodland Garden.	Background or middle of bed; good fresh-cut flower.	Replace old plants after they bloom in July, or flowers will be small next year. Can be grown as annual if started early indoors.

Very Hardy Perennial — Zones 3-8

Propagation	Garden Types	Uses	Notes
By seed.	Sunny garden.	Middle of bed.	Very long-lived, nearly permanent perennial; avoid transplanting. On quiet days, match held below flowers will ignite volatile gas given off by flowers.

Very Hardy Perennial — Zones 3-8

Propagation	Garden Types	Uses	Notes
By division or seed.	Sunny garden.	Vertical accent in background or middle of bed; good for cutting fresh or drying.	Flowers on spike open at top first. Poor drainage in winter cuts short life span. *L. scariosa* needs drier site, is much more drought tolerant.

Tender Annual — Zones —

Propagation	Garden Types	Uses	Notes
Sow seed indoors in late March.	Sunny garden; Bank Garden.	Foreground of bed; edging; good fresh-cut flower.	Seems to be preferred food of rabbits.

Very Hardy Perennial — Zones 4-9

Propagation	Garden Types	Uses	Notes
By division or seed.	Sunny or shady garden; Woodland Garden, Bank Garden.	Middle or foreground of bed; ground cover; edging.	Also called *G. grandiflorum.*

Very Hardy Perennial — Zones 4-9

Propagation	Garden Types	Uses	Notes
By division or seed.	Shady garden; Woodland Garden, Bank Garden.	Middle or foreground of bed; ground cover.	Only species native to North America.

Size	Appearance	Bloom Period	Light Requirements	Growing Requirements

GERANIUM, HARDY   *Geranium sanguineum*

Size	Appearance	Bloom Period	Light Requirements	Growing Requirements
12 in. tall; 12-in. spread.	Pink flowers; fine-textured green foliage.	May–Sept.	Full sun; partial sun; partial shade.	Rich; well-drained soil.

Look for: *G. sanguineum* var. *lancastriense*—clear pink, 6 in. tall, excellent plant form; 'Shepherd's Warning'—clear, rose-pink, 4 in. tall.

GERANIUM, ZONAL   *Pelargonium hortorum* hybrids

Size	Appearance	Bloom Period	Light Requirements	Growing Requirements
18 in. tall; 12-in. spread.	Red, pink, white, or lavender flowers; rounded green foliage.	May–Oct.	Full sun; partial sun; partial shade.	Very adaptable; drought tolerant.

GEUM   *Geum* hybrids

Size	Appearance	Bloom Period	Light Requirements	Growing Requirements
12–24 in. tall; 12-in. spread.	Yellow, orange, or red flowers; low-growing green foliage.	May–June.	Full sun; partial sun; partial shade.	Rich, well-drained soil.

Look for: 'Lady Stratheden' (yellow) and 'Mrs. Bradshaw' (red)—most common; 'Borisii'—good old garden variety with orange flowers.

GLADIOLUS   *Gladiolus* hybrids

Size	Appearance	Bloom Period	Light Requirements	Growing Requirements
36–48 in. tall; 8-in. spread.	Red, pink, yellow, apricot, lavender, or green flowers; straplike green leaves.	June–Oct.	Full sun to partial sun.	Rich, well-drained soil.

GLOBE AMARANTH   *Gomphrena globosa*

Size	Appearance	Bloom Period	Light Requirements	Growing Requirements
6–18 in. tall; 6-12-in. spread.	Purple, white, or rose flowers; green foliage.	June–Oct.	Full sun.	Adaptable to most soils, but avoid rich soils; drought tolerant.

Look for: 'Buddy'—an excellent plant with glowing purple flowers, 6-8 in. tall; *G. haageana*—orange flowers.

GLOBE THISTLE   *Echinops* 'Taplow Blue'

Size	Appearance	Bloom Period	Light Requirements	Growing Requirements
48–60 in. tall; 24-in. spread.	Spherical blue flowers; coarse green foliage.	July–Aug.	Full sun to partial sun.	Well-drained soil.

Propagation	Garden Types	Uses	Notes
Very Hardy Perennial	**Zones 4-9**		
By division, cuttings, or seed.	Sunny or shady garden; Woodland Garden, Bank Garden.	Foreground of bed; ground cover; edging.	Long flowering, very adaptable perennial.
Tender Annual	**Zones —**		
Sow seed indoors in Jan.; also by cuttings.	Sunny or shady garden.	Middle or foreground of bed; edging; good for cutting fresh or drying.	Actually a tropical perennial. Old plants can be trained to several feet tall if kept indoors.
Very Hardy Perennial	**Zones 4-8**		
By division or seed.	Sunny garden; Bank Garden.	Foreground of bed; edging; good fresh-cut flower.	Short-lived perennial. Many hybrids are available.
Annual Bulb	**Zones —**		
Plant corms outdoors when soil has warmed; plant 6 in. deep.	Sunny garden.	Background or middle of bed; good fresh-cut flower.	For succession of flowers, plant every 3 weeks until July. Good for accent in middle of bed among other flowers to cover bare spaces.
Half-Hardy Annual	**Zones —**		
Sow seed 6-8 weeks before planting out, germinates in 20-25 days; soak seeds in hot water to speed germination.	Sunny garden; Bank Garden.	Middle or foreground of bed; edging; good for cutting fresh or drying.	Very easy to grow; prolific bloomer.
Very Hardy Perennial	**Zones 4-9**		
By division.	Sunny garden.	Background or middle of bed; good for cutting fresh or drying.	After first bloom, cut out old stems at soil level to encourage more flowers.

Size	Appearance	Bloom Period	Light Requirements	Growing Requirements

GLORY-OF-THE-SNOW   *Chionodoxa luciliae*

Size	Appearance	Bloom Period	Light Requirements	Growing Requirements
6 in. tall; 3-in. spread.	Blue flowers with white center; straplike green foliage.	April.	Deciduous shade; partial sun; full sun.	Generally adaptable.

GOAT'S-BEARD   *Aruncus dioicus*

Size	Appearance	Bloom Period	Light Requirements	Growing Requirements
72 in. tall; 36-in. spread.	Plumy white flowers; fernlike green foliage.	June-July.	Partial shade; partial sun; full sun.	Rich, moist soil.

GOLDEN STAR   *Chrysogonum virginianum*

Size	Appearance	Bloom Period	Light Requirements	Growing Requirements
8 in. tall; 12-in. spread.	Yellow flowers; green foliage.	May-Oct.	Partial sun to partial shade.	Rich, moist soil.

GRASS, ORNAMENTAL   Various genera

Size	Appearance	Bloom Period	Light Requirements	Growing Requirements
36-72 in. tall; 15-36-in. spread.	Decorative tan to purple flower heads held above foliage; leaves narrow and arching.	July-Nov.	Full sun to partial sun.	Adaptable to most soil and moisture conditions.

Look for: Eulalia grass (*Miscanthus sinensis*)—72 × 36 in., tan flowers last Sept.-Nov.; fountain grass (*Pennisetum alopecuroides*)—36-48 × 18 in., purple flowers last Aug.-Sept.; crimson fountain grass (*P. ruppelii*)—often grown as annual north of Zone 8.

GUINEA FLOWER   *Fritillaria meleagris*

Size	Appearance	Bloom Period	Light Requirements	Growing Requirements
12 in. tall; 4-in. spread.	Checkered purple and white flowers; grasslike green foliage.	April.	Partial shade to partial sun.	Rich, moist soil.

HELIOPSIS   *Heliopsis scabra*

Size	Appearance	Bloom Period	Light Requirements	Growing Requirements
36-48 in. tall; 24-in. spread.	Yellow flowers; green foliage.	June-Sept.	Full sun.	Rich, moist, well-drained soil.

Propagation	Garden Types	Uses	Notes
Very Hardy Bulb	**Zones 3-10**		
By division or may reseed in garden; plant 4 in. deep.	Sunny or shady garden; Woodland Garden, Bank Garden.	Foreground of bed; plant under deciduous shrubs; good fresh-cut flower.	One of the easiest small bulbs to grow. Will easily reseed in favorable locations.
Hardy Perennial	**Zones 5-9**		
By division or seed.	Sunny or shady garden; Woodland Garden.	Background or middle of bed; good for drying.	Native plant; resembles a huge astilbe.
Hardy Perennial	**Zones 6-9**		
By division or seed.	Shady garden; Woodland Garden, Bank Garden.	Foreground of bed; edging; good fresh-cut flower.	Native plant. Good types available with long flowering periods.
Hardy Perennial/Annual	**Zones 6-9**		
By division in spring or by seed.	Sunny garden.	Back, middle, or foreground of bed or edging, depending on height; good for cutting fresh or drying.	Grasses' graceful forms complement other plants or stand well alone.
Very Hardy Bulb	**Zones 3-10**		
By division or may reseed in garden; plant 4 in. deep.	Shady garden; Woodland Garden.	Foreground of bed.	Naturalizes in moist locations.
Very Hardy Perennial	**Zones 3-9**		
By division, cuttings, or seed.	Sunny garden.	Background or middle of bed; good fresh-cut flower.	Color is very strong golden yellow. Watch for red aphids in midsummer. Many varieties available, all good and long blooming.

Size	Appearance	Bloom Period	Light Requirements	Growing Requirements
HONESTY (MONEYWORT) *Lunaria annua*				
24 in. tall; 12-in. spread.	Purple or white flowers; green foliage.	April-May.	Partial sun to partial shade.	Prefers normal soil with adequate moisture.
HOSTA (PLANTAIN LILY; FUNKIA) *Hosta* hybrids				
18-60 in. tall; 12-36-in. spread.	White to purple flowers; large, wide, green, blue-green, or yellow foliage, often variegated.	June-Sept.	Partial sun; partial shade; full shade.	Rich, moist soil.

Look for: 'Aureo-marginata'—24-36 × 36 in., gold-edged; 'Frances Williams'—24 × 36 in., blue-gray edged in gold; 'Ginko Craig'—8-12 × 12 in., white-edged; 'Golden Sunburst'—24 × 24 in., golden yellow; 'Krossa Regal'—60 × 36 in., blue-gray, stiffer, less arching than most hostas.

Size	Appearance	Bloom Period	Light Requirements	Growing Requirements
HYACINTH *Hyacinthus orientalis*				
12 in. tall; 6-in. spread.	Blue, pink, purple, or white flowers; straplike green foliage.	April. Very sweetly scented.	Full sun to partial sun.	Rich soil.
HYACINTH, GRAPE *Muscari armeniacum*				
12 in. tall; 3-in. spread.	Blue flowers; grasslike green foliage.	April-May.	Full sun to partial sun; deciduous shade.	Generally adaptable.
HYACINTH, WOOD (SPANISH BLUEBELL) *Endymion hispanicus*				
20 in. tall; 8-in. spread.	Blue, pink, or white flowers; straplike green foliage.	May.	Full sun; partial sun; deciduous shade.	Very adaptable.

Propagation	Garden Types	Uses	Notes
Hardy Biennial/Annual	**Zones —**		
Sow seed outdoors for bloom the following year, or start early indoors to treat as annual.	Sunny or shady garden; Woodland Garden.	Middle or foreground of bed; good for cutting fresh or drying.	Most prized for wide, rounded, papery seedpods, but also valuable for early flower spikes.
Very Hardy Perennial	**Zones 3-8**		
By division or seed.	Shady garden; Woodland Garden, Bank Garden.	Middle or foreground of bed; ground cover; edging; good fresh-cut flower.	Place in garden according to height of foliage, not flowers. Bloom season and size depends on variety.
Very Hardy Bulb	**Zones 4-10**		
By division; plant 6 in. deep.	Sunny garden.	Foreground of bed; good fresh-cut flower.	Jumbo-sized bulbs with huge flower heads tend to fall over; smaller flower heads of mid-sized bulbs stand better in garden. Size of flower head tends to decrease after first year, giving plant more natural appearance.
Very Hardy Bulb	**Zones 4-10**		
By division or may reseed in garden; plant 4 in. deep.	Sunny or shady garden; Woodland Garden, Bank Garden.	Foreground of bed; edging; good fresh-cut flower.	One of the easiest bulbs to grow; often naturalizes. Very pretty planted with other, larger spring bulbs.
Very Hardy Bulb	**Zones 4-10**		
By division; plant 6 in. deep.	Sunny or shady garden; Woodland Garden.	Middle or foreground of bed; good fresh-cut flower.	Usually sold as *Scilla campanulata* or *S. hispanica*. Very easy to grow and good for naturalizing.

Size	Appearance	Bloom Period	Light Requirements	Growing Requirements
IMPATIENS *Impatiens walleriana*				
8-15 in. tall; 12-in. spread.	Red, pink, purple, or white flowers; green foliage.	Continuous.	Partial sun; partial shade; full shade.	Rich, moist soil.
IMPATIENS, NEW GUINEA *Impatiens* hybrids				
12 in. tall; 12-in. spread.	Red, pink, salmon, or white flowers; green or bronze leaves, variegated with pink and yellow.	Continuous.	Full sun; partial sun; partial shade.	Rich, moist soil.

Look for: 'Sweet Sue' and 'Tangeglow'—both orange flowered and available as seed.

Size	Appearance	Bloom Period	Light Requirements	Growing Requirements
IRIS *Iris* spp.				
5-48 in. tall; 6-18-in. spread.	Available in almost every color; straplike green foliage.	April-July.	Full sun; partial sun; partial shade.	Adaptable but prefers rich soil. Japanese iris must have lime-free soil.

Look for: Bearded—8-36 × 6-12 in., needs sun, blooms April-June; crested—5 × 8 in., needs sun/shade, blooms May; Japanese—36-48 × 12-18 in., needs sunny, moist site, blooms June-July; Siberian—24-48 × 18 in., needs sun, blooms June-July.

Size	Appearance	Bloom Period	Light Requirements	Growing Requirements
LADY'S MANTLE *Alchemilla mollis*				
18 in. tall; 24-in. spread.	Greenish yellow flowers in billowy mass; rounded green foliage.	June-July.	Full sun; partial sun; partial shade.	Rich, moist soil.
LAMB'S-EARS (WOOLLY BETONY) *Stachys byzantina*				
10 in. tall; 12-in. spread.	Insignificant lavender flowers on silvery spikes; low-growing, silver foliage.	June-July.	Full sun; partial sun; partial shade.	Poor, well-drained soil; drought tolerant.

Look for: 'Silver Carpet'—a nonflowering variety.

Propagation	Garden Types	Uses	Notes
Tender Annual	**Zones —**		
Sow seed indoors in Feb.; easily grown from cuttings (simple way to save favorite plant).	Shady garden; Woodland Garden, Bank Garden.	Middle or foreground of bed; edging.	Many varieties are available; tallest grow to 15 in., lowest to 8 in.
Tender Annual	**Zones —**		
By cuttings.	Sunny or shady garden.	Foreground of bed; edging.	Will take more sun than common impatiens. Most varieties are only grown from cuttings.
Very Hardy Perennial	**Zones 3-8**		
By division or seed.	Sunny or shady garden; Woodland Garden, Bank Garden.	Middle or foreground of bed; edging; good fresh-cut flower.	In bearded iris, borers, soft rot, and leaf diseases may be problems but are seldom devastating. Intermediate-height bearded hybrids do best in garden because they need no staking.
Very Hardy Perennial	**Zones 3-9**		
By division or seed.	Sunny or shady garden; Bank Garden.	Foreground of bed; ground cover; edging; good for cutting fresh or drying.	This unusual color combines well with pinks and blues. *A. vulgaris* is very similar in appearance and growing requirements.
Very Hardy Perennial	**Zones 4-9**		
By division or seed.	Sunny or shady garden; Bank Garden.	Foreground of bed; edging.	Useful silver foliage plant for partially shady site. Many gardeners dislike flower spikes, but they give extra texture.

Size	Appearance	Bloom Period	Light Requirements	Growing Requirements

LARKSPUR   *Delphinium ajacis*

Size	Appearance	Bloom Period	Light Requirements	Growing Requirements
24-48 in. tall; 10-in. spread.	Blue, violet, rose, or pink flowers; fine-textured green foliage.	May–July.	Full sun; partial sun; partial shade.	Rich soil, kept on the dry side.

LEOPARD'S BANE   *Doronicum caucasisum*

Size	Appearance	Bloom Period	Light Requirements	Growing Requirements
18 in. tall; 12-in. spread.	Yellow, daisylike flowers; heart-shaped green foliage.	April–May.	Partial sun to full sun.	Rich, moist soil.

Look for: 'Miss Mason'—somewhat longer-lasting foliage.

LIGULARIA   *Ligularia dentata*

Size	Appearance	Bloom Period	Light Requirements	Growing Requirements
48 in. tall; 24-in. spread.	Yellow flowers; large, bold, dark green leaves.	July–Aug.	Partial sun to partial shade.	Rich, moist soil.

Look for: 'Desdemona' and 'Othello'—kidney-shaped leaves; *L. hodgsonii*—smaller, 24-36 in. tall; 'The Rocket'—72 in. tall with 36-in. spread; yellow flowers along elegant, tall, dark stems.

LILY   *Lilium* spp. and hybrids

Size	Appearance	Bloom Period	Light Requirements	Growing Requirements
24-48 in. tall; 8-24-in. spread.	Yellow, orange, pink, red, or white flowers on tall stems; narrow green foliage.	June–Sept.	Full sun to partial sun.	Rich, deep, well-drained soil.

Look for: Hybrid groups include Asiatic—24-60 × 8 in., flowers face up, blooms June; Aurelian—48-72 × 24 in., fragrant, trumpet-shaped flowers, blooms July-Aug.; Oriental—24-84 × 36 in., fragrant, blooms Aug.-Sept.

LILY-OF-THE-VALLEY   *Convallaria majalis*

Size	Appearance	Bloom Period	Light Requirements	Growing Requirements
8 in. tall; 12-in. spread.	White or pale pink flowers; wide green foliage.	May–June. Sweetly scented.	Partial shade to full shade.	Rich, well-drained soil; drought tolerant.

Look for: 'Rosea'—pale pink flowers, hard to come by.

Propagation	Garden Types	Uses	Notes
Hardy Annual	**Zones —**		
Sow seed outdoors in fall or early spring; dislikes transplanting. Once established, self-sown plants appear the following year.	Sunny or shady garden.	Background or middle of bed; good for cutting fresh or drying.	An old-fashioned, spiky accent for the early summer garden. Also called annual delphinium. Sometimes listed as *Consolida orientalis.*
Very Hardy Perennial	**Zones 4-7**		
By division or seed.	Sunny garden.	Middle of bed; good fresh-cut flower.	Foliage goes dormant in summer; cover spot with spreading perennials or annuals. While dormant don't let soil become too dry. Also called *D. cordatum.*
Very Hardy Perennial	**Zones 4-8**		
By division or seed.	Shady garden; Woodland Garden.	Background or middle of bed.	Protect from hot sun or leaves will temporarily wilt; requires constant moisture.
Very Hardy Perennial	**Zones 3-8**		
By division.	Sunny garden; Bank Garden.	Back or middle of bed, depending on height; good fresh-cut flower.	Many types of species and hybrids available.
Very Hardy Perennial	**Zones 2-8**		
By division.	Shady garden; Woodland Garden.	Foreground of bed; ground cover; edging; good fresh-cut flower.	Not evergreen, but a good, tight ground cover. Spreading rhizomes invasive.

Size	Appearance	Bloom Period	Light Requirements	Growing Requirements

LILY-TURF (LIRIOPE)   *Liriope muscari*

Size	Appearance	Bloom Period	Light Requirements	Growing Requirements
12 in. tall; 12-in. spread.	Purple or white flowers; grassy green foliage.	Aug.-Sept.	Partial sun to partial shade.	Very adaptable and tolerant of dry conditions.

Look for: *L. spicata*—less showy, hardier, blooms a month earlier.

LOBELIA   *Lobelia erinus*

Size	Appearance	Bloom Period	Light Requirements	Growing Requirements
8 in. tall; 6-in. spread.	Blue, pink, or white flowers; small green leaves.	May-Oct.	Full sun; partial sun; partial shade.	Rich, moist soil.

Look for: 'Cambridge Blue'—light blue; 'Crystal Palace'—dark blue.

LOOSESTRIFE, PURPLE   *Lythrum salicaria*

Size	Appearance	Bloom Period	Light Requirements	Growing Requirements
36-60 in. tall; 24-in. spread.	Spikes of purple or pink flowers; green foliage.	July-Aug.	Full sun; partial sun; partial shade.	Adaptable; will even grow in very wet soils.

Look for: 'Mordens Pink'—pink, no seeds, 36 in. tall; 'Dropmore Purple'—purple, 36 in. tall; 'Happy'—dark pink, 18 in. tall; 'Fire Candle'—rosy red.

LUNGWORT   *Pulmonaria saccharata*

Size	Appearance	Bloom Period	Light Requirements	Growing Requirements
12 in. tall; 12-in. spread.	Pink buds open to blue flowers; long green leaves speckled with silver.	April-May.	Partial shade to partial sun.	Rich, moist soil.

Look for: 'Mrs. Moon'—prominently speckled leaves; *P. angustifolia*—related species with green leaves and gentian-blue flowers.

LUPINE   *Lupinus* 'Russell Hybrids'

Size	Appearance	Bloom Period	Light Requirements	Growing Requirements
36 in. tall; 18-in. spread.	Blue, pink, purple, white, or yellow flowers; green foliage.	June	Full sun; partial sun; partial shade.	Rich, well-drained soil; prefers acid pH.

Propagation	Garden Types	Uses	Notes
Hardy Perennial	**Zones 6-9**		
By division or seed.	Sunny or shady garden; Woodland Garden, Bank Garden.	Foreground of bed; ground cover; edging; good fresh-cut flower.	Tough, adaptable, evergreen ground cover. Cut away winter-damaged leaves in March.
Half-Hardy Annual	**Zones —**		
Sow seed indoors late Feb.-early March.	Sunny or shady garden; Woodland Garden, Bank Garden.	Foreground of bed; edging; good for cutting fresh or drying.	Prized for clear blue color. Tends to die out in hot weather, so plant in cool northern exposure.
Very Hardy Perennial	**Zones 3-8**		
By division or seed.	Sunny or shady garden.	Background or middle of bed; good fresh-cut flower.	This European species can become a nuisance by seeding profusely and naturalizing in wetland habitats.
Very Hardy Perennial	**Zones 3-8**		
By division.	Shady garden; Woodland Garden.	Foreground of bed; edging; ground cover.	A good, tight, weedproof ground cover.
Very Hardy Perennial	**Zones 4-8**		
By seed.	Sunny garden.	Background or middle of bed.	Short-lived perennial; can be treated as an annual if seed is started early enough indoors. Provide afternoon shade in hot climates.

Size	Appearance	Bloom Period	Light Requirements	Growing Requirements
MARIGOLD	*Tagetes* species			
8-48 in. tall; 8-12-in. spread.	Yellow, orange, or rust flowers; green foliage.	June-Oct.	Full sun.	Adaptable but prefers rich, well-drained soil.
MEADOW RUE	*Thalictrum rochebrunianum*			
36-60 in. tall; 24-in. spread.	Large, airy clusters of lavender flowers; green foliage with fine texture.	July-Sept.	Partial shade; partial sun; full sun.	Rich, well-drained soil.

Look for: 'Lavender Mist'—same as type described above.

Size	Appearance	Bloom Period	Light Requirements	Growing Requirements
MEADOWSWEET, SIBERIAN	*Filipendula palmata*			
48 in. tall; 18-in. spread.	Pink flowers; coarse green foliage.	June-July.	Full sun; partial sun; partial shade.	Rich, moist soil.

Look for: 'Elegans'—most commonly offered form, pale pink; related species *F. purpurea* is similar but with cerise-pink flowers.

Size	Appearance	Bloom Period	Light Requirements	Growing Requirements
MONK'S-HOOD	*Aconitum carmichaelii*			
48 in. tall; 12-in. spread.	Blue flowers; green foliage.	Aug.-Sept.	Partial sun to partial shade.	Rich, moist soil.
MOSS ROSE	*Portulaca grandiflora*			
4-8 in. tall; 8-in. spread.	Yellow, white, red, orange, or pink flowers; small, narrow green leaves give a very fine texture.	June-Aug.	Full sun.	Poor, dry soil.

Propagation	Garden Types	Uses	Notes
Half-Hardy Annual	**Zones —**		
Sow seed indoors in early March, germinates in 1 week; easy to transplant.	Sunny garden.	Background to foreground of bed; edging, depending on variety; good fresh-cut flower.	Many varieties available, varying in color, height, flower size, and foliage. Pest and disease free. Foliage scent unpleasant to some people.
Very Hardy Perennial	**Zones 4-8**		
By division or seed.	Sunny or shady garden.	Background of bed.	Useful for its late summer bloom and contrasting foliage texture (leaves resembling those of columbine).
Very Hardy Perennial	**Zones 3-9**		
By division.	Sunny or shady garden.	Background or middle of bed.	Stiff stems need no staking.
Very Hardy Perennial	**Zones 2-7**		
By division.	Shady garden.	Background or middle of bed; good for cutting fresh or drying.	Also called *A. fischeri.* Avoid hot afternoon sun and hot locations. Very poisonous if eaten.
Tender Annual	**Zones —**		
Sow seed outdoors as soon as soil is warm, germinates in 18-20 days; also by cuttings.	Sunny garden; Bank Garden.	Foreground of bed; edging.	Will self-sow for following year; easily transplanted. Water when young; very drought tolerant later.

Size	Appearance	Bloom Period	Light Requirements	Growing Requirements
NASTURTIUM, DWARF *Tropaeolum minor*				
12 in. tall; 12-in. spread.	Yellow, orange, or cream flowers; rounded green foliage.	June–Oct. Some varieties sweetly scented.	Full sun.	Poor, well-drained, dry soil.
OBEDIENT PLANT (FALSE DRAGONHEAD) *Physostegia virginiana*				
24-36 in. tall; 18-in. spread.	Pink, purple, or white flowers; narrow green foliage.	Aug.–Oct.	Full sun; partial sun; partial shade.	Very adaptable.

Look for: 'Vivid'—lavender-pink, 24 in. tall; 'Bouquet Rose'—rosy pink, 24 in. tall; 'Summer Snow' —white, 36 in. tall; 'Variegata'—white-edged leaves, pink flowers, 36 in. tall.

Size	Appearance	Bloom Period	Light Requirements	Growing Requirements
ONION, GIANT FLOWERING *Allium giganteum*				
36-60 in. tall; 15-in. spread.	Purple flowers in dense ball; strap-like green foliage.	July.	Full sun.	Rich, very well drained soil.
ONION, FLOWERING *Allium aflatunense*				
30 in tall; 8-in. spread.	Lavender ball-shaped flowers; straplike green foliage.	May.	Full sun to partial sun; deciduous shade.	Well-drained soil.
ONION, FLOWERING *Allium albo-pilosum*				
24 in. tall; 8-in. spread.	Silvery-lilac, ball-shaped flowers; straplike green foliage.	May–June.	Full sun to partial sun.	Well-drained soil.

Propagation	Garden Types	Uses	Notes
Half-Hardy Annual	**Zones —**		
Sow seed outdoors after soil has warmed —too early and seeds rot; does not transplant well.	Sunny garden; Bank Garden.	Foreground of bed; edging; good fresh-cut flower.	Flower buds and unripe seeds give peppery flavor to salads, pickles. Watch for black aphids.
Very Hardy Perennial	**Zones 2-8**		
By division.	Sunny or shady garden; Woodland Garden.	Middle of bed; good fresh-cut flower.	Valuable for late bloom. Adaptable to a variety of sites; tends to be invasive. On poor, dry soils is shorter and on heavy soils is less invasive.
Hardy Bulb	**Zones 6-10**		
By division; plant 8 in. deep.	Sunny garden.	Background or middle of bed; good for cutting fresh or drying.	The most dramatic onion and useful for its late bloom season. Often difficult to grow; susceptible to black rot. Good drainage should help.
Hardy Bulb	**Zone 5**		
By division or seed; plant 6 in. deep.	Sunny or shady garden.	Middle of bed; good fresh-cut flower.	One of the easiest flowering onions to grow. Leaves die down promptly after flowering, before the end of May.
Very Hardy Bulb	**Zones 4-10**		
By division; plant 6 in. deep.	Sunny garden; Bank Garden.	Middle or foreground of bed; good for cutting fresh or drying.	Also called *A. christophii*. Flower heads are unusually large for their height.

Size	Appearance	Bloom Period	Light Requirements	Growing Requirements
PACHYSANDRA *Pachysandra terminalis*				
8 in. tall; 8-in. spread.	White flowers; whorled dark green foliage.	April-May.	Partial sun; partial shade; full shade.	Adaptable, but prefers rich soil with acid pH.

Look for: 'Green Carpet'—low, compact; 'Variegata'—white-edged leaves, brightens dark areas.

Size	Appearance	Bloom Period	Light Requirements	Growing Requirements
PANSY *Viola wittrockiana*				
8 in. tall; 8-in. spread.	Blue, yellow, red, white, and purple flowers; green foliage.	April-June. Sweetly scented.	Full sun; partial sun; partial shade.	Rich, moist soil.

Size	Appearance	Bloom Period	Light Requirements	Growing Requirements
PEONY *Paeonia lactiflora*				
24-48 in. tall; 18-in. spread.	Pink, white, or red flowers; coarse, dark green foliage.	June. Sweetly scented.	Full sun to partial sun.	Deep, rich soil; best to prepare 24 in. deep.

Size	Appearance	Bloom Period	Light Requirements	Growing Requirements
PERILLA *Perilla frutescens*				
30 in. tall; 12-in. spread.	Insignificant flowers in spikes; deep reddish purple foliage.	Sept.	Full sun; partial sun; partial shade.	Very adaptable; tolerates dry or moist soil.

Size	Appearance	Bloom Period	Light Requirements	Growing Requirements
PERIWINKLE *Vinca minor*				
6 in. tall; 12-in. spread.	Blue, purple, or white flowers; small, dark green leaves on creeping stems.	April-May.	Partial shade to full shade.	Well-drained soil.

Look for: 'La Grave' ('Bowle's Variety')—blue flowers, 'Miss Jekyll'—white flowers—are the best varieties; 'Multiplex'—double purple flowers.

Propagation	Garden Types	Uses	Notes
Very Hardy Perennial	**Zones 4-8**		
By division or cuttings.	Shady garden; Woodland Garden.	Foreground of bed; ground cover; edging.	Among the best ground covers; virtually weed-proof; tolerant of root competition in shade. A mulch is essential for rapid establishment.
Hardy Annual	**Zones —**		
Sow seed in Aug., grow over winter in cold frame (45°-60°F), plant out in April. South of Zone 6, plant out in fall, mulch lightly.	Sunny or shady garden; Bank Garden.	Middle or foreground of bed; edging; good fresh-cut flower.	Will take light frost; thrives in cool weather; tends to die out in heat of summer.
Very Hardy Perennial	**Zones 3-8**		
By division; very long-lived, so divide only to propagate. Cover eyes on tubers with no more than 1 in. soil.	Sunny garden.	Background or middle of bed; good fresh-cut flower.	Large flowers, to 10 in., available in double, single, anemone, and other forms. In spring, remove mulch and debris to discourage *Botrytis*, which kills shoots and flower buds.
Hardy Annual	**Zones —**		
Sow seed indoors in March, germinates in 8 days. Sow seed outdoors after last frost.	Sunny or shady garden; Woodland Garden.	Middle of bed; good fresh-cut foliage.	Easiest purple-foliaged annual. Reseeds profusely for next year's crop. Foliage has herbal scent.
Very Hardy Perennial	**Zones 3-8**		
By division or cuttings.	Shady garden; Woodland Garden.	Foreground of bed; ground cover; edging.	Useful ground cover and even denser and more effective in rich soil.

Size	Appearance	Bloom Period	Light Requirements	Growing Requirements

PERIWINKLE, ROSE (MADAGASCAR PERIWINKLE)   *Catharanthus roseus*

Size	Appearance	Bloom Period	Light Requirements	Growing Requirements
12-18 in. tall; 12-in. spread.	Pink, white, or rose flowers; dark green foliage.	June-Oct.	Full sun; partial sun; partial shade.	Adaptable to most soils.

PETUNIA   *Petunia hybrida*

Size	Appearance	Bloom Period	Light Requirements	Growing Requirements
18 in. tall; 8-12-in. spread.	Purple, pink, red, and white flowers; green foliage.	May-Oct. Sweetly scented.	Full sun; partial sun; partial shade.	Adaptable to most well-drained soils.

PHLOX, ANNUAL   *Phlox drummondii*

Size	Appearance	Bloom Period	Light Requirements	Growing Requirements
12-18 in. tall; 8-in. spread.	Pink, red, salmon, or purple flowers; fine-textured green foliage.	June-Sept.	Full sun; partial sun; partial shade.	Adaptable.

PHLOX, CREEPING   *Phlox stolonifera*

Size	Appearance	Bloom Period	Light Requirements	Growing Requirements
6 in. tall; 8-in. spread.	Blue, purple, pink, or white flowers; small green leaves; foliage lower than flowers.	May.	Partial sun; partial shade; full shade.	Rich, well-drained soil; prefers acid pH.

Look for: 'Sherwood Purple'—purple, vigorous growth; 'Blue Ridge'—blue; 'Pink Ridge'—best pink-flowered type; 'Alba'—white.

PHLOX, SUMMER   *Phlox paniculata*

Size	Appearance	Bloom Period	Light Requirements	Growing Requirements
36-48 in. tall; 24-in. spread.	Pink, lavender, red, or white flowers; green foliage.	July-Aug. Very fragrant.	Full sun to partial sun.	Rich, moist, well-drained soil.

PHLOX, WILD BLUE (WILD SWEET WILLIAM)   *Phlox divaricata*

Size	Appearance	Bloom Period	Light Requirements	Growing Requirements
15 in. tall; 12-in. spread.	Light blue or white flowers; fine-textured green foliage.	May-June.	Partial shade; partial sun; full sun.	Rich, well-drained soil.

Look for: 'Fuller's White'—good white-flowered form.

Propagation	Garden Types	Uses	Notes
Tender Annual	**Zones —**		
Sow seed indoors early March, germinates in 10 days; also by cuttings.	Sunny or shady garden.	Middle or foreground of bed; edging.	Also called *Vinca roseus.* Very pest and disease resistant.
Half-Hardy Annual	**Zones —**		
Sow seed indoors early March, germinates in 10-12 days.	Sunny garden; Bank Garden.	Middle or foreground of bed; edging.	Flowers can be double, single, or ruffled. Cascading forms available. Rejuvenate midsummer by cutting back, feeding, and watering.
Half-Hardy Annual	**Zones —**		
Best when seeds sown early indoors in March, or sow outdoors when trees leaf out.	Sunny garden; Bank Garden.	Foreground of bed; edging; good fresh-cut flower.	Use care in transplanting.
Very Hardy Perennial	**Zones 3-8**		
By cuttings or division.	Shady garden; Woodland Garden, Bank Garden.	Foreground of bed; ground cover; edging; good fresh-cut flower.	Flowers with azaleas and likes the same growing conditions. Spreads by stolons but easily pulled if it creeps out-of-bounds.
Very Hardy Perennial	**Zones 3-8**		
By division or cuttings.	Sunny garden.	Background or middle of bed; good fresh-cut flower.	Many varieties available in various colors. Provide good air circulation to reduce powdery mildew; some varieties more resistant than others.
Very Hardy Perennial	**Zones 3-8**		
By division or seed.	Shady or sunny garden; Woodland Garden, Bank Garden.	Foreground of bed; edging; good fresh-cut flower.	Native plant. Dies down in summer.

Size	Appearance	Bloom Period	Light Requirements	Growing Requirements

PINK, ALLWOOD   *Dianthus allwoodii*

Size	Appearance	Bloom Period	Light Requirements	Growing Requirements
12 in. tall; 8-12 in. spread.	Pink, purple, or white flowers on stems above the foliage; fine-textured gray-green foliage.	May-June. Sweetly scented.	Full sun to partial sun.	Sandy, well-drained soil.

Look for: 'Blanche'—double, white-fringed petals; 'Doris'—double, salmon pink with deep pink eye; 'Helen'—deep salmon pink; 'Ian'—compact, double, crimson.

PINK, MOSS   *Phlox subulata*

Size	Appearance	Bloom Period	Light Requirements	Growing Requirements
4 in. tall; 12-in. spread.	Blue, pink, or white flowers; fine-textured green foliage.	April-May.	Full sun to partial sun.	Sandy, well-drained soil; prefers alkaline pH, but adaptable.

PLUMBAGO (LEADWORT)   *Ceratostigma plumbaginoides*

Size	Appearance	Bloom Period	Light Requirements	Growing Requirements
6 in. tall; 12-in. spread.	Blue flowers; small green leaves.	Aug.-Sept.	Full sun; partial sun; partial shade.	Well-drained soil.

POPPY, OPIUM   *Papaver somniferum*

Size	Appearance	Bloom Period	Light Requirements	Growing Requirements
36-48 in. tall; 6-in. spread.	White, pink, or red flowers, coarse, ragged silvery foliage.	June-Aug.	Full sun.	Adaptable but prefers light, well-drained soil.

POPPY, ORIENTAL   *Papaver orientale*

Size	Appearance	Bloom Period	Light Requirements	Growing Requirements
24-48 in. tall; 18-in. spread.	Red, orange, pink, or white flowers; coarse, ragged green foliage.	June.	Full sun to partial sun.	Well-drained soil.

Propagation	Garden Types	Uses	Notes
Very Hardy Perennial	**Zones 4-8**		
By cuttings or layering.	Sunny garden; Bank Garden.	Foreground of bed; edging; good fresh-cut flower.	Will continue to rebloom if dead-headed. Available in single or double (with extra petals) forms.
Very Hardy Perennial	**Zones 3-8**		
By cuttings or division.	Sunny garden; Bank Garden.	Foreground of bed; ground cover; edging.	Very fine, stiff foliage forms low mat. Flowers appear among foliage.
Hardy Perennial	**Zones 6-9**		
By division or cuttings.	Sunny or shady garden; Bank Garden.	Foreground of bed; ground cover; edging.	Plant spring bulbs underneath. Turns bronze in fall. Rhizomes somewhat invasive.
Hardy Annual	**Zones —**		
Sow seed outdoors after danger of heavy frost; avoid transplanting. Repeat sowings for longer bloom.	Sunny garden.	Background or middle of bed; good for cutting fresh or drying.	Available in carnation-flowered, peony-flowered, or tulip-flowered forms. For arrangement, cut flowers in bud and sear stem. Not the opium-producing variety.
Very Hardy Perennial	**Zones 3-8**		
By division, root cuttings, or seed.	Sunny garden.	Background or middle of bed; good for cutting fresh or drying.	Foliage dies down in July, reappears in Sept.; plan for other flowers to hide this gap. For arrangement, cut flowers in bud and sear stem. White varieties short-lived.

Size	Appearance	Bloom Period	Light Requirements	Growing Requirements

POPPY, SHIRLEY (CORN POPPY)   *Papaver rhoeas*

Size	Appearance	Bloom Period	Light Requirements	Growing Requirements
30-36 in. tall; 12-in. spread.	Pink, red, salmon, or white flowers; green foliage.	June-Aug.	Full sun to partial sun.	Light, well-drained soil.

PRIMROSE, POLYANTHUS   *Primula polyanthus*

Size	Appearance	Bloom Period	Light Requirements	Growing Requirements
10 in. tall; 8-12-in. spread.	All colors of flowers; green foliage in rosette form.	April-May. Sweetly scented.	Partial shade to partial sun.	Rich, moist, well-drained soil.

QUEEN-OF-THE-PRAIRIE   *Filipendula rubra*

Size	Appearance	Bloom Period	Light Requirements	Growing Requirements
48-72 in. tall; 36-in. spread.	Pink flowers; coarse green foliage.	June-July.	Full sun to partial sun.	Rich, moist soil.

Look for: 'Venusta' ('Magnifica')—deepest pink, most common; 'Venusta Alba' ('Magnifica Alba') —white, shorter at 36-60 in.

RED-HOT-POKER   *Kniphofia* hybrids

Size	Appearance	Bloom Period	Light Requirements	Growing Requirements
18-36 in. tall; 18-in. spread.	Orange, yellow, red, and white flower spikes; long, narrow, grasslike green foliage.	June-Sept.	Full sun to partial sun.	Rich, moist, well-drained soil.

Look for: 'Earliest of All'—coral, 30 in. tall; 'Royal Standard'—flowers have red top, yellow bottom, 36 in. tall; 'Primrose Beauty'—pale yellow, 30 in. tall.

SAGE, MEALY-CUP   *Salvia farinacea*

Size	Appearance	Bloom Period	Light Requirements	Growing Requirements
24-36 in. tall; 12-in. spread.	Blue or white flowers; green foliage.	June-Oct.	Full sun; partial sun; partial shade.	Adaptable.

Look for: 'Victoria'—popular blue variety for bedding and cutting, 18 in. tall.

SAGE, RUSSIAN   *Perovskia atriplicifolia*

Size	Appearance	Bloom Period	Light Requirements	Growing Requirements
36 in. tall; 18-in. spread.	Lavender-blue flowers; fine-textured silvery foliage.	July-Aug.	Full sun.	Poor, well-drained, dry soil.

Propagation	Garden Types	Uses	Notes
Hardy Annual	**Zones —**		
Sow seed in fall where winters are mild, elsewhere in early spring, germinates in 15 days; does not transplant well.	Sunny garden.	Middle of bed; good for cutting fresh or drying.	Dead-head for prolonged bloom. Self-sows abundantly for future years. Repeat sowings for longer bloom. For arrangements, cut flowers in bud, sear stem.
Very Hardy Perennial	**Zones 3-8**		
By division or seed.	Shady garden; Woodland Garden.	Foreground of bed; edging; good fresh-cut flower.	Prefers constantly moist soil with afternoon shade in hot climates. The most common type of primrose.
Very Hardy Perennial	**Zones 3-9**		
By division or seed.	Sunny garden.	Background of bed; good for cutting fresh or drying.	Rarely needs staking in spite of its height.
Hardy Perennial	**Zones 5-9**		
By division or seed.	Sunny garden.	Middle or foreground of bed; good fresh-cut flower.	Often listed as tritoma. In northern areas mulch for winter protection.
Hardy Annual	**Zones —**		
Sow seed indoors in late Feb.; also by cuttings or division.	Sunny or shady garden.	Middle or foreground of bed; good for cutting fresh or drying.	Actually a perennial that is hardy in the South.
Very Hardy Perennial	**Zones 3-9**		
By division or cuttings.	Sunny garden.	Middle of bed; good fresh-cut flower.	Must have full sun and good drainage to do well.

Size	Appearance	Bloom Period	Light Requirements	Growing Requirements
SAGE, SCARLET (SALVIA)	*Salvia splendens*			
12-36 in. tall; 8-12-in. spread.	Scarlet, salmon, purple, or white flowers; green foliage.	June-Oct.	Full sun; partial sun; partial shade.	Very adaptable to most soils.

    Look for: 'Carabiniere'—scarlet, 12-14 in. tall; 'Laser Purple'—purple, 10-12 in. tall; 'Carabiniere White'—white, 12-14 in. tall; 'Rose Flame'—salmon pink, 24 in. tall.

Size	Appearance	Bloom Period	Light Requirements	Growing Requirements
SALVIA (SAGE)	*Salvia superba*			
18-36 in. tall; 18-in. spread.	Purple flowers; green foliage.	June-Aug.	Full sun.	Poor, well-drained soil.

    Look for: 'East Friesland' and 'May Night' ('Mainacht')—both excellent, 18-24 in. tall.

Size	Appearance	Bloom Period	Light Requirements	Growing Requirements
SEA HOLLY	*Eryngium alpinum*			
30 in. tall; 18-in. spread.	Stiff, steely blue flowers; coarse green foliage.	July-Aug.	Full sun to partial sun.	Poor, sandy, well-drained, dry soil.

Size	Appearance	Bloom Period	Light Requirements	Growing Requirements
SEDUM	*Sedum* 'Autumn Joy'			
24 in. tall; 15-in. spread.	Pink flowers in flat head; fleshy green foliage.	Aug.-Sept.	Full sun to partial sun.	Poor, well-drained soil; drought tolerant.

Size	Appearance	Bloom Period	Light Requirements	Growing Requirements
SIBERIAN BUGLOSS (HARDY FORGET-ME-NOT)	*Brunnera macrophylla*			
15 in. tall; 18-in. spread.	Airy clusters of tiny blue flowers; coarse, heart-shaped green foliage.	April-May.	Partial shade; partial sun; full sun.	Rich soil.

Propagation	Garden Types	Uses	Notes
Tender Annual	**Zones —**		
Sow seed indoors in late Feb.	Sunny or shady garden.	Middle or foreground of bed; edging.	One of the longest-blooming annuals, continuing well into fall.
Very Hardy Perennial	**Zones 4-9**		
By division or cuttings.	Sunny garden; Bank Garden.	Middle or foreground of bed.	An excellent purple perennial for the sunny June border.
Very Hardy Perennial	**Zones 3-8**		
By division or seed.	Sunny garden; Bank Garden.	Middle of bed; good for cutting fresh or drying.	Flowers very stately looking and sculptural. *E. planum* is disappointing in comparison to *E. alpinum.*
Very Hardy Perennial	**Zones 3-9**		
By division or cuttings.	Sunny garden; Bank Garden.	Middle or foreground of bed; good for cutting fresh or drying.	One of the best perennials available today. Performs best in poor soil. Seed heads are attractive all winter.
Very Hardy Perennial	**Zones 3-8**		
By division or seed.	Sunny or shady garden; Woodland Garden.	Foreground of bed; ground cover; edging.	Also called *Anchusa myosotidiflora;* leaves make good ground cover in summer. Reseeds freely in garden.

Size	Appearance	Bloom Period	Light Requirements	Growing Requirements
SNAPDRAGON *Antirrhinum majus*				
24-36 in. tall; 6-12-in. spread.	Flowers come in all colors except blue; green foliage.	June-Oct. Faint sweet scent.	Full sun; partial sun; partial shade.	Well-drained soil.
SNEEZEWEED *Helenium autumnale*				
24-72 in. tall; 18-in spread.	Yellow, orange, rust, and red flowers; green foliage.	Aug.-Sept.	Full sun.	Rich, moist soil.

Look for: 'Bruno'—mahogany red, 24 in. tall; 'Butterpat'—butter yellow, 36 in. tall; 'Riverton Beauty'—yellow with bronze center, 48 in. tall.

Size	Appearance	Bloom Period	Light Requirements	Growing Requirements
SNOWDROP *Galanthus nivalis*				
6 in. tall; 4-in. spread.	Hanging white flowers; straplike green foliage.	Feb.-March.	Deciduous shade; partial sun; partial shade.	Rich, moist soil; plant 4 in. deep.
SOLOMON'S SEAL *Polygonatum biflorum*				
24-36 in. tall; 12-in. spread.	White flowers; broad green leaves; flowers hang along arching stems under foliage.	May-June	Partial shade to full shade.	Adaptable, but prefers rich, well-drained soil.

Look for: *P. odoratum* var. *thunbergii* 'Variegatum'—striking variegated type from Japan.

Size	Appearance	Bloom Period	Light Requirements	Growing Requirements
SPEEDWELL, SPIKE *Veronica spicata*				
15 in. tall; 12-in. spread.	Blue, pink, or white flowers; green foliage.	June-Aug.	Full sun to partial sun.	Well-drained soil.

Look for: 'Blue Peter'—deep blue; 'Red Fox'—the best pink variety, deep rose-pink.

Propagation	Garden Types	Uses	Notes
Half-Hardy Annual	**Zones —**		
Sow seed indoors in early March, germinates in 2 weeks.	Sunny or shady garden.	Middle of bed; good fresh-cut flower.	May overwinter with mulch in South. To rejuvenate in summer, cut back, feed, and water. Susceptible to rust disease. Varieties vary in height, flower form; stake taller varieties.
Very Hardy Perennial	**Zones 3-9**		
By division, cuttings, or seed.	Sunny garden.	Background or middle of bed; good fresh-cut flower.	Nonallergenic but blooms during hay fever season. If crowded by other plants, may die out. Pinch mid-June for compactness.
Very Hardy Bulb	**Zones 3-9**		
By division; may reseed in garden.	Shady garden; Woodland Garden.	Plant under deciduous shrubs; edging; good fresh-cut flower.	Transplant and divide when in bloom or just after blooming.
Very Hardy Perennial	**Zones 3-8**		
By division; may reseed in garden.	Shady garden; Woodland Garden.	Background or middle of bed.	Useful vertical accent in the shady garden.
Very Hardy Perennial	**Zones 3-8**		
By division, cuttings, or seed.	Sunny garden; Bank Garden.	Middle or foreground of bed; good fresh-cut flower.	Most need staking or they will flop.

Size	Appearance	Bloom Period	Light Requirements	Growing Requirements
SPEEDWELL, WOOLLY *Veronica incana*				
18 in tall; 12-in. spread.	Blue flowers; low-growing silver foliage.	June-July.	Full sun.	Sandy, well-drained soil.
SPIDER FLOWER *Cleome hasslerana*				
36-60 in. tall; 15-in. spread.	Purple, pink, or white flowers; green foliage.	June-Oct.	Full sun; partial sun; partial shade.	Very adaptable.
SPIDERWORT *Tradescantia andersoniana*				
24 in. tall; 18-in. spread.	Blue, white, or pink flowers; grasslike green foliage.	June-Aug.	Full sun; partial sun; partial shade.	Adaptable.
Look for: 'Blue Stone'—deep blue, 12 in. tall; 'Pauline'—pale pink; 'Innocence'—white, 24 in. tall.				
SQUILL, SIBERIAN *Scilla sibirica*				
6 in. tall; 4-in. spread.	Blue or white flowers; straplike green foliage.	March-April.	Partial sun to partial shade; deciduous shade.	Adaptable; plant 4 in. deep.
Look for: 'Spring Beauty'—larger flowered and usually the variety sold.				
STERNBERGIA *Sternbergia lutea*				
6 in. tall; 4-in. spread.	Yellow, crocus-like flowers; straplike green foliage.	Sept.-Oct.	Full sun to partial sun; deciduous shade.	Rich, well-drained soil, kept dry in summer; plant 6 in. deep.
STRAWFLOWER *Helichrysum bracteatum*				
18-36 in. tall; 8-12 in. spread.	Stiff yellow, orange, or pink flowers; green foliage.	July-Sept.	Full sun.	Very adaptable; drought tolerant.

Propagation	Garden Types	Uses	Notes
Very Hardy Perennial	**Zones 3-8**		
By division, cuttings, or seed.	Sunny garden; Bank Garden.	Foreground of bed; edging; good fresh-cut flower.	Foliage is lower than flower; use in front of bed.
Half-Hardy Annual	**Zones —**		
Sow seed indoors 8-10 weeks before setting out; sow outdoors in early spring in areas with long summer.	Sunny or shady garden.	Background or middle of bed.	Easy to grow; self-sows vigorously.
Very Hardy Perennial	**Zones 4-9**		
By division or seed.	Sunny or shady garden; Woodland Garden, Bank Garden.	Middle or foreground of bed.	Often sold as *T. virginiana*. Shorter forms are desirable since they are less likely to need staking.
Very Hardy Bulb	**Zones 2-8**		
By division; may reseed in garden.	Shady garden; Woodland Garden, Bank Garden.	Plant under deciduous shrubs; edging; good fresh-cut flower.	Very easy spring bulb. Does not like hot climates.
Moderately Hardy Bulb	**Zones 7-10**		
By division or seed.	Sunny or shady garden; Woodland Garden, Bank Garden.	Foreground of bed; edging; good fresh-cut flower.	Leaves appear in fall and last all winter. In the North, choose a south-facing location and mulch with salt hay.
Half-Hardy Annual	**Zones —**		
Sow seed indoors mid-March or outdoors when trees leaf out.	Sunny garden.	Background or middle of bed; good for cutting fresh or drying.	Outstanding flower for drying. Cut just before center of flower opens, hang upside down to dry. Shorter varieties need less staking.

Size	Appearance	Bloom Period	Light Requirements	Growing Requirements
SUMMER SNOWFLAKE	*Leucojum aestivum*			
15 in. tall; 6-in. spread.	Hanging white flowers; straplike green foliage.	April–May.	Full sun to partial sun; deciduous shade.	Rich, moist soil.
SUNDROP	*Oenothera tetragona*			
18 in. tall; 12-in. spread.	Yellow butter-cup-like flowers, often red in bud, atop straight stems; green foliage.	June–July.	Full sun to partial sun.	Very adaptable to any well-drained soil.

Look for: *O. fruticosa, O. fruticosa* 'Youngii,' and *O. pilosella*—similar to *O. tetragona.*

SUNFLOWER, MEXICAN	*Tithonia rotundifolia*			
48–72 in. tall; 48-in. spread.	Bright orange flowers; large green leaves.	July–Sept.	Full sun.	Well-drained, moist to dry soil.

Look for: 'Torch'—preferred variety, earlier blooming with larger flowers.

SWEET WILLIAM	*Dianthus barbatus*			
12–18 in. tall; 10-in. spread.	Red, pink, white, or rose flowers; green foliage.	June–Aug. Sweetly scented.	Full sun to partial sun.	Rich soil.
SWEET WOODRUFF	*Asperula odorata*			
8 in. tall; 12-in. spread.	White flowers; whorls of light green foliage.	April–May.	Partial shade to full shade.	Rich, well-drained soil.

Propagation	Garden Types	Uses	Notes
Very Hardy Bulb	**Zones 4-10**		
By division; may re-seed in garden; plant 6 in. deep.	Sunny or shady garden; Woodland Garden.	Middle or foreground of bed; good fresh-cut flower.	Good for wet, poorly draining soils. Called summer snowflake because it blooms after the spring snowflake (*L. vernum*).
Very Hardy Perennial	**Zones 4-9**		
By division.	Sunny garden.	Middle or foreground of bed.	Shallow rhizomes spread rapidly but are easily removed to keep under control. Overwinters as low evergreen rosettes.
Half-Hardy Annual	**Zones —**		
Sow seed indoors in April for earlier bloom, germinates in 10 days; sow outdoors as early as last frost date.	Sunny garden.	Background of bed; good fresh-cut flower.	Rich soils and excess water encourage overly large plants that break apart.
Hardy Biennial/Annual	**Zones —**		
As annual, sow seed indoors 6-8 weeks before planting out for Aug. bloom; as biennial, sow May to July, will bloom June of the next year.	Sunny garden; Bank Garden.	Foreground of bed; edging; good fresh-cut flower.	Reseeds in garden.
Very Hardy Perennial	**Zones 4-8**		
By division, cuttings, or seed.	Shady garden; Woodland Garden.	Ground cover.	Used to flavor May wine. Beware of spreading, invasive rhizomes. Looks like miniature pachysandra, but not evergreen.

Size	Appearance	Bloom Period	Light Requirements	Growing Requirements

TOBACCO, FLOWERING   *Nicotiana alata*

Size	Appearance	Bloom Period	Light Requirements	Growing Requirements
36 in. tall; 24-in. spread.	Pink, red, white, or green flowers; green foliage.	June-Oct. Sweetly scented.	Full sun; partial sun; partial shade.	Well-drained, moist soil.

Look for: 'Nicki Series'—short and compact, 16-18 in. × 12 in.; 'Domino Series'—10-14 in. × 10 in., longer blooming than Nicki.

TRILLIUM (WAKE ROBIN)   *Trillium grandiflorum*

Size	Appearance	Bloom Period	Light Requirements	Growing Requirements
15 in. tall; 12-in. spread.	White flowers; whorls of rounded green leaves.	April-May.	Full shade.	Rich, well-drained soil.

TULIP   *Tulipa* hybrids

Size	Appearance	Bloom Period	Light Requirements	Growing Requirements
6-30 in. tall; 8-in. spread.	Flowers come in all colors; green foliage.	March-May. Some varieties sweetly scented.	Full sun to partial sun.	Rich, well-drained soil; prefers neutral pH; plant 6-10 in. deep.

Look for: Darwin hybrids—20-26 in. tall, large flowers, late April; Darwin and Cottage—20-26 in., some fragrant, early to mid-May; Fosteriana hybrids—10-20 in., large flowers, late April; Greigii hybrids—8-12 in. tall, mottled leaves, late April; Kaufmanniana hybrids—5-8 in. tall, early April; Single and Double Earlies—12-14 in. tall, usually fragrant, early April.

TURTLEHEAD   *Chelone lyoni*

Size	Appearance	Bloom Period	Light Requirements	Growing Requirements
36 in. tall; 18-in. spread.	Pink flowers; green foliage on straight stems.	Aug.-Sept.	Partial sun to partial shade.	Rich, moist soil.

VERBENA   *Verbena hybrida*

Size	Appearance	Bloom Period	Light Requirements	Growing Requirements
8-12 in. tall; 10-in. spread.	Pink, red, lavender, purple, or white flowers; finely cut green foliage.	June-Sept. Some varieties sweetly scented.	Full sun to partial sun.	Adaptable and will tolerate dry soils.

Propagation	Garden Types	Uses	Notes
Hardy Annual	**Zones —**		
Sow seed indoors in March.	Sunny garden; Bank Garden.	Middle or foreground of bed; edging; good for cutting fresh or drying.	Flowers open in evening, release sweet fragrance. Flowers close on hot days. Cut back for rebloom. Prefers shade protection from hot sun.
Very Hardy Perennial	**Zones 4-8**		
By division or seed.	Shady garden; Woodland Garden, Bank Garden.	Foreground of bed.	One of the prettiest native woodland flowers.
Very Hardy Bulb	**Zones 3-7**		
By division.	Sunny garden; Bank Garden.	Middle or foreground of bed; good fresh-cut flower.	Many hybrids provide range of bloom season, color, size, and form. In deep South, bulbs must be precooled before planting.
Very Hardy Perennial	**Zones 4-9**		
By division or seed.	Sunny or shady garden; Woodland Garden.	Background or middle of bed; good fresh-cut flower.	Flower shape resembles a turtle's head. *C. obliqua* is similar to *C. lyoni.*
Half-Hardy Annual	**Zones —**		
Sow seed indoors 8-10 weeks before planting outdoors.	Sunny garden; Bank Garden.	Foreground of bed; edging; good fresh-cut flower.	Heat tolerant.

Size	Appearance	Bloom Period	Light Requirements	Growing Requirements
VIRGINIA BLUEBELL	*Mertensia virginica*			
36 in. tall; 12-in. spread.	Blue flowers; green foliage.	April-May.	Partial shade.	Rich, moist soil.
WILD INDIGO, BLUE	*Baptisia australis*			
48 in. tall; 24-48-in. spread.	Blue pealike flowers; green foliage creates finely textured effect.	June.	Partial sun to full sun.	Prefers moist soil with acid pH.
WINTER ACONITE	*Eranthis hyemalis*			
3 in. tall; 3-in. spread.	Yellow buttercup-like flowers; deeply cut green foliage.	Feb.-March.	Deciduous shade to partial shade.	Rich, moist soil; prefers acid pH.
WISHBONE FLOWER	*Torenia fournieri*			
8-14 in. tall; 6-8-in. spread.	Bluish purple flowers; green foliage.	June-Oct. Sweetly scented.	Partial sun to partial shade.	Moist, well-drained soil.
WORMWOOD, SILVER KING	*Artemisia* 'Silver King'			
24-36 in. tall; 12-in. spread.	Insignificant flowers; silver foliage with a fine, fernlike texture.	—	Full sun.	Poor, well-drained, sandy soil.
WORMWOOD, SILVER MOUND	*Artemisia* 'Silver Mound'			
12 in. tall; 18-in. spread.	Insignificant flowers; silvery foliage with fine, feathery texture.	—	Full sun.	Poor, sandy, well-drained soil. Best when planted on mound of sandy soil.

Propagation	Garden Types	Uses	Notes
Very Hardy Perennial	**Zones 3-8**		
By division or seed.	Shady garden; Woodland Garden.	Middle of bed; good fresh-cut flower.	Early-blooming native plant; pink buds open blue. Foliage dies down in summer. Plant in late summer to early fall.
Very Hardy Perennial	**Zones 3-8**		
By division or seed.	Sunny garden.	Background of bed; good fresh-cut flower.	Prefers not to be moved; a large, long-lived perennial that needs staking.
Very Hardy Bulb	**Zones 4-9**		
By division or seed; plant 4 in. deep.	Shady garden; Woodland Garden, Bank Garden.	Plant under deciduous shrubs and trees; foreground of bed.	Needs a cool, shady location in summer. Soak corm in water overnight before planting for better results. Can reseed.
Tender Annual	**Zones —**		
Sow seed indoors in early March. Sow outdoors after frost; blooms will be later.	Shady garden; Woodland Garden, Bank Garden.	Foreground of bed; edging.	Easy to transplant. Prefers humidity. Rejuvenate by cutting back. Often reseeds for the following year.
Very Hardy Perennial	**Zones 4-8**		
By division or cuttings.	Sunny garden.	Background or middle of bed; good for cutting fresh or drying.	Needs staking to stay neat. Pinch for bushy shape. Roots invasive in light soils.
Very Hardy Perennial	**Zones 4-8**		
By division or cuttings.	Sunny garden; Bank Garden.	Foreground of bed; edging; good for cutting fresh or drying.	A tight mound in early summer but stems may lean, leaving open center in summer; can be cut back when new growth shows at base.

Size	Appearance	Bloom Period	Light Requirements	Growing Requirements
YARROW, FERNLEAF *Achillea* 'Coronation Gold'				
36 in. tall; 18-in. spread.	Deep yellow flowers in flat head; green foliage with fern-like texture.	June–Aug.	Full sun.	Poor, well-drained, dry soil.
YARROW, MOONSHINE *Achillea* 'Moonshine'				
24 in. tall; 18-in. spread.	Light yellow flowers in flat heads; fernlike silvery foliage.	June–Aug.	Full sun.	Well-drained, dry soil.
ZINNIA *Zinnia elegans*				
12-36 in. tall; 8-15-in. spread.	Orange, yellow, pink, red, or white flowers; green foliage.	June–Oct.	Full sun to partial sun.	Adaptable to most well-drained soils.
ZINNIA, CREEPING *Sanvitalia procumbens*				
6 in. tall; 12-in. spread.	Deep yellow flowers; small green foliage.	June–Oct.	Full sun.	Light, well-drained, dry soil.

Propagation	Garden Types	Uses	Notes
Very Hardy Perennial	**Zones 3-8**		
By division.	Sunny garden.	Background or middle of bed; good for cutting fresh or drying.	In poor soil, shorter stems need no staking.
Hardy Perennial	**Zones 4-8**		
By division.	Sunny garden; Bank Garden.	Middle or foreground of bed; good for cutting fresh or drying.	In light, poor soil, plant growth needs no staking.
Half-Hardy Annual	**Zones —**		
Sow seed indoors early March, germinates in 5 days. Sow in May for late summer bloom.	Sunny garden.	Background to foreground of bed, depending on height; shorter varieties for edging; good fresh-cut flower.	Hybridized into many shapes, sizes, and heights. Cactus types have attractive, ragged petals. Good air circulation helps reduce mildew. Pinch young plants for bushiness.
Hardy Annual	**Zones —**		
Sow seed outdoors in late fall or early spring. Many young seedlings will survive winter. Thin in spring.	Sunny garden; Bank Garden.	Foreground of bed; edging.	Not necessary to start ahead indoors.

Hardiness Zone Map

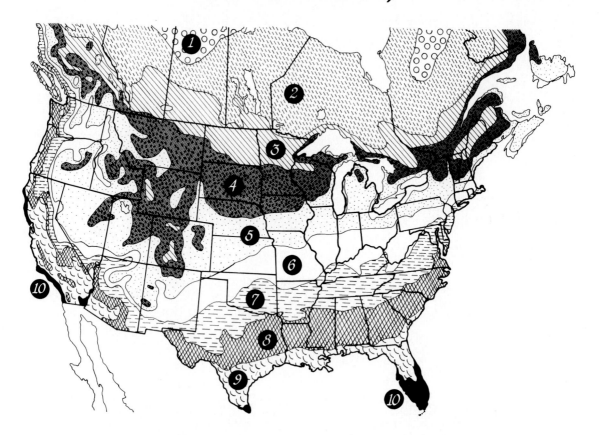

Average Minimum Temperatures for Each Zone

Zone 1	below -50°F		Zone 6	-10° to 0°
Zone 2	-50° to -40°		Zone 7	0° to 10°
Zone 3	-40° to -30°		Zone 8	10° to 20°
Zone 4	-30° to -20°		Zone 9	20° to 30°
Zone 5	-20° to -10°		Zone 10	30° to 40°

Resources Guide

Drip Irrigation Systems

Aquatic Irrigation Systems
619e East Gutierrez
Santa Barbara, CA 93103

Clapper's
1125 Washington Street
West Newton, MA 02165

Gardener's Supply Company
128 Intervale Road
Burlington, VT 05401

International Irrigation Systems
1555 Third Avenue
Niagara Falls, NY 14304

Submatic Irrigation Systems
P.O. Box 246
Lubbock, TX 79408

Flower Sources

Kurt Bluemel, Inc.
2543 Hess Road
Fallston, MD 21047

Bluestone Perennials, Inc.
7211 Middle Ridge Road
Madison, OH 44057

W. Atlee Burpee Company
300 Park Avenue
Warminster, PA 18974

Busse Gardens
635 East Seventh Street
Route 2, Box 13
Cokato, MN 55321

Carroll Gardens, Inc.
444 East Main Street
Box 310
Westminster, MD 21157

The Country Garden
Route 2, Box 455A
Crivitz, WI 54114

The Crownsville Nursery
1241 Generals Highway
Crownsville, MD 21032

The Garden Place
6780 Heisley Road
Mentor, OH 44060

J. L. Hudson, Seedsman
P.O. Box 1058
Redwood City, CA 94064

International Growers Exchange, Inc.
17142 Lahser Road
Detroit, MI 48219

Lamb Nurseries
East 101 Sharp Avenue
Spokane, WA 99202

251

Milaeger's Gardens
    4838 Douglas Avenue
    Racine, WI 53402

Park Seed Company
    Highway 254 North
    Greenwood, SC 29647

Powell's Gardens
    Route 2, Box 86
    Princeton, NC 27569

Thompson & Morgan, Inc.
    Farraday & Gramme Avenues
    P.O. Box 1308
    Jackson, NJ 08527

Andre Viette Farm and Nursery
    State Route 608
    Route 1, Box 16
    Fisherville, VA 22939

Wayside Gardens
    Garden Lane
    Hodges, SC 29695-0001

White Flower Farm
    Route 63
    Litchfield, CT 06759-0050

Garden Tillers

Mantis Manufacturing Corporation
    1458 County Line Road
    Huntingdon Valley, PA 19006

General Gardening Tools and Accessories

Gardener's Eden
    P.O. Box 7307
    San Francisco, CA 94120

David Kay, Inc.
    26055-D Emory Road
    Warrensville Heights, OH 44128

Walter F. Nicke
    Box 667G
    Hudson, NY 12534

Plow and Hearth
    560 Main Street
    Madison, VA 22727

Smith & Hawken
    25 Corte Madera
    Mill Valley, CA 94941

Organic Pest Controls

Agri-Systems International
    125 West Seventh Street
    Wind Gap, PA 18091

Mellinger's, Inc.
    2310 South Range Road
    North Lima, OH 44452

Natural Gardening Research Center
    Highway 46
    P.O. Box 149
    Sunman, IN 47041

Necessary Trading Company
    Main Street, Box 305
    New Castle, VA 24127

Reuter Laboratories, Inc.
    8450 Natural Way
    Manassas Park, VA 22111

Safer Agro-Chem, Inc.
    384 Brooks Road
    Memphis, TN 38116

Plant Labels

Gardener's Supply Company
    See Drip Irrigation Systems *for
        address*

Mellinger's, Inc.
    See Organic Pest Controls *for address*

Walter F. Nicke
    See General Gardening Tools and
        Accessories *for address*

Paw Paw Everlast Label Company
    P.O. Box 93-C
    Paw Paw, MI 49079

Smith & Hawkin
　See General Gardening Tools
　　and Accessories *for address*

Wayside Gardens
　See Flower Sources *for address*

Plant Supports

Kinsman Company
　River Road
　Point Pleasant, PA 18950

Rain Gauges

W. Atlee Burpee Company
　See Flower Sources *for address*

Mellinger's, Inc.
　See Organic Pest Controls *for address*

Otis S. Twilley Seed Company
　P.O. Box 65
　Trevose, PA 19047

Soil Block Presses

Brookstone
　300 Vose Farm Road
　Peterborough, NH 03458

W. Atlee Burpee Company
　See Flower Sources *for address*

Gardener's Supply Company
　See Drip Irrigation Systems *for*
　　address

Green River Tools
　5 Cotton Mill Hill
　P.O. Box 1919
　Brattleboro, VT 05301

Soil Thermometers

W. Atlee Burpee Company
　See Flower Sources *for address*

Computemp
　Rodco Products Company
　P.O. Box 944
　2565 Sixteenth Avenue
　Columbus, NE 68601

Gro-Tex
　South Berwick, ME 03908

Mellinger's, Inc.
　See Organic Pest Controls *for address*

Spraying Equipment

W. Atlee Burpee Company
　See Flower Sources *for address*

Mantis Manufacturing Corporation
　See Garden Tillers *for address*

Weeding Tool

W. Atlee Burpee Company
　See Flower Sources *for address*

Recommended Reading

Attracting Songbirds

McKinley, Michael. *How to Attract Birds.* San Francisco, Calif.: Ortho Books, 1983.

Pistorius, Alan. *The Country Journal Book of Birding and Bird Attraction.* New York: W. W. Norton, 1981.

Proctor, Dr. Noble. *Garden Birds.* Emmaus, Pa.: Rodale Press, 1986.

Schutz, Walter E. *How to Attract, House and Feed Birds: Forty-Eight Plans for Bird Feeders and Houses You Can Make.* New York: Macmillan, 1974.

Simonds, Calvin. *Private Lives of Garden Birds.* Emmaus, Pa.: Rodale Press, 1984.

Terres, John K. *Songbirds in Your Garden.* New York: Thomas Y. Crowell, 1968.

Borders, Sidewalks, and Patios

Brimer, John Burton. *The Homeowner's Complete Outdoor Building Book.* New York: Popular Science Books, 1985.

Garden Construction. San Francisco, Calif.: Ortho Books, 1985.

Garden Projects. New York: Arco, 1985.

Lees, Carlton B. *New Budget Landscaping: Designing Your Outdoor Space for Use, Comfort, and Pleasure.* New York: Popular Science Books, 1985.

Proulx, E. Annie. *Plan and Make Your Own Fences and Gates, Walkways, Walls, and Drives.* Emmaus, Pa.: Rodale Press, 1983. (This book has gone out of print; check your local library.)

Composting

Minnich, Jerry, Marjorie Hunt, and the editors of *Organic Gardening* magazine. *The Rodale Guide to Composting.* Emmaus, Pa.: Rodale Press, 1979.

General Flower Gardening

Bloom, Alan. *Perennials for Your Garden.* Beaverton, Ore.: International Specialized Book Services, 1981.

Cox, Jeff, and Marilyn Cox. *The Perennial Garden.* Emmaus, Pa.: Rodale Press, 1985.

254

Crockett, James U. *Bulbs*. New York: Time-Life Books, 1971.

Fell, Derek. *Annuals: How to Select, Grow, and Enjoy*. Tucson, Ariz.: HP Books, 1985.

Harper, Pamela, and Frederick McGourty. *Perennials: How to Select, Grow, and Enjoy*. Tucson, Ariz.: HP Books, 1985.

Hebb, Robert. *Low-Maintenance Perennials*. Jamaica Plain, Mass.: Arnold Arboretum of Harvard University, 1975.

Taylor's Guide to Annuals. Boston: Houghton Mifflin, 1986.

Taylor's Guide to Perennials. Boston: Houghton Mifflin, 1986.

Identifying Pests and Diseases

Carr, Anna. *Rodale's Color Handbook of Garden Insects*. Emmaus, Pa.: Rodale Press, 1979.

Cravens, Richard H. *Pests and Diseases*. Alexandria, Va.: Time-Life Books, 1977.

Forsberg, Junuis L. *Diseases of Ornamental Plants*. Rev. ed. Urbana, Ill.: University of Illinois Press, 1975.

Martin, Alexander C. *A Golden Guide: Weeds*. New York: Golden Press, 1972.

Yepsen, Roger B., Jr., ed. *The Encyclopedia of Natural Insect and Disease Control*. Emmaus, Pa.: Rodale Press, 1984.

Landscaping

Brookes, John. *Room Outside: A Plan for the Garden*. New York: Viking-Penguin, 1970.

Dirr, Michael A. *A Manual of Woody Landscape Plants*. Champaign, Ill.: Stipes, 1978.

Douglas, William Lake, et al. *Garden Design*. New York: Simon & Schuster, 1984.

Ingels, Jack E. *The Landscape Book*. New York: Van Nostrand Reinhold, 1983.

Loewer, Peter. *Gardens by Design*. Emmaus, Pa.: Rodale Press, 1986.

Pierceale, G. M. *Residential Landscapes*. Reston, Va.: Reston, 1984.

Rose, Graham. *The Low Maintenance Garden*. New York: Viking-Penguin, 1983.

Sunset editors. *Landscaping Illustrated*. Menlo Park, Calif.: Sunset Books-Land Publishing, 1984.

Whitcomb, Carle. *Know It and Grow It*. Tulsa, Okla.: Oil Capital Printing, 1975.

Magazines for Flower Gardeners

American Horticulturist, 7931 East Boulevard Drive, Alexandria, VA 22308

Avant Gardener, P.O. Box 489, New York, NY 10028

Horticulture, 300 Massachusetts Avenue, Boston, MA 02116

Hort Ideas, Route 1, Gravel Switch, KY 40328

National Gardening, National Gardening Association, Depot Square, Peterborough, NH 03458

Rodale's Organic Gardening, Rodale Press, Inc., 33 East Minor Street, Emmaus, PA 18049

The Green Scene, The Pennsylvania Horticultural Society, 325 Walnut Street, Philadelphia, PA 19106.

Scented Flowers and Foliage

Verey, Rosemary. *The Scented Garden.* New York: Van Nostrand Reinhold, 1981.

Wilder, Louise Beebe. *The Fragrant Garden.* Mineola, N.Y.: Dover, 1974.

Using Color in the Garden

Crockett, James U. *Crockett's Flower Garden.* New York: Little, Brown, 1981.

Hobhouse, Penelope. *Color in Your Garden.* New York: Little, Brown, 1986.

Jekyll, Gertrude. *Colour Schemes for the Flower Garden.* Salem, N.H.; Merrimack Publishers' Circle, 1985.

Phillips, Phoebe. *The Flower Garden Planner.* New York: Simon & Schuster, 1984.

Using Flowers

Okun, Sheila. *A Book of Cut Flowers.* New York: William Morrow, 1983.

Thorpe, Patricia. *Everlastings: The Complete Book of Dried Flowers.* New York: Facts on File, 1985.

Wiita, Betty. *Dried Flowers for All Seasons.* New York: Van Nostrand Reinhold, 1982.

Woodland, Meadow, and Bank Gardens

Bruce, Hal. *How to Grow Wildflowers and Wild Shrubs and Trees in Your Own Garden.* New York: Alfred A. Knopf, 1976.

Jekyll, Gertrude. *Wall, Water, and Woodland Gardens.* Salem, N.H.: Merrimack Publishers' Circle, 1985.

Martin, Laura C. *The Wildflower Meadow, A Gardener's Guide.* Charlotte, N.C.: East Woods Press, 1986.

Penn, Cornelia. *Landscaping with Native Plants.* Winston-Salem, N.C.: John F. Blair, 1982.

Phillips, Harry R. *Growing and Propagating Wildflowers.* Edited by J. Kenneth Moore. Chapel Hill, N.C.: University of North Carolina Press, 1985.

Schenk, George. *The Complete Shade Gardener.* Boston: Houghton-Mifflin, 1984.

Sperka, Marie. *Growing Wildflowers: A Cultivator's Guide.* New York: Charles Scribner's Sons, 1984.

Plant Name Index

Botanical Name	Common Name	Botanical Name	Common Name
Colchicum spp.	Colchicum	*Geranium himalayense*	Geranium, hardy
Coleus hybridus	Coleus (Flame nettle)	*Geranium maculatum*	Geranium, hardy
		Geranium sanguineum	Geranium, hardy
Convallaria majalis	Lily-of-the-valley	*Gomphrena globosa*	Globe amaranth
Coreopsis lanceolata	Coreopsis (Tickseed)	*Gypsophila paniculata*	Baby's breath
		Helenium autumnale	Sneezeweed
Coreopsis verticillata	Coreopsis, thread-leaf	*Helichrysum bracteatum*	Strawflower
		Heliopsis scabra	Heliopsis
Cosmos bipinnatus	Cosmos	*Helleborus orientalis*	Lenten rose
Cosmos sulphureus	Cosmos, Klondyke	*Hemerocallis* hybrids	Daylily
		Heuchera sanguinea	Coral bells
Crocus chrysanthus	Crocus, snow	*Hibiscus moscheutos*	Rose mallow
Crocus vernus hybrids	Crocus, Dutch	*Hosta* spp. and hybrids	Hosta (Plantain lily; Funkia)
Crocus zonatus	Crocus, autumn		
Dahlia hybrids	Dahlia, bedding	*Iberis sempervirens*	Candytuft, hardy
Dahlia hybrids	Dahlia	*Impatiens* hybrids	Impatiens, New Guinea
Delphinium ajacis	Larkspur		
Delphinium elatum hybrids	Delphinium (Larkspur)	*Impatiens balsamina*	Balsam
		Impatiens walleriana	Impatiens
Dianthus allwoodii	Pink, allwood	*Iris cristata*	Iris, crested
Dianthus barbatus	Sweet William	*Iris germanica*	Iris, bearded
Dicentra eximia	Bleeding heart, fringed	*Iris kaempferi*	Iris, Japanese
		Iris reticulata	Iris, netted
Dicentra spectabilis	Bleeding heart, common	*Iris sibirica*	Iris, Siberian
		Kniphofia hybrids	Red-hot-poker (Tritoma)
Dictamnus albus	Gas plant		
Digitalis purpurea	Foxglove	*Lamium maculatum*	Dead-nettle
Doronicum caucasisum	Leopard's bane	*Leucojum aestivum*	Snowflake, summer
Dryopteris marginalis	Fern, marginal shield		
		Liatris pycnostachya	Gay-feather
Echinacea purpurea	Coneflower, purple	*Ligularia dentata*	Ligularia
		Lilium 'Asiatic Hybrids'	Lily, Asiatic hybrid
Echinops 'Taplow Blue'	Globe thistle		
Endymion hispanicus	Hyacinth, wood (Spanish bluebell)	*Lilium* 'Aurelian Hybrids'	Lily, Aurelian hybrid
		Lilium 'Oriental Hybrids'	Lily, Oriental hybrid
Epimedium spp.	Barrenwort		
Eranthis hyemalis	Winter aconite	*Liriope muscari*	Lily-turf (Liriope)
Eryngium alpinum	Sea holly		
Eupatorium coelestinum	Ageratum, hardy	*Lobelia cardinalis*	Cardinal flower
Euphorbia myrsinites	Spurge, myrtle	*Lobelia erinus*	Lobelia
Filipendula palmata	Meadowsweet, Siberian	*Lobularia maritima*	Alyssum, sweet
		Lunaria annua	Honesty (Moneywort)
Filipendula rubra	Queen-of-the-prairie		
		Lupinus 'Russell Hybrids'	Lupine
Fritillaria imperialis	Crown imperial	*Lycoris squamigera*	Amaryllis, hardy (Resurrection lily)
Fritillaria meleagris	Guinea flower		
Funkia spp. and hybrids	Hosta (Plantain lily; Funkia)		
		Lythrum salicaria	Loosestrife, purple
Gaillardia grandiflora	Blanket flower (Gaillardia)		
		Mertensia virginica	Virginia bluebell
Galanthus nivalis	Snowdrop	*Mirabilis jalapa*	Four-o'clock
Gazania ringens	Gazania	*Miscanthus sinensis*	Grass, eulalia

Botanical Name	Common Name	Botanical Name	Common Name
Monarda didyma	Bee balm (Bergamot)	*Pulmonaria saccharata*	Lungwort
		Rudbeckia fulgida	Black-eyed Susan (Coneflower)
Muscari armeniacum	Hyacinth, grape		
Myosotis sylvatica	Forget-me-not	*Rudbeckia hirta* hybrids	Daisy, gloriosa
Narcissus hybrids	Daffodil (Narcissus)	*Salvia farinacea*	Sage, mealy-cup
		Salvia splendens	Sage, scarlet (Salvia)
Nicotiana alata	Tobacco, flowering	*Salvia superba*	Salvia (Sage)
Oenothera tetragona	Sundrop	*Sanguinaria canadensis*	Bloodroot
Pachysandra terminalis	Pachysandra	*Sanvitalia procumbens*	Zinnia, creeping
Paeonia lactiflora	Peony	*Scilla sibirica*	Squill, Siberian
Papaver orientale	Poppy, oriental	*Sedum* 'Autumn Joy'	Sedum
Papaver rhoeas	Poppy, Shirley (Corn poppy)	*Sempervivum* spp. and hybrids	Hen-and-chickens
Papaver somniferum	Poppy, opium	*Senecio cineraria*	Dusty miller
Pelargonium hortorum hybrids	Geranium, zonal	*Stachys byzantina*	Lamb's-ears (Woolly betony)
Pennisetum alopecuroides	Grass, Japanese fountain		
Pennisetum ruppelii	Grass, crimson fountain	*Sternbergia lutea*	Sternbergia
		Tagetes spp.	Marigold
Perilla frutescens	Perilla	*Thalictrum rochebrunianum*	Meadow rue
Perovskia atriplicifolia	Sage, Russian	*Thymus serpyllum*	Thyme, lemon
Phlox divaricata	Phlox, wild blue (Wild sweet William)	*Tiarella cordifolia*	Foam flower
		Tithonia rotundifolia	Sunflower, Mexican
Phlox drummondii	Phlox, annual	*Torenia fournieri*	Wishbone flower
Phlox paniculata	Phlox, summer	*Tradescantia andersoniana*	Spiderwort
Phlox stolonifera	Phlox, creeping	*Trillium grandiflorum*	Trillium (Wake robin)
Phlox subulata	Pink, moss		
Physostegia virginiana	Obedient plant (False dragonhead)	*Tritoma* hybrids	Red-hot-poker (Tritoma)
		Tropaeolum minor	Nasturtium, dwarf
Platycodon grandiflorus	Balloon flower	*Tulipa* hybrids	Tulip
Polygonatum biflorum	Solomon's seal	*Verbena hybrida*	Verbena
Polystichum acrostichoides	Fern, Christmas	*Veronica incana*	Speedwell, woolly
Portulaca grandiflora	Moss rose	*Veronica spicata*	Speedwell, spike
Primula japonica	Primrose, Japanese	*Vinca minor*	Periwinkle
		Viola wittrockiana	Pansy
Primula polyanthus	Primrose, polyanthus	*Zinnia elegans*	Zinnia

Index

Page numbers in *italic* indicate entries in The Best Plants Chart; page numbers in **boldface** indicate illustrations and photographs.

Insect(s). *See also names of individual insects*
    beneficial, 152, 154-55
Insect control. *See* Backyard pest management (BPM)
Insecticides, 151
Integrated pest management, 150. *See also* Backyard pest management
Iris, 22, 46, 168, *218-19*
    bearded, 44, **84,** 85, 104, 105, 167, 169, *218*
    crested, **82,** 83, 119, *218*
    Japanese, **120,** 121, *218*
    netted, 65, 73, 75, 77, 79, 83, 85, 119
    Siberian, 44, 45, 48, 62, **72,** 73, **76,** 77, *218*
J Japanese anemone, 61, **72,** 73, **74,** 75, 77, 79, 83, 169, *188-89*
Japanese beetles, control of, 153, 154, 156
Japanese juniper, dwarf, **84, 118,** 119
Japanese holly, 85, 119
Japanese iris, **120,** 121, *218*
Japanese juniper, dwarf, **84,** 85, **118,** 119
Japanese painted fern, 64, **74,** 75, **78,** 79, **82,** 83, 104, 105, **118,** 119, **120,** 121
Japanese primrose, **120,** 121
Juniper, 51
    dwarf Japanese, **84,** 85, **118,** 119
K Klondyke cosmos, 202-3
L Lacewing, 155
Ladybugs, 8-9, 154-155, 157
Lady fern, **80,** 81, 83, 121
Lady's mantle, **118,** 119, *218-19*
Lamb's-ears, 46, 64, **72,** 73, **76,** 77, *218-19*
Lamb's-quarters, 157-58, 159
Lamium, **74,** 75, **78,** 79, **80,** 81, 83, 121
Larkspur, 73, 77, *206-7. See also* Delphinium
Lavender, 58, 67
Leadwort. *See* Plumbago
Leaf hoppers, control of, 153
Leaf miners, control of, 153
Leaf mold, 118, 173
Leaf rollers, control of, 156

Leafy spurge, 158
Leaves
    as compost, 132, 133
    as humus source, 130
    as mulch, 126, 136-37, 138
Lemon thyme, 85
Lenten rose, 75, 83
Leopard's bane, *220-21*
Leucothoe, drooping, 60, **74,** 75, **82,** 83
Light, for seedlings, 175
Light conditions, 14-16, **15,** 63, 64, 65
    deciduous shade
      definition of, 185
      flowers suitable for, *186-87, 188-89, 194-95, 198-99, 202-3, 204-5, 214-15, 216-17, 226-27, 238-39, 240-41, 242-43, 246-47*
    full shade, 15, 61, 62, 97
      Decorative Home Garden for, 28
      definition of, 16
      flowers suitable for, *190-91, 196-97, 216-17, 218-19, 228-29*
      Herbaceous Flower Border for, 29, 80, **80,** 81, 94, 104, 105
      Woodland Garden for, 30, **31,** 81-83, **82**
    full sun, 15, **15**
      Bank Garden for, 84-85, **84**
      Decorative Home Garden for, 28, 71, **72,** 73, 86-87, 94
      definition of, 16
      flowers suitable for, 61, 62, 63, 64, 65, *186-87, 188-89, 190-91, 192-93, 194-95, 196-97, 198-99, 200-201, 202-3, 204-5, 206-7, 210-11, 212-13, 214-15, 218-19, 222-23, 224-25, 226-27, 228-29, 230-31, 232-33, 234-35, 236-37, 240-41, 242-43, 244-45, 246-47, 248-49*
      Herbaceous Flower Border for, 29, 74, 76-78, 90-91, 94, 99, 100, 101, 106, 113, 116
    partial shade, 15, **15**
      Bank Garden for, 118, **118,** 119